IDEAS for TRAINING MANAGERS and SUPERVISORS

Useful Suggestions, Activities, and Instruments

by Patrick Suessmuth

UNIVERSITY ASSOCIATES, INC.
7596 Eads Avenue   La Jolla, CA 92037

Contents

Preface

Too many of today's best training ideas never reach most training directors. These may be ideas that develop spontaneously in training situations, or practical processes and techniques that are devised by resourceful trainers for their own use. Some of these ideas are passed on at seminars and conferences, but too many of them do not get far beyond the person who created them.

In 1969, I decided to remedy this situation by writing a bimonthly column in *Canadian Training Methods*. I started the column as a means of forcing myself to put out for others what I personally was finding useful and interesting. In the process of sharing this information, I received many ideas from the readers and I incorporated those ideas and the names of their originators into the column.

This book is an edited compilation of those "Training Ideas Found Useful" columns.

I suggest that you *don't* read this book from cover to cover. A better approach would be to go to the table of contents and pick one of the articles that interests you and read it. With any kind of luck, it should offer you further reinforcement for many of the things you are already doing or trigger some new idea you can use or try in the next session you have to instruct.

Do you have an idea or innovation that you developed yourself? If you want to join in this sharing, send your idea, simulation, activity, or whatever to me in its rough form. Explain its purpose, how it works, and the background of the people you used it with (educational level and type of job held). Add anything else you think we should know and I'll happily consider including it, with full credit to you, in my column.

Patrick Suessmuth

Canadian Training Methods
Chesswood House Publishing
542 Mt. Pleasant Road, Suite 301
Toronto, Canada

PRINTING HISTORY

The printing history of the original "Training Ideas Found Useful"
columns (arranged by chapter number) includes the following:

Chapter

 1 *Canadian Training Methods*
     (CTM), Vol. 3, No. 4, page 23
    Training, 9(11), 52
 2 *CTM, 7*(1), 14
 3 *CTM, 8*(2), 38
 4 *CTM, 10*(1), 22
 5 *CTM, 2*(3), 26
 6 *CTM, 5*(2), 20
    ERI News, March 1974, 6
 7 *CTM, 10*(2), 38
 8 *CTM, 4*(6), 23
    Training, 10(10), 42
 9 *CTM, 8*(5), 28
10 *CTM, 9*(6), 21
11 *CTM, 5*(5), 22
    Training, 13(6), 20
12 *CTM, 7*(2), 40
    Training, 13(8), 41
13 *CTM, 8*(3), 26
14 *CTM, 9*(4), 20
15 *CTM, 8*(6), 22
16 *CTM, 4*(4), 22
17 *CTM, 4*(5), 27
    Training, 11(5), 32
18 *CTM, 2*(6), 28
    Training, 9(5), 33
    Church School Builder,
       27(7), 10
    Youth Leadership, 4(2), 17
    Key, 15(2), 39
19 *CTM, 4*(1), 26
    Training, 11(10), 46
20 *CTM, 4*(2), 24
    Training, 11(2), 41
21 *CTM, 8*(4), 25
22 *CTM, 3*(1), 30
    Training, 9(6), 39
23 *CTM, 3*(6), 27
    Training, 9(9), 55
24 *CTM, 6*(1), 24

25 *CTM, 5*(4), 26
26 *CTM, 6*(3), 25
    Learning Resources, 1(3), 26
27 *CTM, 2*(4), 24
28 *CTM, 6*(2), 41
29 *CTM, 6*(4), 25
    ERI News, May 1974, 8
30 *CTM, 7*(6), 24
31 *CTM, 7*(4), 19
32 *CTM, 7*(5), 23
33 *CTM, 8*(1), 23
34 *CTM, 4*(3), 27
    Training, 10(1), 31
35 *Training, 10*(3), 38
    Adapted from "Training" in the
       text, *Experiential Exercises &*
       Cases in Management, by
       F. E. Kast & J. E. Rosenzweig,
       page 153
36 *CTM, 5*(6), 25
37 *CTM, 2*(5), 16
    Training, 10(2), 60
    Focus, (Newsletter of the
       Community Film Council of
       Greater Nashville), June 1973
38 *CTM, 3*(2), 22
39 *CTM, 3*(5), 24
    Training, 10(5), 48
40 *CTM, 5*(1), 22
41 *CTM, 3*(3), 28
42 *CTM, 5*(3), 34
43 *CTM, 6*(5), 19
44 *CTM, 6*(6), 24
45 *CTM, 7*(3), 23
46 *CTM, 9*(5), 24
47 *CTM, 6*(5), 19
48 *CTM, 9*(1), 24
49 *CTM, 9*(2), 44
50 *CTM, 9*(3), 23
    CTM, 9(5), 24

Part

Setting Up Courses

1

A Capsule Guide for a Novice Trainer

A few days ago we were approached by a man about to teach his first course. He is a professional in his area of competence, the writing of architectural specifications, but he has no instructing experience. Taking time out for an instructor training course is an impossibility for him at this time and he requested that we give him some pointers on how to handle a classroom. We responded with the capsule instructor's guide that follows.

SET OBJECTIVES

Establish the criteria for success. In specific terms, what will the students be able to do after they have completed your course? Outline concisely the point you want to reach in terms of student development.

This is extremely important and the success of the whole course depends on the clarity of these objectives. Clearly defined instructional objectives that are expressed in terms of student involvement make it possible for the instructor to gauge at any point in the course just how effectively he is moving toward his objective.

The clearly defined objective makes content relevancy possible. The instructor should ask about all planned content: Will this put me closer to my instructional objective? If some of the hitherto planned content does not move students closer to the achievement of the objective, then this content falls into the category of "nice-to-know" instead of "need-to-know" and is relegated to a time after the planned objective has been reached.

Marit Stengels, Training Officer, Royal Insurance Group, was co-author of this column.

1

The following are examples of specific instructional objectives:

a. *Instructor training course.* All participants will be able to make a presentation using participation and positive reinforcement in such a way that when they finish their presentations they will know what the students are able to do.

b. *Skill training.* All participants will be able to type seventy words a minute using an electric typewriter.

Some examples of nonspecific objectives:

a. *Clerical training.* Students will have a knowledge of the forms used to process a claim. (This does not specify how much knowledge and precisely what the student will be able to do with that knowledge.)

b. *Report Writing.* Students will learn the format of the formal report. (This does not specify what they will be able to do with the format.)

Examples of critical and noncritical content in a course:

a. *Instructor training course objective.* All participants will be able to make a presentation using participation and positive reinforcement in such a way that when they finish their presentations they will know what the students are able to do.

b. *Planned content.*
   1. History of teaching;
   2. Student presentations;
   3. Student critiques;
   4. Questioning techniques;
   5. Positive reinforcement;
   6. Principles of learning.

Neither "history of teaching" nor "principles of learning" would move students closer to the instructional objective. In this case, these two topics are said to lack content relevancy, e.g., they're noncritical and therefore should be left out.

ASK QUESTIONS

To have participation, ask questions that require more than a yes/no answer–or a recall answer.

It's an accepted fact that the lecture method is limited and the student only learns things he is involved in. Learning is a process synonymous with doing. Participation in a classroom is generated by questions requiring more than yes/no answers. If properly used, the questioning technique is infallible at spurring participation.

A checklist for asking meaningful questions includes:

a. Are students required to do more than recite by rote or answer yes or no?

b. Are you prepared to encourage students to question the meaning of your questions?

c. Are your questions spurring the class into asking you more and more questions?

d. Does each question put the class closer to the instructional objective?

e. Does your lesson plan contain a strong note to yourself to turn *all* student questions back to other students for them to answer?

In the classroom it is usually difficult to get the class going at first. Ask a question. Wait. The silence will be agonizing and fifteen seconds will seem like fifteen minutes. But wait. Don't answer your own question. The temptation will be great but don't do it. Rephrase your original question and invite an "opinion" rather than a "correct answer." In this way, the student doesn't have to risk being wrong, because an opinion is always right. For example, instead of asking, "Why are white filaments used instead of black?," ask, "Does anyone here think he knows why white filaments are used instead of black?" A student has less to lose if he tries to answer the second question.

Accept all student answers, even wrong ones, without resorting to saying, "No, that's wrong," or "No," or shaking your head.

If a student gives you a wrong answer, you have several alternatives. You can say to the rest of the class, "Do the rest of you agree?," "Why?," or "Why not?," or you can accept and modify the student's answer.

For example, a student's answer to the question, "Who is the prime minister of Canada?," might be "Mr. Diefenbaker." Your reply could be "Yes, Mr. Diefenbaker was Canada's prime minister in the fifties and at times he may still appear to think he is. Who was the man who was prime minister after him?" "And who was prime minister after him?" There is always an alternative to saying "No" to a student answer.

Attempting to use questioning for the first time in conducting a class is undeniably a very difficult thing for a novice instructor. Extensive planning can eliminate many of the difficulties that will occur but it isn't until the instructor is actually in front of the class that he grasps what it's all about. The instructor's role is to ask questions that will lead students to their ultimate instructional objectives, to let students talk if they are on the topic (headed for the objective), and to insert questions that will put students back on topic if they wander off the topic.

In the classroom, the professional's function is chiefly as an instructor and *secondly* as a resource person for his own area of competence.

The pecking order is not on an expert-to-novice basis. Rather it is on a basis that assumes each member of the class has his own unique set of resources, and the expert will help the class exploit its own resources to reach the instructional objective.

The easiest way for a new instructor to implement questioning techniques is to make overhead projectuals of the questions he plans to ask. He can shuffle, add to, and adjust these questions once the class is in progress.

POSITIVE REINFORCEMENT

If you run your course using only the one criterion of positive reinforcement, you'll be half-way safe. Because, to use a lot of positive reinforcement, you must have something to reinforce. If you set up a course depending on the use of position reinforcement, participation is an automatic must.

Reinforce *every* meaningful student achievement no matter how small. Reinforce immediately after achievement occurs. Do not reinforce in anticipation of successful achievement. Wait until it happens. Accept all student responses, but reinforce those that indicate progress toward the objective. Do not use negative reinforcement. It will not eliminate the undesired actions of your students nor will it move them to correct these actions. Research is proving that undesired behavior stems from:

a. A failure to reinforce desired behavior;
b. Bizarre side effects from excessive negative reinforcement or punishment.

If students are motivated to learn, e.g., if they are involved and have a stake in what's going on in the classroom, positive reinforcement serves as a signal that they have made progress toward their objectives.

The amount of reinforcement must be proportionate to the student's achievement. Exaggerated praise doesn't work because it breaks the rules. The student knows the value of his own accomplishment and he is likely to be quite perceptive about patronizing overtones in exaggerated praise.

Negative reinforcement will cause the student either not to respond at all, or to respond only in cases when his certainty of being right is 100 percent. It's chilling to realize that an instructor can immobolize an enthusiastic participating class into stubborn silence with a few minutes of careless negative reinforcement.

Some people hold the idea that there is a question of ethics involved in the use of positive reinforcement. Our view does not concur with this.

Positive and negative reinforcements have always occurred randomly in all human relations; both occur randomly on a day-to-day basis to each and every one of us, sometimes with devastating effects, e.g., the traditional school system.

Learning the dynamics of the process of positive reinforcement gives you more control of your behavior and you have fewer unintentional effects to cope with in your personal relationships.

People who respond to your positive reinforcement do so because the reinforcement is part of a reciprocal arrangement; in a classroom, reinforcement is balanced by achievement.

If you use positive reinforcement clearly and honestly, it constitutes half of a working relationship and requires the cooperation of the other person. The system is self-balancing.

SUMMARY

The three essentials from which any instructor, new or experienced, can build and improve his instructional skills are:

1. Questioning;
2. Using positive reinforcement;
3. Having a clear results-oriented objective.

Questioning sets the atmosphere for participation. Positive reinforcement keeps the participation going and on the topic. The objective controls the participation preventing the session from getting off the topic.

These three essentials properly woven together should help any instructor provide stimulating and meaningful training sessions.

2

Criteria for Selecting Trainers

Many of us have to select trainers. This article will not tell you how to select an instructor, but it will outline the criteria for selection that are used by a number of different trainers. It is important to be aware of the distinction of selecting vs. criteria before you read this, because all of us who have provided these outlines realized that we assess a large number of these criteria quite subjectively. So, if you find yourself saying, "That's good but how do you recognize it or measure it?," the answer sometimes is that we do it but don't know how.

In preparing this article, I first set down my hiring criteria, and then I called the other trainers quoted here and exchanged criteria with them. We found it helpful and hope you will too.

The first set of criteria is my own, designed to get instruction-oriented, bright people who can eventually become industrial training consultants. I have rank-ordered my criteria with the first one being most important and the tenth being least important. The first four are "musts." That is, no one is hired unless all four criteria are met. The remaining six are nice to have, but applicants who don't have them will not be ruled out of the competition.

FIRST SET

First Criterion

Wants to be a trainer, or as interviewees say, "wants to teach." This is the first criterion because, if the person doesn't want to teach, the job is wrong for him. It is a simple divider of potential instructors but an effective one. I have found that people who aren't sure whether or not they want to teach rarely make it as instructors. If you are trying to conserve your organization's resources, then you don't want to take on someone who might make a trainer but most likely won't. The least doubt expressed by a person about instructing as a career should serve as a warning of a higher potential of getting a poor instructor if that person is hired. I use this criterion throughout the interview, constantly listening to pick up any tentativeness about instructing as a career. If I pick up that tentativeness, I push the negative aspects of the instructing job.

Second Criterion

Relates well with people. As I write this, I realize I don't know how I assess it. Part of it is tied to how the individual comes across in the interview—which I realize is highly subjective.

That an instructor needs to relate well with people should be self-evident. I place this criterion second because every instructor has to deal with all types of people under all kinds of conditions. Some conditions are such that the person will be tried to his or her limits and still will have to deal civilly with the student. All of us, I'm sure, easily can remember a student who tried our patience, probably in some cases to the breaking point. This being the case, when looking for a new instructor, it is essential to find people who relate to others effectively enough to accept people for what they are. They must not revert to behaviors of attacking or easily offending people.

Third Criterion

Intelligence. Using participation in teaching automatically means that the instructor has to be fast to adapt and adjust student answers to the context of the lesson being taught. This requires intelligence. Insight is even better. The teacher must have enough insight into both the subject and the students to be able to understand how a student arrived at the answer voiced, and to use this insight to change the lesson to relate to the student's thought pattern.

Fourth Criterion

Know what he or she wants in a job. This may not seem important enough to rank fourth, but I think it is. At this point I'm not talking about tasks or subtasks composing the job; I'm talking about the elements that Maslow has placed in the Needs Hierarchy. I listen to hear that the person is looking for a job that will make demands of him—a job that will use everything he has. If a person is looking for a job that provides money and security, the two basic needs on Maslow's Hierarchy, I know he hasn't had the right kind of experience to make it in instructing.

To be able to teach the current industrial management psychology and believe in what one is saying, a person has to know that money and security aren't all a job offers. They must know this so that they can relate many of the ideas they use in teaching to the fact that people aren't puppets but want to be and should be challenged and involved to the utmost in their learning.

Fifth Criterion

Willing to change self, i.e., be changeable. I include this because all instructors are faced regularly by defects in their own personality. These defects need changing. A person who can't or won't change his or her personality won't make it as an instructor. All people have difficulty changing themselves; therefore, in looking for new instructors one should be selecting people who can change and adjust their personal characteristics as they learn about them. To assess this, one need only listen for statements relating how the interviewee sees himself and how he is changing.

Sixth Criterion

Outgoing, showmanship, flair. This may seem totally irrelevant. It isn't, because flair is something that all instructors need. Without it they come across flat and dull. Being outgoing helps create first impressions, and since instructors are constantly meeting new groups, it is an essential ingredient. It also helps an instructor to break-the-ice with new groups.

Thus far, this criterion has proven to be unteachable in instructor training. A person who is not outgoing and whose basic personality lacks any showmanship finds it difficult to be free and easy in his/her delivery to a class, and no amount of training seems to bring it out. A person without flair seems to be strained in classroom activities of a participative nature, especially when attempting to lighten the activity.

The first six criteria are the most important. Without some part of them, a person has a higher chance of failing as an instructor. I see these first six as essentials and the next four criteria are nice to have.

Seventh Criterion

Analytical. Analysis is not essential in an instructor until one asks the instructor to look into training needs. It is not essential until one gives the instructor freedom to teach what he wants to teach. As long as he teaches from a manual, the skill of analysis isn't necessary.

Once an instructor has to analyze who, what, and how he will teach, this criterion is needed. Most new instructors lean initially on more experienced teachers who have done most of the analytical work for them. This skill can be and usually is developed with time and experience in instructing. If a person enters instructing with a highly perceptive and analytical mind, it is a distinct plus.

Eighth and Ninth Criteria

Self-aware, secure within self. These two criteria are interrelated with criterion five because they show a person's self-knowledge. This self-awareness and self-security are vital to an instructor. Awareness is vital because being aware of anything is a big step in any change process. Security within oneself is vital because it allows changes in one's personality characteristics and ideas.

Tenth Criterion

Experience. Not in teaching. I expect all the people I hire to need training to be good instructors. By "experience," I mean experience in what they are going to have to teach. If it's management, then they must be experienced managers. If it's welding, then they must have experience in welding. Note that I put this experience criterion as tenth, not first. This is definitely not essential. A person can learn or gain it with time.

SECOND SET

The second set of criteria comes from John Michaluk and Gord Appleton, both training officers at the Royal Bank of Canada. They break their criteria into two distinct sections, one being absolutes, the other being nice to have.

Absolute Criteria

A. Must be in the salary range $X to $Y. If applicants are not in this range, either they are too junior or the training section just can't afford to pay them. Hence, there is no point in those people trying for the job.

B. Sound technical banking skills. This criterion is not to be confused with people skills; it means technical. For example, the person knows what a letter of credit means and how to use it.

C. The individual has been a good supervisor as seen by his senior managers. This is done partly via feedback in the performance appraisal system.

D. The person has to be an effective oral communicator—in other words, can speak in front of others.

E. Has a car and is willing to travel.

F. The person can project. This is the same as the outgoing, show-manship, flair criterion previously outlined.

These absolutes are in no particular order. All are musts. If the trainer-to-be doesn't have them, then he or she isn't hired. Some of these criteria may seem almost universal; it one relates them to a strong policy of promotion from within they make sense.

Nice-to-Have Criteria

Rather than rank ordering these nice-to-have criteria, as I did the first set, Michaluk and Appleton have given each criterion a weight. This weight is one of relative importance. The weight scale is from 1 to 5, with one being the least weight and 5 being the highest. When they interview a person, they assess him or her on a similar 1 to 5 scale for each criterion. This assessed value is multiplied by the weight factor for each criterion. For example, if the person being interviewed is highly em-pathic in the interview, he would be assessed at the 5 level. Multiplying this value of 5 times the 3 weight of empathy gives an overall value for empathy of 15 for that person. The assessed values multiplied times the weight for all nice-to-have criteria are then added up and the total value of the individual can be compared with those of other people assessed the same say—hence, a choice with some rationality behind it can be made.

Criteria and Weight

A. Empathic (weight 3).

B. Emotionally mature and stable (weight 3).

C. Perceptiveness (weight 4).

D. Ability to organize and plan as demonstrated in his past work (weight 2).

E. Is a decision maker *vs.* a fence sitter (weight 3).

F. Familiar with the organization of the bank and its interpersonal relationships in great detail. This is included so that in dealing with a class of students from various areas in the bank, the person can draw on the interrelationship of one area to another to show various effects of the points the students are trying to master (weight 1).

G. Willing to work irregular hours (weight 2).

H. Self-motivated and independent. The reason for this is two-fold: first, in the training section they will not be told everything they have to do, although in the past they have; second, to do a good job in a laissez-faire environment requires this type of person (weight 5).

I. Creative and innovative (weight 5).

J. Involved in personal growth courses, such as university extension courses, etc. (weight 4).

K. Some past instructing or teaching experience, be it in a church group, scouts, or whatever (weight 1).

L. Desire to instruct (weight 5).

THIRD SET

This set is the simplest and easiest of all to use. It comes from Marit Stengels, Training Officer, Royal Insurance Group. It has only the following six criteria:

The first criterion is high interpersonal skills. Without this criterion being met, the person is not hired. It is the only definite, absolute or "must" criterion that Marit Stengels uses.

The next four criteria are important but not definites or absolutes. They are all of equal importance and hence are lumped together. They are (2) basic technical knowledge of insurance, (3) intelligent, (4) interested in training and (5) analytical. The last and bottom of the list is (6) ability to write. This is included because the trainer's job at Royal Insurance Group includes the development of training manuals and materials, hence writing skills are necessary.

CONCLUSION

It is hoped that these three sets of trainer selection criteria will help you to establish your own set for use in selecting trainers for your organization.

3

Choosing a Lesson Format

One of the hardest aspects of designing a lesson is deciding which format your lesson should follow. This article will explore the various styles available to classroom situations. Programmed instruction will not be considered because when PI is being used the instructor does not have a problem of design. The methods we are considering are: individualized study; pairs; small groups; class discussion; question and answer; show and tell; lecture; and printed material. These have been listed in order of their effectiveness in creating learning, as I see it. (For another view on this, see Peterson, 1972.)

DETERMINING FACTORS

To determine which format would be most effective in developing a lesson, the following four factors have to be considered:

1. frequency of use;
2. complexity of task;
3. time available for lesson; and
4. number of people performing the task.

Before doing the quiz in Figure 3.5, you will find an explanation of these factors helpful.

Frequency of use. This refers to the number of times the task is repeated and how frequently the student has to recall and use what was taught. In most jobs, frequency of use varies from task to task. For example, a line man in a public utility may (a) climb hydro poles three or more times a day—a high frequency use of his skill in pole climbing, (b) replace a pole about once a month—a moderately low frequency use of his pole replacement skills, and (c) face a specific emergency situation once every six months or more—a definitely low frequency use of the skills involved here.

You may have to break a task up into a number of subtasks in order to assign a frequency of use to each.

This is the *key* question to ask in designing a lesson for this factor: What is the time in hours, days, weeks between the repetitions of the task? Mark it on the scale in Figure 3.1.

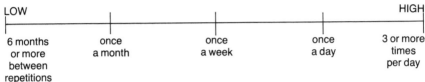

Figure 3.1. Frequency of use scale.

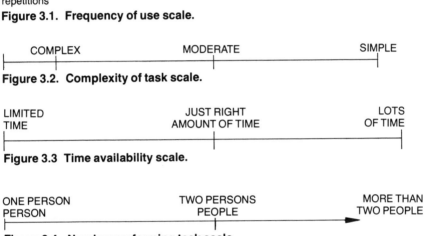

Figure 3.2. Complexity of task scale.

Figure 3.3 Time availability scale.

Figure 3.4. Number performing task scale.

Complexity of task. Here, you are asked to determine how simple or complex the task to be learned will be *for the learner*. For example, (a) sharpening a pencil is a simply learned task, (b) learning to tie a knot is relatively simple, but (c) winding a transformer, repairing a malfunctioning calculator, or dealing with an irate customer are all complex tasks to master.

This is the *key question* to ask when considering this factor: What is the complexity level of the task I'm instructing? Mark it on the scale in Figure 3.2.

Time available for lesson. Time is money, the experts agree, and—like money—nobody ever has quite enough. So what to do when you know the time available isn't sufficient to teach the material you have? Your choices are simple: you can extend the time, cut out some of the material, i.e., teach less, or "cover" the material and hope for the best. If your material is important and must be learned, you can consider only the first two.

This is the *key question* to ask: Do I have adequate time available to ensure real learning of the task being taught? Mark your answer on the scale in Figure 3.3.

Number performing the task. The number of workers doing the task also affects how you should design the training. If the task is done by a group of people working together, then the training is done using groups that will make up the work teams. If the work is done by two people working together, then the training should be done in pairs. The same is true of the individual situation. If the task is such that one person does it working alone at the work station, then having the task learned by a group or class working together has to be ineffective.

This is the *key question*: How many people work at this task? Mark it on the scale in Figure 3.4.

Now try the quiz in Figure 3.5. The way I determined my answers for the situations in Figure 3.5 is developed in the next section.

TECHNIQUES TO USE

1. Individualized study
2. Pairs
3. Small groups
4. Class discussion
5. Question and answer
6. Show and tell
7. Lecture
8. Printed material

SITUATION 1

Frequent use
Complex material
Lots of time
Does task alone

Circle no. of technique to use:

1 2 3 4 5 6 7 8

SITUATION 2

Frequent use
Complex task
Limited time
Does task alone

Circle no. of technique to use:

1 2 3 4 5 6 7 8

SITUATION 3

Used every 6 months
Complex material
Limited time
Does task with one other person

Circle no. of technique to use:

1 2 3 4 5 6 7 8

SITUATION 4

Used every 6 months
Complex material
Lots of time
Does with one other person

Circle no. of technique to use:

1 2 3 4 5 6 7 8

SITUATION 5

Used weekly
Moderate complexity
Time just right
Does task alone

Circle no. of technique to use:

1 2 3 4 5 6 7 8

Figure 3.5. Quiz

DETERMINING TECHNIQUES

To determine which techniques to use in teaching a particular task, use
Figure 3.6 in the following manner:

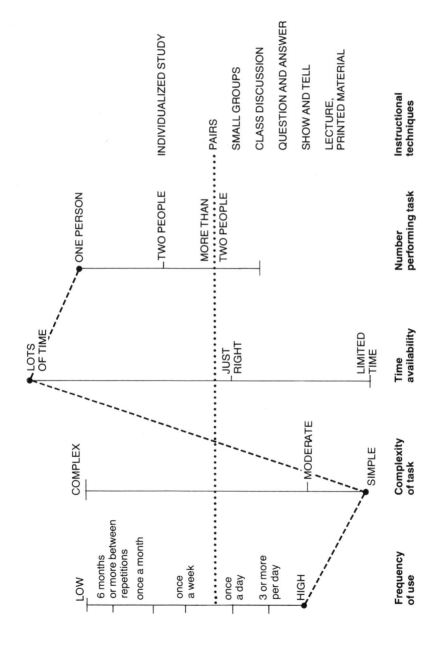

Figure 3.6. Determining the instructional technique to use for teaching a particular task

1. Mark a dot representing the use level on the frequency of use scale;
2. Mark the complexity level on the complexity-of-task scale;
3. Mark the time level on the time-availability scale;
4. Mark the people level on the number of people-performing-the-task scale;
5. Join the dots with a dashed line (see the sample line in Figure 3.6);
6. Visually evaluate the middle position between the dots—an eyeball average;
7. Draw the average line through the scales and extend it to the technique column (see the sample line in Figure 3.6);
8. Read the technique to use.

Repeat the procedure for the next instructional task.

In Figure 3.6, I have used the seven steps for Situation 1 that told me the most effective method for that situation is pairs. The answers for the other situations are (2) class discussion; (3) class discussion; (4) individualized study, (5) individualized study.

SUGGESTED READING

Peterson, R. J. Effectiveness of educational techniques compared, *Canadian Training Methods*, January-February, 1972, 13.

Preparing an Instructor's Manual

You have been asked by your organization to prepare a course to be presented by others who may or may not have had training in instructional techniques. This training idea will set out some guidelines we have used successfully in the past in putting together an instructor's manual. We will not cover how to determine the topic or the needs to be covered. What we intend to cover is the format, the layout, and the typing considerations in putting the instructor's manual together. The following are eleven tips we have found useful in preparing our instructor's manuals.

TIPS

1

In specifying elapsed lesson time in your manuals, do not use times such as *10:30* or *11:00*; use *1½* or *2 hr*. The reasons for this are:

    A. Course revisions will throw out the timings for all subsequent parts of the course manual;

    B. Timetable changes from course to course will alter the times;

    C. Student feedback can slow or speed up parts of the course and hence make exact timings meaningless.

Ken Barlow, Records Manager for the Ontario Ministry of Revenue, was co-author of this column. His records management background was instrumental in the development of many of the ideas expressed here. Ken has also been helpful to me in the design of evaluation forms, laying out copy for training manuals, and in comparing training concepts and ideas, as well as being instrumental in establishing the current information returns system I am using in the writing of most of these columns.

2

Time for a specific activity, such as a group activity to define the steps to problem solving, should be specified in the procedures of the lesson. The lapsed-time column is specifically for the timings on the lesson as a whole.

3

Use small (lower case) letters rather than capitals in your manuals. Small letters are more readable than capital letters. You shouldn't use capitals for the body of your manual for the following reasons:

A. People's eyes are more familiar with small letters.

B. Research comparing small-letter and capital-letter material shows that the eye actually scans only the top half of a printed line. With capitals, the eye has to scan the complete height of the letter, making reading more labored. Figure 4.1 visually highlights this research for you.

THE COMMUNICATION OF HIS FINDINGS IS THE

PRODUCT OF A MANAGEMENT-SERVICES

CONSULTANT'S SERVICE TO HIS CLIENT

The communication of his findings is the product of a

management-services consultant's service to his client.

Figure 4.1. Which is easier to comprehend: the text in capitals or in lower case letters?

C. Small letters provide far greater variation in form, too. Using small letters may seem like a trivial point in terms of manual preparation, but it isn't so trivial when one considers situations in which flustered instructors under classroom pressure situations are referring to the manual for help.

To further emphasize the small-letter vs. capital-letter situation, compare your reaction to the two typed passages in Figure 4.2. I'm sure you will prefer the lower case copy.

Students grow up in a school environment full of fear. If I want to be a human being interacting with human beings called students, I must take the risk of trusting them in ways that I have not trusted them before. If I know what they will do, I am not really taking a risk at all. I must somehow find ways of taking as many risks as they are taking. I must become as vulnerable as they are. (W. D. Romey, Risk-Trust-Love: Learning in a Humane Environment. Columbus, OH: Merrill, 1972, p. 155)

STUDENTS GROW UP IN A SCHOOL ENVIRONMENT FULL OF FEAR. IF I WANT TO BE A HUMAN BEING INTERACTING WITH HUMAN BEINGS CALLED STUDENTS, I MUST TAKE THE RISK OF TRUSTING THEM IN WAYS THAT I HAVE NOT TRUSTED THEM BEFORE. IF I KNOW WHAT THEY WILL DO, I AM NOT REALLY TAKING A RISK AT ALL. I MUST SOMEHOW FIND WAYS OF TAKING AS MANY RISKS AS THEY ARE TAKING. I MUST BECOME AS VULNERABLE AS THEY ARE. (W. D. ROMEY, RISK-TRUST-LOVE: LEARNING IN A HUMANE ENVIRONMENT. COLUMBUS, OH: MERRILL, 1972, P. 155.)

Figure 4.2. A comparison of lower case and capital letters

Group Activity: 2-3/4 hrs.

Visual 5   On flip-chart paper, build a list of techniques and

            ideas to use when one is reducing conflict using the

            Resolving Style of Conflict Correction.

            Allow the groups to start to work.

Pass out   Pass out to each group the following:

paper   — 3 or 4 sheets of flip-chart paper

and pens   — 1 felt pen per group

Remember, you can set pens and paper on the floor beside

each group. Don't plop them down in the middle of the

group and interrupt the participants' work on Visual 5.

After the pens and paper are passed out you can put strips

of masking tape on the walls, two strips per page for each

page you estimate the teams are going to post.

When groups are done, have them post their lists, using the

strips of masking tape.

Tell the groups to read each other's lists. You can read the

lists too, if you haven't already done so when the groups

were writing them.

**Figure 4.3. A sample lesson plan page using some of the layout techniques
discussed in this article**

4

Research has shown that our eyes travel about four inches when reading a line comfortably. Lines greater than this in length require increasingly greater amounts of eye movement. A normal typed page usually contains lines of about seven or more inches in length. Therefore, in preparing instructor's manuals, we suggest the following guidelines for easy readability:

- A line of 4 inches or 40 typed characters provides the easiest to read material;
- 5½ inches or 55 typed characters provide lines with moderate eye movement;
- A width greater than 6 inches or 60 typed characters per line should be avoided at all costs.

5

Use lots of white space to separate things. Some guidelines found useful in the use of white space are:

A. Double space when typing;

B. Double space to separate paragraphs;

C. Triple space for major changes, change of activities, group activities, etc.

The use of new pages should be reserved for the start of new topics or modules. Using new pages to separate activities leads to excessively bulky manuals.

While on the point of white space, it is interesting to note that the normal typewriter provides a space of 1/6 inch per line. Hence a triple double space provides only one inch of space between items.

6

Use boxes around notes to the instructor. This technique will separate the training material from the author's instructional notes, which are included to help instructors understand the lesson's procedures. Although time consuming to prepare, these boxes are immeasurably valuable to the instructor using the manual. See Figure 4.3 for an example of this boxing of instructional notes.

7

Figure 4.4 shows the basic layout of a page in the instructor's manual. You will note that no lines have been drawn to separate Aids, Procedure, and Lapsed Time columns. The reason for this is that our experience has shown the lines to be distracting from the total effect of the layout. We reserve lines for boxes and the wording on (a) visuals, (b) slides, or (c) chalkboard.

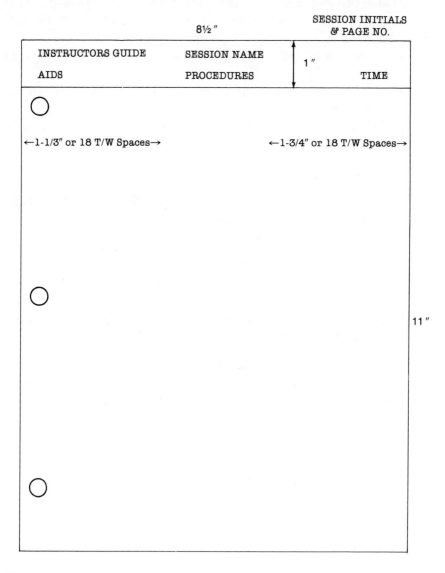

Figure 4.4. Scaled down representation, with measurements, for layout of the second page in each session

8

If you are using slides or visuals that contain wording, we also recommend the total content of the aid be included, in quotes, in the procedures section of the manual. We also recommend that the wording be underlined, as well as put in quotation marks.

9

Page headings vary depending on whether they are on the first, second, or subsequent pages of a topic.
The first page should contain:

A. Title of the course;

B. Topic of the session or module;

C. Purpose and/or objective of the topic;

D. Training aids and lesson materials;

E. Pre-topic preparation required (a) by the instructor before teaching the topic, (b) of the student before coming to the session;

F. Summary of the topic;

G. Coded page number in the upper outside corner.

The second page should contain:

A.   Session name in the center of the page;

B. Title for (a) Aids column, (b) Procedures column, (c) Lapsed Time column;

C. Coded page number in the upper outside corner.

The subsequent pages should contain:

A. Title of the manual in the upper inside corner;

B. Coded page number in the upper outside corner.

Nothing else is needed on these subsequent phases because the pattern of the manual will suffice to identify the different columns.

10

Coding page numbers. We recommend that the pages by numbered by sessions. Don't number the pages sequentially throughout the whole manual because changes will distort your numbering and require the whole manual to be readjusted. Some sample page codings and numbers for conflict resolving are CR-1, CR-2, CR-3, etc.; for decision making, DM-1, DM-2, etc.

11

Variety in your typed material makes the copy more interesting. A solid page of typed material doesn't invite one to plunge into reading the copy. Tips you can use to vary your copy are demonstrated in the following:

A. Type TWO OR THREE words in capitals;

B. LETTER SPACE two or three words in capitals. This means you place one space unit between each letter of each word and two extra spaces between words;

C. Underline a few key words;

D. Use periods . . . or dashes—in your copy;

E. USE HEADINGS.
    The use of headings and titles in various places within your main copy helps improve the look and people's desire to read your page;

F. Use Subtitles. Subtitles are used by indenting them into the line, capitalizing the key words, and underlining the whole subtitle;

G. Indent portions of your copy from 5 to 7 spaces:
    when you are quoting or when you want to emphasize a sentence or paragraph;

H. "Use quotation marks to highlight certain things";

I. In your typing use parentheses (brackets) around words or phrases;

J. And finally, here is a completely different one for you. Use indentations of 6 to 8 spaces for the bulk of your paragraph's copy.

A STANDARDIZED FORMAT

A standardized format in your manual's instructions will help all instructors to understand more easily the directions provided. We suggest the following headings and related definitions be included as one of the introductory pages to the instructor's manual.

Meaning of Headings

Ask: precedes a question for the instructor to ask the class.

Desired Response: precedes an expected answer, but not necessarily the only form the answer from the class may take.

Answer: precedes the exact and only answer to the preceding question.

Group Activity: precedes an exercise or some activity where the class is broken up into groups of from three to five people each. Group activities involving more than a maximum of five people per group will have the number of people per group specified.

Individual Activity: precedes a task that is to be done by each individual personally without help or collaboration with others.

Take-up: precedes a description of the techniques the instructor should use in processing, that is, having the class share the results of the activity that the class has been working on.

Boxed areas are not labeled because the box encloses the author's notes to the instructor on the material in the manual; the boxed information is not usually given to or explored with the class. You might call it private notes to the instructor.

5

Why Use Professional Writers?

Much of the time, money, and effort spent on preparing training materials is wasted. This is especially true of printed materials, be they case studies, reading notes, or actual training manuals.

Why aren't these materials doing the job they were designed to do? There's a myriad of good reasons . . . undefined objectives, inappropriate media for the actual objectives, and poor visual presentation. This list could go on and on with valid reasons for failure of material.

One of the most powerful causes of failure in printed material is poor writing.

Most companies would not even consider promoting a payroll clerk to the job of Actuary nor a secretary to the job of systems analyst unless they were specifically qualified. Yet, when it comes to needing a writer, all too often a disastrous assumption is made that anyone who speaks the language and knows the subject matter can communicate this knowledge effectively in writing. This simply is not so. Vocational competence does not add up to competence in communicating the related facts. And any assumption that it does leads to a proliferation of poor, ineffective material.

Training materials written by nonprofessional writers are in great supply and they make interesting reading. The following is an excerpt from a set of reading notes handed out at the end of a communications class.

Sidestepping Difficult Material
This often comes as the result of an unfortunate habit, acquired over a long period of time.

Marit Stengels was co-author of this column.

Many of us, when allowing the privilege of selecting either easy or more difficult material, all too readily decide on the former.

We select light, entertaining radio programmes, we watch television shows that demand little or no concentration; our choice of reading material provides but slight mental challenge, and our conversational encounters relate only to the most casual subjects.

Once this habit of selecting only the "easy" becomes established, then an enforced encounter with more difficult material often produces a listening challenge too great for us to meet.

School life provides an excellent, although unfortunate, example. With a well established habit of listening only to the "easy," the student suddenly faces more challenging material—material that he can no longer ignore.

A little self examination, honestly administered, will show us just how far we may have succumbed to this insidious bad listening habit.

What's wrong with what you just read? Better question: If you were the student, how would you feel? The passage is insulting and ends in a cliche of paternal condescension. But rather than attempting a critique of this segment, look at it rewritten.

Are You Listening?

Morris Bean, President of Bean and Co. in Ohio recalls dozing off during an industrial marketing expert's speech on the finer points of the art.

"I suddenly came to and became aware that I wasn't listening because I wasn't interested. And I realized I wasn't interested because I didn't know much about the subject. I then started listening."

How many times have you tuned out for somewhat the same reasons that Morris Bean did?

Most of us do quite often. Our school system firmly accustoms us to the habit of tuning out. Passive listening is reinforced by the casual content of radio and television. Thus, when you're confronted with something unknown, you have two choices. You can tune out or you can make a firm decision to listen actively.

The second choice is the far more advantageous. You can only estimate the value of what you are about to hear. To make any judgements about what a speaker has to say, you have to hear him. And that requires a decision to listen.

You can make your own comparison of the original segment and the rewritten version. Keep in mind that for any printed material to be effective, it must be as concise as possible, relate to the reader's needs, and interest him as well. It must also accomplish its objective, in this case, trying to get the reader to understand the need for active listening, *without talking down to him*.

While many companies still aren't doing so, they can and should use a professional writer in many areas of training and employee development.

Powers Regulators is an example of a place where this concept worked successfully. Some months before the scheduled date of a supervisory seminar for field people, the company contracted a writer to prepare a made-to-order case study for this seminar. The writer took the objective, researched the type of work these supervisor did and came up with a case study, implementing a role-play, which fitted specifically into these men's work situations and problems.

This case study had phenomenal success: because the men could relate to it, because it seemed to be a direct attack on the problems they were having, and because it was realistic to them. Involvement was total, excitement ran high, and the men could see direct application of the knowledge they were picking up.

Compare this type of reaction to the usual attitude to case studies, the standardized ones appearing in many courses.

At Powers Regulators, the case was successful because it fitted the situation. Moreover, it was professionally prepared. Many writers are excellently equipped to deal with conflict situations and to set up realistic human encounters. It's their life's work and it's reasonable that they should be able to do a far better and more effective job of it.

When you're going into print with training materials, you can't afford not to hire a professional writer.

Writer on Permanent Staff

Evaluate your needs, and if they warrant it, hire a fulltime writer.

If your company can't use a writing staff of two or more, make sure the writer you do hire is experienced. This isn't the area in which to let a novice flounder.

Service Organizations

Most large cities have management consultant firms that offer writing along with any other service you might wish to use. Community colleges can also be of assistance in this area.

If you don't have a large or continuing amount of writing to produce, hiring the service is the most economical way to do it. Screening individual writers can cost time and money. In the case of single assignments, it is especially true that while a consulting firm's fee may seem higher, it's more economical. The same holds true for some of the longer assignments.

You can choose your consulting firm through the help of the yellow pages in the phone book. A great help in screening these firms is knowing who their other clients are and seeing the kind of work they've done in the past.

Figure 5.1. What to look for in the writer you hire

Experience in writing to specific objectives:
Discuss the writer's sample writing with him in terms of objectives.

Diversified Experience:
The more areas a writer has worked in successfully, the greater the probability that he'll be able to adapt to writing for your needs.

English:
Look for easy-reading, idiomatic writing in the sample work he shows you. Stiff, long-winded, and hyper-grammatical writing spells out failure for a training manual.

Professional Attitude:
If you hire someone who would rather do, in his terms, "creative writing but there's no money in it," you may run into problems.

Figure 5.2. Working with the writer you hire

Before you assign anything to be written, determine your objectives. What exactly do you want to accomplish with this manual, case study, or film?

Give the writer all the material available on his assigment and give him necessary access to the resource people on the subject. Keep him up-to-date and informed at all times.

Make sure that the writer has a very clear picture of his responsibilities and the amount of authority he will be allowed to exercise.

Edit only when necessary, and explain why to the writer when you do so. Don't do any editing that you can't give solid reasons for. If editing is necessary, the best course is to tell the writer why something is not appropriate, and let him rewrite it.

Free-lance Writers

If you don't have enough work for a fulltime writer, and feel that a consulting firm would not be suitable for your purposes, hire a free-lance writer for specific tasks.

Finding a suitable free-lance writer is the biggest problem here. The yellow pages of the phone book in most large cities have a category for writers. Always ask to see sample work of any writer you contact.

And until you are satisifed that a particular writer can do the required job in your company, arrange for his first assignment to be a small one. Some writers will be willing to do that first assignment on speculation if it is not too long.

If no writers are listed in your yellow pages or you would prefer to find a writer another way, you can advertise or make inquiries at a library concerning writers' associations in your area. In Canada, you can contact the Canadian Authors Association, 22 Yorkville Avenue, Toronto 5.

Once you do find someone suitable, hang on to him! He becomes more and more valuable to you as he becomes familiar with your particular operation.

What an individual free-lance writer will charge varies, depending on how much work he has, how good his writing is, and how well he has been able to market his writing skill.

In calculating what a writer will cost you, you have to reckon in terms of savings, because you're producing more effective material if you use a good writer. And that's what this is all about:

Producing training materials that work.

How to Improve on JIT

This article had to be written. Why? Because JIT has outlived its usefulness. Recent educational technological developments have made JIT basically obsolete.

I realize that at this point I have probably split my reading audience. There is one group that knows about JIT and will be concerned about such a rash opening statement. The other group is made up of readers who haven't heard about JIT and want to know what it is.

What is JIT?

JIT stands for Job Instruction Training, which came into prominence during the Second World War. Its prominence developed because the war created a situation in which large numbers of unskilled people entered the work force. Their lack of skill and need for training to handle complex industrial tasks lead to the development of JIT.

What JIT accomplished, in terms of the war effort, was to greatly increase the efficiency of the job-instruction learning process. The increased efficiency that developed because of job instructor training cannot be disputed. In the 40s it worked better than anything available at that time in teaching skills on-the-job.

It even works today. But in the light of advances in educational technology, it needs redesigning, even though many trainers still revere its four-step method.

Figure 6.1 outlines the four-step method of Prepare the Learner, Present the Operation, Try Out Performance, and Follow-up. It also outlines How to Get Ready to Instruct as related to the setting up of any training plan that has already been prepared.

HOW TO GET READY
TO INSTRUCT

Have a Time Table:

Indicate how much skill you expect him to have, by what date.

Break Down the Job:

List important steps;
Pick out the key points (safety is always a key point)

Have Everything Ready:

Prepare the right equipment, materials, and supplies.

Have the Workplace Properly Arranged:

Set it up just as the worker will be expected to keep it.

If the Learner Hasn't Learned, the Teacher Hasn't Taught.

HOW TO INSTRUCT

Step 1. Prepare the Worker

Put him at ease.
State the job; find out what he already knows about it.
Get him interested in learning the job.
Place him in the correct position.

Step 2. Present the Operation

Tell + show + illustrate one important· step at a time.
Stress each key point; give reasons why.
Instruct slowly, clearly, completely, and patiently, giving no more than he can master.
Repeat—Question (Why, What, Where, When, Who, How); Check.
Make sure the learner really learns.

Step 3. Try Out Performance

Have him do the job; correct his errors.
Have him explain each key point.
Make sure he understands.
Continue until you know that he knows.

Step 4. Follow-up

Put him on his own; designate to whom he goes for help.
Check frequently; encourage questions.
Taper off extra coaching and close follow-up.

Figure 6.1. The traditional four-step JIT format

What's Wrong with JIT?

The four-step method is obsolete. JIT, in its original form, just doesn't fit into today's theories of adult education. When JIT originated, the emphasis was on what the instructor did whereas today the emphasis is on what the student does. In other words, educational technology has changed since JIT was originated and the main change has been from *instructor orientation* to *student orientation*.

Student orientation means we should design the learning steps to optimize student or worker involvement in the learning. This entails skipping the first two steps, Prepare the Worker and Present the Operation, and plunging the worker right into the third step, Try Out Performance. Put the worker right at the job, then reinforce right behaviors and correct wrong behaviors.

This may seem a bit drastic, but consider the following situation in which the instructor follows the steps of JIT.

The instructor is teaching an artillery class. It is early morning. The troops are out on the parade square, about to learn the parts of the 105 mm howitzer. To top this situation off, it is pouring rain and everyone is standing there, absolutely miserable. But the sergeant instructor has to go through the Prepare the Student phase because that's one of the steps. This means that the troops, rather than getting on with the job, have to bear with the instructor for five or ten minutes while he "prepares them to learn" a process that goes something like this:

"Gentlemen, this is a gun. You can observe that it is a gun because of the two wheels, the sight mechanism and the barrel here, and the breech block here. I am sure you all have some familiarity with guns. You've seen them in the movies. You've seen them in books and you have all, no doubt, wondered about the actual mechanism of guns many times when you have looked at them. Now this particular gun . . ." and on and on, to prepare the learner.

What's the learner thinking? Something like: "Is that drop of water going to penetrate right through my neck and trickle down my back or is it not . . .?" But he is being prepared to learn.

Then, having completed "preparing the learner," the instructor moves on into "presenting the operation." This show-and-tell session goes something like this: "Now, as I was saying earlier, this is the breech block. Observe the breech block. To open it, you take the handle here. Gripping it firmly with the right hand, slide—now notice—I say slide and push at the same time to release the breech block mechanism . . ." Meanwhile the troops are still standing there in the rain—learning. "Ah! that drop of water has penetrated down my back and it is about to enter my underpants . . ."

Results of Steps 1 and 2

Obviously, nothing has been learned in that situation. So what should be done? Well, consider the average student. Consider yourself in the above situation, having to learn about the 105 mm howitzer. What would you want to occur? The only thing I can think of is "let me get at that gun so that I can get in out of the rain."

This *let-me-get-at-it attitude* is true of almost all learning situations. Students always want to get at the machine or tool or experiment they are to learn. So let them. Eliminate steps 1 and 2. Most students want to get the learning over with so that they can become useful and productive.

Although you may feel my rain example is a bit extreme, doesn't a worker who is standing in a plant beside a new piece of equipment have somewhat similar feelings? I think so. In fact, I feel, he becomes curious about it, as do most people faced with new learning situations. They want to try things out, so why not take advantage of their curiosity by putting them directly into the learning situation?

Damage and Safety

Plunging the worker or student into the learning situation leads to questions such as: what happens when we turn the student loose? What damage could he do to the equipment, himself, and others? Consider the 105 mm howitzer. Could he fire it accidentally, or jam it, or damage it? Certainly he could, and this leads us to one of the tasks of the instructor in this learning situation. The instructor must be constantly on the alert to prevent accidents. This means he watches what all the students do. He prethinks his lesson in terms of student behaviors that could result in personal injury or damaged equipment. He considers where he must stand to be able to see, react, and prevent accidents.

Reducing the Risks

I imagine a number of us are now reacting with the conclusion that this danger problem is too great a risk to take. That's understandable but, from my point of view, it is unacceptable because we haven't, until recently, adequately considered our students' behavior.

At this point, let's go back to the 105 mm howitzer and weigh for ourselves what we would do if we were plunged right into the lesson on the howitzer, especially if we had never used the gun and were totally unfamiliar with it.

More than likely, each of us would take a careful, slow, plodding approach. We would look the gun over carefully, considering whether we should touch it. We might even look at what others were doing. We would watch the instructor to see if he approved of what we were doing. We would want to know how we were doing. We would have questions to ask and answers we would need.

In other words, we are not likely to jump in with both feet and create a dangerous situation. This doesn't mean we wouldn't create some dangerous situations inadvertently, but in general, accidents or damage wouldn't happen. What this does mean is that if we plunge the student into the lesson he is going to be careful, cautious, and consider each thing he does. He is also going to be looking to the instructor to find out how he is doing.

Another thing to consider by omitting steps 1 and 2 in the instructional process is who is at fault if the student goes wrong? The student? Certainly not. The teacher has to be at fault because he hasn't told the student how to do anything. All the teacher has done is to tell the student to go ahead and figure it out as best he can. The student realizes that under this set of conditions he can't be wrong and hence feels freer to try things. He realizes he can't be accused of not having listened or of not following orders, since none were given in this new learning environment. The person at fault if a student goofs has to be the instructor; he wasn't performing his new role adequately.

The Instructor's Role

Every student is likely to seek information on how he is doing during the Tryout Performance. This desire on the part of students to find out how they are doing leads us to what the intructor's role should be (or what the instructor should be doing while the student trys to learn under these conditions).

I have already mentioned that the instructor must: (a) be alert to prevent accidents, watching what all students are doing, (b) have prethought his lesson in terms of student behaviors, (c) have positioned himself to see, react, and prevent accidents. There are two more elements in the instructor's role: (d) reward, praise, or reinforce correct student behaviors, and (e) ask the students leading but thought-provoking questions.

Reinforcing and questioning the student are the keys to this revamped JIT approach. The trainer must reinforce the students in doing the things that they are doing and that the trainer wants them to continue doing. The key to reinforcing is to *catch the students when they are right*, and let them know you have seen them doing the right thing. When students ask, "Should I do this or should I do that?," the instructor can reinforce the correct action. If the student says, "What do I do now?," the trainer should respond with a question that will cause the student to explore various aspects he hadn't considered up to that point.

Using this new approach, the instructor can interact with the student's learning process, letting the student know that he is in an area that he should explore carefully. The instructor must reward, reward, and then reward some more. One should remember that all of us like to be told we are right, and the more often we are told that we are right the better we feel and the better we will work on the task at hand. Students are the same. They *never* get enough rewards in any learning situation.

Through this rewarding-questioning kind of approach (or developmental approach), the instructor can very quickly and safely shape the new skills that he wants.

The New JIT

Where does this leave us in comparing the original JIT steps and the new approach after I have completely bypassed the "prepare the learner" and "present the operation" steps? In a way they are included in the Tryout Performance step.

I feel that the four steps, as originally stated, were not meant to have equal weight. They get it today, but they shouldn't. If we wish to give the four steps proper weight, we should give almost all of the weight to step 3, the Tryout Performance part. This would decrease the emphasis that steps 1 and 2 now receive.

When the four steps are printed, all we should be able to read easily is the third step. To read steps 1 and 2, we should have to use a magnifying glass to make out what they say. This would create the right weighting. Step 4, Follow-up, can be printed in a size that can just be read but only by looking closely with the naked eye.

The Future JIT

In conclusion, now that I have destroyed the original four steps, let me propose a new four-step method in which steps 1 and 2 are at least comparable in stature to step 3.

Step 1. Analyze the training problem, (see Mager, 1970);
Step 2. Set behavioral training objectives (see Mager, 1962);
Step 3. Let the student do the task;
Step 4. Follow-up.

REFERENCES AND READINGS

Mager, R. F.*Preparing Instructional Objectives*. Belmont, CA.: Fearon, 1962.

Mager, R. F., & Pipe, P. *Analyzing Performance Problems; or You Really Oughta Wanna*. Belmont, CA.: Fearon, 1970.

7

A Lesson Design for Real World Training: Recruiting Salesmen

The design presented here is simple and highly adaptable to many training situations. It breaks conventional training boundaries. The concepts or key points involved have been printed in italics for easier reviewing of the main parts. The theme of this design is: *make the student aware of the information he has about the task at hand, and have him use it to determine how to do the task*.

In the conversation that follows, note the way Mr. B, who is with a major life insurance company, has set up the learning situation so that the students have to do the task using their own information—information they all have in their heads *before* the training starts. The training design involves a deep consideration of the students and their reactions to a learning situation, but let's hear it from Mr. B as he talked about it in a recent conversation.

Pat: Mr. B, I'd like to know what, initially, made you feel there was a need to redesign a program to teach managers techniques for recruiting salesmen.

Mr. B: I decided to redesign a program that already had six sessions giving the students the *practical* side of management with the company's philosophy of recruiting and managing a branch. This local program was basically a series of six lectures on how to recruit, how to train men, how to supervise men, and how to motivate men.

Pat: For the training, recruiting, motivating. . . .

Mr. B: And for the supervision. Right. The result was that out of six people who completed the course, two or three left the company altogether and the other three didn't recruit anyone.

Pat: So you had six people out of six who didn't recruit.

Mr. B: Right. The program didn't work. To be able to recruit you have to be able to get names. We'd told them how to get names: what to say, where to look, when to do it, how to set time tables—the whole bit. They had copies of all this, but *nothing happened with the lectures*.

Pat: *Although you taught salesmen recruiting, no recruiting of potential salesmen took place.*

Mr. B: Right. *You've got to do more than just tell them how to do it. They've got to do it themselves. The only way they are going to know they can recruit is to have done it during the course.* I decided to try taking them right out onto the street to do recruiting. I had read about a successful branch manager who went out every morning from 8:00 to 10:00 and contacted shop owners, asking them if they knew of anyone who would be interested in a career in life insurance. This simple idea had worked for this fellow, so I thought I could transfer it to the recruiting situation.

Pat: *So you looked at what a successful person was doing–and then said, "Let's try that."*

Mr. B: I could not tell our trainees how to recruit or give them a copy of the book because we had done that in the previous program. They had the book. They could have read it and said, "This is how this man is successful and I can do the same thing," but they didn't do it.

Pat: Your previous students had the information but didn't use it.

Mr. B: In my mind, they lacked the self-confidence to try something. *So I included in the precourse letter the idea of approaching merchants. I asked the trainees to come with a five-minute talk they could give on the street.*

Pat: You sent a precourse letter asking them to prepare a talk they would use when meeting a storeowner?

Mr. B: Right. I also included three or four pages of background on nominator soliciting (this is what it is called).

Pat: So your design for the first day was to say, "Now, let's go out on the street and into that store and *try it*."

Mr. B: When they came into the first session at 8:30 in the morning, I welcomed them and asked if they wanted to know anything about what was going to happen over the next three days. There were no questions, so I said, "Do you have your talks prepared?" They all said, "Yes." When I asked if they wanted to try out their talks before they went on the street, they all looked at each other, so I repeated the question.

Pat: *You were creating an element of safety there for those who had never done this. What was their reaction then?*

Mr. B: *Silence. Everyone just sat there. They couldn't believe it. Then one man said, "Did you really want us to prepare a talk to give on the street?"* I said, "Yes," and another fellow said, "I didn't understand your letter too clearly." So I took out a copy of the letter, read it over again, and said, "What is it you don't understand?" Silence. Then I said, "Take fifteen or twenty minutes either to work and prepare a talk or to fix up your talk, because you are going to give it on the street in less than half an hour."

Pat: Had they basically rejected trying it out on each other or was the half-hour period going to give them a chance to shift it and try things among themselves?

Mr. B: They were starting to face the reality that they were going out on the street.

Pat: Although you had indicated in the precourse letter that the trainees should come in prepared to face the real world, they didn't interpret it as being the *real* world.

Mr. B: Right. *They just thought, "This is another training course that is going to be sheltered, that is going to be away from what I do every day.* I'm going to do it here in the classroom and then never again because I don't live in this (classroom) world."

Pat: Right. It's not that they didn't come in prepared; they didn't come in prepared to face the "real world." *The thrust of really going out to face the world seems to change the whole student position.*

Mr. B: Yes. After they prepared their talks, I asked, "Would you like to try them before going out?" *I was very positive with them as each person tried his talk. I tried to support them.*

Pat: You felt you had to encourage them in this trial period. These men who had never done any recruiting were being asked to prepare for recruiting based on their previous experience?

Mr. B: Yes. I didn't want to give them anything I had designed because if they used it, it might not be successful for them or it might be successful and they would see it as mine. *I wanted to show them that they could do it, that what they were developing could be useful and successful. I had to have faith in them, more than they had in themselves.*

Pat: So this is a problem you had in the original design of the new lesson. Is this a safe area for me to try things in?

Mr. B: Yes.

Pat: When they practiced on each other you saw that they had reasonable models and your faith in them was supported?

Mr. B: Right.

Pat: They also were showing signs of needing rewarding encouragement from you.

Mr. B: Right. I had to reward them at that point, building them up enough to go out and do a reasonable job. *The other thing I thought about when I was designing this session was: what's the worst thing* *that can happen if I send these people out on the street? The worst that could happen would be their discovery that they couldn't do the job.*

Pat: Oh? You weren't concerned from the company's standpoint at all?

Mr. B: My first concern was whether the trainees couldn't do the job. Later in the session, they admitted their fear that they couldn't do the job and they were afraid of facing it. The other fear I had was that they might embarrass the company. However, I concluded that since they are salesmen to begin with, they could sell. They had enough confidence, poise, knowledge, and background not to embarrass the company.

Pat: The *background* of these people was solid enough to enable them to perform under pressure, even without preparation. Preparation was only to help them feel more secure.

Mr. B: Right. They practiced their talks, and I built them up. We had coffee, they discussed their fears, and this relaxed them even more. Then I assigned each trainee to what I called an observer, someone from the department who would just go along. The trainee would introduce the observer as his associate.

Pat: The observer then becomes a support and help to the trainee if needed.

Mr. B: The observer also was given a questionnaire. Each time the trainee and observer completed making a call on a businessman, they would go outside and fill in the questionnaire, making notes to share with the others and myself when they returned.

Pat: Instead of another established person from the organization, you could have had two trainees go together?

Mr. B: Yes, I tried that in a later course.

Pat: Did it work, too?

Mr. B: Yes. It worked even better.

Pat: Why? Any comments on that?

Mr. B: Well, both trainees felt they were in the same boat. No one was watching them. There was no pressure. They had felt pressure even in the classroom preparation session because I was an observer.

Pat: *You found they worked better with a peer than with a more experienced person.*

Mr. B: They got better results and they were more confident about going in. No one was judging them.

Pat: Other than themselves?

Mr. B: *They tried harder with another trainee than with an observer.*

On the first day, when they went out, I didn't want any names. I didn't want any interviews. All I asked them to do was to try ten approaches in an hour.

Pat: You wanted ten approaches in an hour?

Mr. B: Sure; they were only five minutes each. That's only fifty minutes and they were going from store to store.

They were instructed to introduce themselves to the store manager, introduce the associate, and explain that they were in the recruiting field and were not there to sell anything. They were to explain their recruiting problem—finding the kind of individual they described for the job they had. Then they'd ask, "Do you know anyone who would fit this kind of career?" If the owner hesitated, they would add, "Since you have businessmen and salesmen calling on you, you probably have a stack of business cards you could go through to find some names." This was a standard approach. The goal was ten of these approaches for that day.

Pat: You didn't put it on the basis of how many names they came back with?

Mr. B: Not until the second day. On the first day, I felt that if they could make the ten approaches by themselves, they would feel they had accomplished something.

Pat: In other words, you are saying that one of the biggest hurdles was just to approach anyone?

Mr. B: Yes.

Pat: So your first day's design set up no pressure to get anybody.

Mr. B: The success of this one was making the ten approaches. They *all* made ten approaches. No, I'm sorry: one didn't. He was more scared than the others, and he was rejected on his first approach. The second time, he went to the office of someone he knew and spent half an hour talking. He still came back with two names, though. However, he didn't go on from there to face strangers, nor did he make the ten approaches. All the others did.

Pat: Your design indicated that they would have problems approaching people and this person exemplified that idea. Given an hour, he just couldn't face people. Did he overcome it?

Mr. B: On the second day, he went out and made between ten and fifteen approaches.

Pat: You're also saying that this man, although he failed, still came back with two names, which wasn't a requirement at all?

Mr. B: His coming back with two names spurred the others on; they saw someone coming back with names even though it wasn't structured that way.

Pat: Was he the only one who came back with names?

Mr. B: No. Two others came back with one each. We got four names.

Pat: I assume your session is now at about noon on the first day.

They came back after lunch for a debriefing?

Mr. B: Yes. All I asked was "What happened?" Each person stood up and explained the problems he had.

Pat: Did some have solutions that helped the others?

Mr. B: Yes. Those who didn't get names asked the others how they did it. When one person would say, "I did this and this and this," the others asked, "Well show us; let's do it." As it turned out, I was sitting back and they were role playing with each other and talking over ideas.

Pat: Did they suspect that the next day would be the real thing?

Mr. B: No. Not until the end. They thought it was a one-shot affair.

Pat: It's interesting that they were already into getting names, which is what you wanted them to do the next day.

Mr. B: Right. Eventually I said, "We are going to do it again tomorrow, so if you like, you can take fifteen or twenty minutes now to redesign your talks using some of the others' ideas." They did this and practiced their talks. *In this practice, I asked questions about what they were doing*: "Why was Henry successful?", "Why Bob?", "Why weren't you successful?", "What do you think about your talk?". Asking these questions enabled them to come up with answers such as "I wasn't prepared enough," "I stumbled," "I didn't know what to say," "My nervousness showed," and I didn't know how to help myself."

Pat: *The one who only made two calls would never have made any calls under the other type of training.*

Mr. B: None at all. His fear level was too high.

Pat: Then the program continued on day two with the trainees out again—trying this time to get names?

Mr. B: We started at 8:30 A.M. I asked if they had any questions before we went out on the street. A couple of them said, "It's snowing outside. We can't go out when it's snowing." I ignored that. Another person said, "Let's go to the boat show this morning. There are lots of people there." I had to confront them with "You are going out on the street and each individual has to get one name." Off they went with their observers. When they came back each had at least one name. Altogether they had nineteen names.

Pat: That's more than three each.

Careful consideration of the thoughts expressed in the previous dialogue should allow you to redesign some of the training you do to more directly relate it to the real world.

Other Results

Mr. B: After the second day, the trainees were saying: "This really works," "I really can recruit," "I'm not as scared as I was," "I was really upset about facing the job."

Pat: They could say all those things because they actually had done it.

Mr. B: Yes. They had recruited. From the nineteen names, five or six interviews to hire salesmen resulted.

Two more highlights:

Pat: Putting them at this task took more time. The old training on this name solicitation took a morning, didn't it?

Mr. B: Yes. A half day was spent with someone talking to the students about sources of names.

Pat: Well, you now spend a day and a half on the same issue. Although you've tripled the time, you've gone from no names solicited to four obtained on day one and nineteen on day two. With this experience, do you feel you could do it in less time now?

Mr. B: Yes. This was the first time I'd tried something like this. I might get it done in a day now.

Pat: *So one requirement for changing to this type of training is enough time to try using it.*

Mr. B: *You've got to have the time to do it. Also, I think the program can be continued this way.*

Pat: You could have gone from there to phoning and interviewing actual people. Instead of talking about it, you could have carried the training into a real world context and even tried training a new recruit.

Mr. B: That's right. This is what it opened up.

Pat: Let's push it. Had your trainees been on any other training programs?

Mr. B: Yes. They wondered why they hadn't had any training of this type before. They even asked for this design in their sales training.

Pat: They said this, even though their initial reaction to it was to fight it?

Mr. B: They did.

Pat: *So the major problem you had as a trainer, once you got it rolling, was being firm enough to push it.*

Mr. B: *Exactly. If you back off, the game is over.* It's the funniest thing. They wanted all their future management training changed into practical things they could use.

In a training session, I asked each representative to come and do a twenty-minute training session for the others. After they would train, we would talk about it, and then we would do it again. One of the representatives went back home and changed the training he did. He conducted a training session on telephone selling, in which the trainees really picked up the phone and called a customer. Their training included feedback and discussion of what happened. As a result, sales increased dramatically.

Pat: Someone took the concept we are talking about here and used it in sales training sessions. *Instead of talking about selling, they found that doing the real thing seemed to help them.*

Mr. B: Yes. They talk about how they will phone somebody and ask for an appointment, and then they do it while all of them are sitting there. Then they talk about the experience.

Pat: So, this person took the concept of *"let's not talk about it; let's have a real world here-and-now experience."*

Mr. B: You've got it.

Pat: That's an element that we haven't even mentioned. The *now* concept.

Mr. B: It seems that the students want the real world thing.

What's Wrong with This Lesson?

READ THIS LESSON DESIGN

Lesson Topic
Cost Improvement Program.

Lesson Objective
Each student will implement a Cost Improvement Program in his department within two months of this lesson.

Student's Background
One to seventeen years of management experience.

Lesson Outline

A. Ask the students: "What are the problems in installing a Cost Improvement Program?"

B. List the student responses on a chalkboard.

C. Break the class into groups and have each group develop ways to overcome the problems.

D. Have each group present its recommendations. (Write these recommendations on a chalkboard for all to see and compare.)

E. Establish a common plan from collected recommendations.

F. Develop an implementation program.

G. Do appropriate in-plant follow-up.

TAKE THIS QUIZ ON THE LESSON

Check either *Yes* or *No* for each question.

Yes No

___ ___ 1. Should the lesson have its timing specified?

___ ___ 2. Does the lesson approach its objective well?

___ ___ 3. Is student participation ensured in the lesson?

___ ___ 4. Would the lesson be interesting and involving for the students?

___ ___ 5. Does the lesson plan provide suitable guidance for the instructor who prepared it?

___ ___ 6. Is the lesson objective stated in behavioral terms?

___ ___ 7. Does the lesson's design ensure that the instructor won't talk too much?

___ ___ 8. Should the lesson have an introduction preceding the opening question, "What are the problems in installing a Cost Improvement Program?"

___ ___ 9. Have the students had practice in this lesson, in solving problems in a Cost Improvement Program?

___ ___ 10. Is the whole lesson well summarized or concluded?

___ ___ 11. Does the lesson take a positive approach to teaching the implementation of a Cost Improvement Program?

___ ___ 12. Should the lesson be restructured to ensure reaching the objective?

_____

No self-rating chart is available for this quiz to permit you to compare your responses with those of other trainers. I can say that if you got eleven right, your thinking and reactions are somewhat like mine. I said eleven instead of twelve because I changed one of my answers in preparing this article; that, I felt, was wrong.

The following trainers helped me field test the quiz: Gord Bonner, Consumers Glass; Ann Richie, Ontario Provincial Police; Bob Peterson, Ontario Hydro, and John Whitley, Eatons of Canada. Their average number correct was 6.7. How did you fair in relation to them?

EXPLORING THE QUESTIONS

Now that you have done the quiz, consider each question in turn. This exploration of each question should help to determine what's wrong with the cost improvement lesson.

Question 1: Should the lesson have its timing specified?
Answer: No

I expect a number of you said yes and in a way you, too, are correct. I'll delve into why yes is also correct after I explain why I said no. Because of the way this lesson is structured, it is next to impossible, even with many years of training experience, to predict how long each part will take. If you do set a time to finish each part, there is a good chance that this time pressure will force you to cut off some meaningful dialogues. This pressure to keep to the schedule would destroy the lesson, reduce student thinking, and hinder your freedom to explore the subject freely and deeply with your students.

Timing in a lesson imposes a restraint that has to affect the instructor's presentation.

Now I haven't said timing isn't important, I have said *it is a restraint*. Timing is necessary, but in this lesson it should be for the whole lesson, not for its parts. This, of course, presents problems. The main problem is: what if I don't cover it all? What if we only get to the end of Part C in the three hours the lesson was scheduled to take? My solution is to continue the lesson the next time the class meets. Obviously, if they used three hours effectively and only reached the end of Part C, the students probably need more time to internalize and adequately consider the subject area.

Remember, the lesson's objective is to implement the program. You probably can cover the subject in half an hour, if you really put it to the class. Whether they then implement it is another story. If the lesson takes two classes instead of the one you expected (which is the yes side of this question) then you have to: (a) drop some future lesson, (b) hope some other parts go faster than expected, (c) schedule more classes. But don't rush the lesson, learning, or development that is occurring.

Question 2: Does the lesson approach its objective well?
Answer: No.

The lesson does not approach the objective at all. The objective states that each student will *implement*. The lesson does not implement the cost improvement program. The closest the outline comes to implementation is in Part F when the class discusses the steps to be used in implementing the program. It may seem a moot point to say this lesson only establishes the program, but the truth of the situation is that there is a gigantic gulf between establishing a program as outlined in this lesson and actually implementing a cost improvement scheme.

As for how *well* the lesson approaches the objective, all you have to ask is: couldn't the session start just as well at Part C? That's right— leave out Parts A and B, they accomplish little. Start with Part C and the overall performance of the lesson will improve.

The word *performance* is important. In this lesson we have a performance objective not a knowledge development or theory objective. Yet in the lesson as structured, there is little performance. The students don't install and run a cost improvement system. They only theorize about such a system. What should be done is a restructuring of the whole lesson. A careful look at the objective shows that *the objective is not a classroom objective at all*. This whole lesson isn't needed at all. The session should occur right within the job structure, not in a classroom. It is a program unto itself. It may help to have group conferences to discuss overlapping concepts and exchange ideas but it certainly doesn't require a classroom effort to implement it. What is required is some darn good coaching on the job by the organization's managers.

Questions 3 and 4: Is student participation ensured in the lesson? Would the lesson be interesting and involving for the students?

The explanation of these two is tied together. Both questions, although appearing to have yes answers, should be answered no to be right.

To explain these two no answers is tricky. The best way to explain the rationale of why the lesson doesn't ensure participation or interest is to say the lesson totally lacks a nuts-and-bolts approach. It plays games rather than getting down to the real task.

How can it gain real participation and interest when all it deals with is theory? Trainees in an industrial setting want to deal with reality, and reality to them is the actual work situation. To create reality in any lesson, present class members with some problem from their work place and relate it to theory. Then stand back and watch as the theory is attacked, explored, criticized, destroyed, and eventually restructured to provide a valid solution to the problem. The participation, involvement, and interest that result when reality manages to *slip into* a session are totally different from what occurs in most of our training sessions.

Most sessions we trainers put on *never* slip into reality. We avoid it. Reality, one can say, has almost no place in the classroom. Reality threatens us. Reality often destroys the appearance of a smoothly running, properly conducted class. Reality leads to confusion, to students going out to the plant or office to get things. Reality leads to a total lack of teacher-centeredness in the classroom. In fact, someone looking in might say, "Who's in charge of that class?" Finally, reality usually causes the content for the session to be pushed to the side and only marginally drawn on—and then only as it relates to the ideas being worked out in the class.

Question 5: Does the lesson plan provide suitable guidance for the instructor who prepared it?

Answer: Yes.

An easy question for most of us, thrown in to keep up our morale.

Question 6: Is the lesson objective stated in behavioral terms?

Answer: Yes.

I say that yes with some trepidation. I tried out the quiz on a number of trainers (see the footnote for their names), and of all the questions this one led to the most controversy for me personally. I had originally said yes to this question, but in trying it out I got a number of no answers. Fortunately, I asked the trainers why they said no and learned in each case that they felt the objective needed a percentage figure for the actual cost improvement. In other words the *no* people felt that the objective should have read: "Each student will implement a cost im-provement program *that will result in a 5% reduction in the overall costs* in his department within two months of this lesson."

The *yes* person finally restored my confidence after the series of no answers. When I again asked why, he said, "It is in behavioral terms." I then confronted him with the *no* people's logic and a mass discussion followed. (The discussion was fun and I'm sorry I didn't record it, or I would present it here).

The upshot of the conversation was that we were right. The answer to this question was yes—but the yes could be qualified. That is, the answer is yes *but* the wording of the objective could be more specific.

One other personal thing I discovered while trying out this question was the danger that lies in trying to assess the validity of objectives you have written yourself. I found that I am inclined to see my own objec-tives as being great. How to overcome this problem of gloating over one's own objectives is a mystery to me. The best technique, although hard to take, is to show the objectives to others. That is a sure way to improve them.

Question 7: Does the lesson's design ensure that the instructor won't talk too much?

Answer: No.

No lesson, no matter how well it is designed to provide for student involvement, will prevent an instructor from talking. Any instructor will talk if he wants to. No lesson design alone can stop him. To reduce instructor talk requires a personal commitment by the instructor himself. Without this commitment, any instructor will talk too much. In other words, this lesson will get the involvement of the students, but it will not stop the instructor from talking.

Question 8: Should the lesson have an introduction preceding the opening question, "What are the problems in installing a cost improvement program?"

Answer: No.

To deal adequately with why *no* is right would require a whole column by itself. Briefly, the key points are:

First, the question does introduce the lesson; it tells us the aim of the session. It motivates the students and gets them involved. It provides an outline of what is coming. It certainly gives us the topic, and if the question has been properly developed it links the lesson to the students' backgrounds and experiences.

Second, one might feel that some input is necessary for the students before plunging them into the task. The answer is a *definite no*.

To illustrate this point, Marit Stengels tells the following story of a recent experiment she tried.

A group of adult students, taking a course to upgrade them to the grade twelve level, was given a case study on management techniques. The students were not managers and they had no previous instruction or experience with management techniques, but they solved the case. In fact, they solved it almost as well as a group of managers would have. Conclusions from this experiment lead to many questions about management training, but more relevant here is the lack of input *from the instructor*. This lack of input is critical because the more starting input the instructor provides, the less learning the student will achieve.

This leads to the third reason: the more the student discovers for himself, the better is the lesson's overall design, because it provides a real learning experience for the student.

Question 9: In this lesson, have the students had practice in solving problems in a cost improvement program?

Answer: No.

If you said yes, I agree with you if you add one word—*hypothetically*. In other words, the hypothetical answer is yes, but in terms of reality the answer is no. Because the lesson begs for reality, no is the only answer.

The lack of reality is highlighted in this session by the absence of any attempt in the lesson outline to relate the students' involvement to the actual job situations.

Question 10: Is the whole lesson well summarized or concluded?

Answer: Yes.

This is true because of the repetition within the session itself. This cyclical type of repetition is best illustrated in this lesson by Part E, the establishing of a common plan. In their effort to design a common course of action, the students are obviously going to refer to the recommendations that were posted in Part D. Summarizing and concluding activities also occur in the transition from establishing a common plan in Part E to developing an implementation plan in Part F. All this repetition and recycling over the same area can only make an instructor's summarizing and concluding statements appear irrelevant to the students.

Question 11: Does the lesson take a positive approach to teaching the implementation of a cost improvement program?

Answer: No.

What could be more negative than opening with "What are the problems. . . ." If the students hadn't seen any problems before, they surely should after this part of the lesson. It teaches them what adversities have to be overcome, which is negative, rather than delving into ways and means of implementing the program, which would be positive.

This opening could also create a classic behavior problem for the teacher. Students may react to this session on implementing a cost improvement program with the feeling, "Why should I start this? Haven't I got enough problems to deal with already?"

I say classic because, as usual, the students will hide their problems from the instructor. Thus, we have the classic instructional problem: the students are not communicating their feelings and reactions and the teacher is unaware of the existence of their reactions to his lesson and the development of their problems. Result: little learned.

Question 12: Should the lesson be restructured to ensure reaching the objective?

Answer: A very loud yes; do restructure.

The least that can be done is to knock out Parts A and B and start the lesson at C. If possible, redesign the lesson to bring in reality and get rid of its hypothetical nature.

This lesson, like many others, should start where it ends. Begin the lesson at Part F with the statement, "Let's figure out how we can improve our cost figures." This can frighten us as trainers because that is all there is to the lesson plan. There is nothing else. One must hope that the students will respond, will take up the task. They usually do, *if* the trainer and his organization want meaningful training.

Part

2

Learner-Centered Teaching

Questions on a Learning Situation

The purpose of this article is to take a look at a very familiar learning situation that is removed from the job, but probably has been experienced by everyone. Figure 9.1 outlines the situation, the questionnaire asks questions about it. You may read Figure 9.1, and then answer the questions before comparing your answers with mine, or you may read straight through, answering as you go. If you have any violent disagreements, or if you have any positive comments, I'd be glad to hear from you.

1st: Read This

**THE SITUATION
UNDER CONSIDERATION**

You are at a friend's place for an evening. It is decided to play a game like monopoly or bridge. Only your host knows how to play the game. The set-up, rules, tricks, things to watch for, and how the game is played are explained in full detail to you by your host. Finally you interrupt, saying, "I'm lost—let's play one round and see how it goes."

Figure 9.1

2nd: Answer These Questions on the Situation

THE QUESTIONNAIRE

Check the answer(s) you feel are right

1. Who controls the learning?
   ___ The host   ___ The novice player
2. More explaining by the host would have made the new player able to play the game.
   ___ True ___ Questionable ___ False
3. The host would have succeeded in his explanation if he had used a more participative approach, i.e., asked questions, leading the novice player to think up answers.
   ___ True ___ Questionable ___ False
4. Why did the novice interrupt the host?
   ___ Frustration
   ___ Failure to absorb information
   ___ Not listening carefully
   ___ Desire to learn
   ___ The host was a friend, so it was easier than if the instructor were a stranger
   ___ His mind was wandering
   ___ The explanation proved too complicated to understand and absorb
5. Interrupting the host's explanation of how to play with "I'm lost, let's play . . ." will so disrupt the host, he won't be able to instruct properly.
   ___ True ___ Questionable ___ False
6. Learners learn by doing; few of us will argue with that statement. To teach how to play the game, the key to any lesson plan would be to get the novice playing.
   ___ True ___ Questionable ___ False
7. The situation in Figure 9.1 presents a parallel to most instructional situations.
   ___ True ___ Questionable ___ False
8. Figure 9.1 briefly outlines the essence of effective instructing.
   ___ True ___ Questionable ___ False
9. Learning "to play games" like bridge, chess, etc., is easier than most organizational learning requirements.
   ___ True ___ Questionable ___ False
10a If, some evening, you find yourself confronted by a novice wanting to join you in your favorite game, you would normally instruct him/her to play by:
   ___ 1. An explanation of rules, tricks, steps, etc., followed by trying to play.
   ___ 2. An explanation with some dialogue between the two of you, followed by trying to play.
   ___ 3. An explanation for three minutes only and then trying to play.
   ___ 4. Starting right in trying to play, adding brief explanations only as needed.
10b Go through the above and decide how you would do it as a trainer, not as a friend or host. Write a *b* next to your choice.
11. The host's starting position in relation to the knowledge level of the learners in Figure 9.1 is similar to many instructional situations in that the students know:
   ___ Nothing
   ___ Little
   ___ Basic things
   ___ A moderate amount
   ___ Most of how to play

3rd: Read on

1. Who controls the learning?

Answer: The novice player.

The instructor—in this case, the host—never controls learning. As an instructor, I want to control the learning, but I don't. I never do. The learner does; he determines how and if he will absorb what is being instructed. Control of learning rests with the student totally. The instructor's job is to help the student reach the learning objective. What the instructor controls is the situation, not the learning. If the question was who controls the learning *situation*, the answer would be the host.

2. More explaining by the host would have made the new player able to play the game.

Answer: False.

I don't like the answer false for this question. It isn't strong enough. The answer should be no; never will more explanation help. Why not? Well, if the first explanation leads to "I'm lost. . . .," so will the re-explanation—unless it's radically different, which most people find impossible to do. The original position is usually so strong that it just naturally takes over in the second explanation. If a student is lost after the initial explanation, the normal thing for an instructor to do is to start all over again and re-explain. For example, in teaching bridge, the normal instructor starts by outlining the high card point values, bidding system etc. But if the novice doesn't grasp the concept of trump, he will be lost and no amount of explanation on the fine points of bridge will help. The learner needs a chance to express how much he does understand and he needs to be able to ask his *own* questions.

3. The host would have succeeded in his explanation if he had used a more participative approach, i.e. asked questions, leading the novice player to think up answers.

Answer: False.

Participation for participation's sake is not a particularly valuable training strategy. Questions from the host at the start of a new game will have to be so simple as to be of no help at all or so difficult that the whole exchange will become a guessing game. What the novice needs is not questions but a small bit of information and a chance to ask his own questions.

Participation does not equal learning; participation *may* produce learning, but only if it is specifically and exactly tuned in to the students' learning needs.

4. Why did the novice interrupt the host?

Answer: All the answers are appropriate.

I won't try to explain all these individually. The general explanation is to put yourself in the learner's shoes. When masses of information come at a learner, it is difficult to both absorb one piece and listen to the next. It is so difficult that most of us eventually give up trying and either announce that we're lost or begin to daydream. As an example of this, about half way through a lecture I attended, the lecturer said, "I see a number of blank looks—are there any questions?" Silence. Finally one brave soul said, "I don't understand enough even to ask a question!"

5. Interrupting the host's explanation of how to play with "I'm lost, let's play. . . ." will so disrupt the host, he won't be able to properly instruct the game.

Answer: False.

When teaching a game, most people have no trouble adapting to this format. They had probably planned a free round anyway and when the novice asks for it, the swing is not too difficult. Unfortunately, when this happens in the training world, most trainers are inflexible. They answer, "We'll get to that later" or "I'm coming to that" and carry on with their original lesson plan. If class pressure is strong enough and the instructor is especially sensitive, the lesson may get halted and re-planned at this point, but usually the original lesson plan is too firmly fixed to be altered. Wouldn't it be nice if every lesson plan included several large *stop* signs, so that student positions could be considered? Yes, and the plan should also have had a variety of paths pre-planned—a kind of built-in flexibility.

6. Learners learn by doing; few of us will argue with that statement. To teach how to play the game, the key to any lesson plan would be to get the novice playing.

Answer: True.

I assume that everyone checked true to the question, and I'd like to explain why I used this simple, obvious question. Almost every lesson plan pays lip service to the learn-by-doing concept. They begin with an outline, explanation, lecture, description, or theoretical input on the thing to be learned. The end of the lesson has the actual "playing." This is backwards. In 400 B.C., Sophocles said, "One must learn by doing the thing, for though you think you know it, you have no certainty until you try."

The ordinary lesson sets up a situation in which the instructor *thinks* the student knows but has no certainty. By changing the lesson so that the beginning of the task coincides with the beginning of the lesson, the instructor actually sees the student doing, and knows where to make inputs and which inputs to make. Both instructor and student have certainty.

7. The situation in Figure 9.1 presents a parallel to most instructional situations.

Answer: False.

Well, it does to a point. The last sentence should be deleted to make the situation parallel to most instructional situations. Most students are far too polite to interrupt an instructor. Most of us have been well trained to sit quietly and hope for enlightenment and if it doesn't come, to do our grumbling after class when the authority figure isn't listening.

8. Figure 9.1 briefly outlines the essence of effective instructing.

Answer: False.

No student should ever be put in the position of having to interrupt an instructor with "I'm lost." An instructor should sense this long, long before a student gets up the courage to voice it. The essence of effective instructing is to have students use the time successfully.

9. Learning "to play games" like bridge, chess, etc., is easier than most organizational learning requirements.

Answer: False.

Learning to play a game is just as hard as most learning requirements of an organization. There are three reasons for this:

1. Games involve having as many concepts, skills, knowledge of rules and even the proper attitude, as do real-world learning situations;

2. Games seem easier because the objectives are always clearly defined;

3. Games are simple to the player that knows them, but they are not simple to a person who has not played them before.

10a. If, some evening, you find yourself confronted by a novice wanting to join you in playing your favorite game, you would normally instruct him/her to play by:

_____ *1. An explanation of rules, tricks, steps, etc., followed by trying to play.*

___ *2. An explanation with some dialogue between the two of you, followed by trying to play.*

___ *3. An explanation for three minutes only and then trying to play.*

___ *4. Starting right in trying to play, adding brief explanations only as needed.*

10b. Go through the above and decide how you would do it as a trainer, not as a friend or host.

Answer: I hope you chose 3 or 4 for both questions.

11. The host's starting position in relation to the knowledge level of the learners in Figure 9.1 is similar to many instructional situations in that the students know:

Answer: Either a moderate amount or most of how to play.

What the students know and what the students can do are two different things. Most students have played games: different games with different rules. A sharp instructor realizes this and uses it. Assuming a student knows little or nothing slows the learning.

Some of you are probably thinking that by assuming the students know a moderate amount or most of how to play, the instructor will overestimate the student's capabilities. You are correct, *if*—and that's a big *if*—you instruct by explaining or lecturing. Both of these methods fail to relate to the student's real capabilities.

Instructing by involving the students in "playing" reveals their deficiencies exactly. It allows *all* student skills and knowledge to be applied.

10

On Learner-Centered Courses

Some fascinating problems develop when one decides to try learner-centered teaching. For example, one has to:

- Determine the meaning of *learner-centered* versus *instructor-centered*;
- Overcome a personal tendency to see the learning situation from the instructor's viewpoint;
- Decide how to measure the learner-centeredness of one's instructing; and
- Face the major problem of how to change aspects of one's instruction from being instructor-centered to being learner-centered—when one has no idea what should be changed.

To illustrate this, consider a situation in which you learn that your instructing style does not allow learners to express their feelings about each other, the learning process, or the content of the course. You should readily recognize this as not being a learner-centered situation because if it were your instructing would allow full expression of feeling by the learners. In fact, you probably would want to encourage this expression.

Having made this discovery, you face a problem. How do you change your instructing to allow student feelings to be expressed?

Just saying to the class at various times, "What are your feelings?" or "Feel free to tell me your reactions at any point," *does not work*. Even saying to a class, "Please feel free to ask questions at any time," doesn't work. Some thoughts on how to cope with the problem of getting students to express their feelings are presented in the last section of this article.

Let's assume you are going to begin a course next week. Also assume that you really need this course to be able to do your job better.

For each pair of alternatives shown in the following questionnaire, check which you would prefer as a characteristic of the course:

1. __ A. Goals set by the instructor, in advance, to meet needs that he has identified.

    B. Goals set by you (the learner), with assistance from the trainer, to meet your needs as they evolve.

2. __ A. All learners go through the same learning experiences. At any one time all learners attend the same sessions and do the same things.

    B. There is a wide variety of activities. At any one time, various learners will be doing different things to suit their own needs at that point in time.

3. __ A. The sequencing, or order in which things are taught, is fixed in advance by the instructor according to his preferences and programming planning techniques.

    B. The sequencing is very flexible; it is not determined in advance, but according to the felt needs of you the learner. Similar items may be learned in different sequence by different learners.

4. __ A. Decisions are made by the instructor, who maintains control over the course.

    B. Decisions are made by you the learner or jointly by the instructor and learners. Hence, joint control over the course.

5. __ A. The instructor evaluates the course in terms of the extent to which the instructor's goals are met.

    B. The instructor evaluates the course in terms of the extent to which learners feel their goals are met.

6. __ A. Relatively few teaching-learning methods are used. Methods are selected by the instructor according to his preferences or ideas.

    B. A wide variety of teaching-learning methods are selected by learners according to their individually preferred methods and learning styles.

7. __ A. The instructor is distant, having a closed formal relationship with you as a learner.

    B. The instructor develops a close, open, personal relationship with you.

8. ___ A. The class members do not trust each other. People are relatively distant from each other.

     B. The class is trusting, supportive, close, and its members develop meaningful relationships with each other.

9. ___ A. The instructor is seen in a role, rather than as a person.

     B. The instructor is seen as a person, rather than in a role.

10. ___ A. It is generally not considered legitimate for people to express feelings about each other, the learning process, or the content of the course.

     B. Full expression of feelings is permitted and encouraged.

11. ___ A. An expository, lecturing, question-and-answer approach to teaching is used. Information and ideas are presented to learners by the instructor.

     B. A discovery approach to learning is used. Situations and resources are provided for learners to generate, experience, and discover ideas for themselves.

12. ___ A. Ideas are presented as though they are definite, authoritative, and the "right" answers.

     B. The emphasis is on the fact that there is no right answer, that each person's opinion is valid as it relates to himself and his specific situation.

I expect that you answered this the same way I did. (See Figure 10.1 for how three classes, totaling 28 people, answered it.) In personally doing the questions, I checked only *B* answers. When one interprets the quiz it is apparent that the *A* items are all instructor-centered, while the *B* items are all learner-centered. Hence, if you checked only *B's*, you wanted a learner-centered course. Where you checked *A*, you might like to personally explore your reasons for preferring an instructor-centered item. If you checked a fair number of *A's* (four or more) you may be at odds with the definition of learner-centeredness used in this article and probably should discontinue your reading until your definition of what you want in a course is more in agreement with mine.

How three classes, totaling 28 people, answered this quiz.

1. A	5	3. A	14	5. A	1	7. A	2	9. A	1	11. A	2
B	23	B	14	B	27	B	26	B	27	B	26
2. A	9	4. A	2	6. A	8	8. A	0	10. A	0	12. A	1
B	19	B	26	B	20	B	28	B	28	B	27

Figure 10.1.

For the purposes of everything that follows, learner-centered instruction is defined by the *B* items, instructor-centered by the *A* items. Using this definition, Figure 10.2 is a questionnaire that assesses how learner-centered a course's instructing is. The rest of this article goes into (1) the background of the questionnaire, (2) how to score it, and (3) interpreting the data.

Figure 10.2. A Scale for Measuring the Degree of Learner-Centeredness of a Course

This questionnaire is designed to obtain your views about the nature of this course. It consists of 48 statements; in front of each statement there is a space for a number.

Please put a number in the space in front of each statement, according to the following scales.

+3 if the course definitely or nearly all the time was like this.
+2 if the course, generally or most of the time, was like this.
+1 if the course, over-all, was something like this.
−1 if the course, over-all, was not really like this.
−2 if the course generally, or most of the time, was not like this.
−3 if the course definitely or nearly all the time, was not like this.

_____ 1. The teaching-learning process involved the learner discovering things for himself.
_____ 2. People felt free to speak and express their opinions.
_____ 3. Each course member attended the same sessions.
_____ 4. Ideas, concepts, procedures, etc. were presented by the instructor as facts, as proven, as valid ways of doing things.
_____ 5. The goals of the course were set by the learners, based on their own important issues.
_____ 6. A large number of different learning methods were used.
_____ 7. The instructor evaluated the course by the extent to which participants found it useful.
_____ 8. Course members formed real friendships with the instructor.
_____ 9. Issues of values, emotions or feelings were avoided.
_____ 10. The course was based on a pre-planned content or syllabus.
_____ 11. The sequence or order in which things were learned was largely determined by the learners themselves.
_____ 12. The course was controlled by the instructor.
_____ 13. At any one time, all course members would be doing the same thing.
_____ 14. The teaching-learning process involved instructor explanation with learner grasp.
_____ 15. Different learning methods were used to suit the requirements of different learners.
_____ 16. The instructor judged the course by the extent to which he felt participants successfully learned the laid-down content.
_____ 17. The instructor presented ideas, concepts, procedures, etc., as speculative, not definitely proven or known for certain to be true.
_____ 18. The instructor often admitted his own uncertainties, weaknesses and problems.
_____ 19. There was much exploration and discussion of values, feelings and emotions associated with the subject matter.
_____ 20. There was little variety in the learning methods used.
_____ 21. Everybody, participants and instructor, had an equal say in the way the course was run.

___ 22. At any one time, different learners or groups of learners would be doing different things.

___ 23. There was little trust and support throughout the group as a whole.

___ 24. The order in which things were learned varied according to the requirements of individual participants.

___ 25. The course members had very little to say in deciding what was taught on the course.

___ 26. The instructor judged the course according to the feelings of the participants.

___ 27. The emphasis was on presenting neat, cleared up end results of thinking and research.

___ 28. People were discouraged from becoming emotional.

___ 29. The course was run by a co-operative group of learners and instructor.

___ 30. The sequencing, or order in which things were taught, was fixed in advance.

___ 31. The content was not determined in advance, but evolved during the course itself.

___ 32. The instructor measured the effectiveness of the course according to the extent to which participants acquired the specific knowledge and skills.

___ 33. The emphasis was on the generation of knowledge, rather than passing it on.

___ 34. The instructor made all the decisions about the way the course was to be run.

___ 35. It was stressed that to many problems there is no 'right' answer and that each individual must solve problems in the way that he/she thinks is best.

___ 36. The instructor quite often discussed his out-of-work life and activities with course members.

___ 37. The instructor stuck to his favorite learning methods and used these whenever possible.

___ 38. Emotional issues were brought out into the open and discussed.

___ 39. The instructor avoided talking about his own thoughts, feelings and emotions.

___ 40. Each participant went through the same sequence of learning.

___ 41. The relationships between learners and instructor were formal, based largely on role or status.

___ 42. The instructor never discussed his own problems with course members.

___ 43. Individual participants were able to 'do their own thing' if they wished.

___ 44. Facts, ideas, concepts etc., were presented, put over by the instructor to the learner.

___ 45. The instructor treated the participants as friends and equals.

___ 46. Participants did not really respect each other's views and opinions.

___ 47. The instructor did not really care what happened to participants.

___ 48. There was much co-operation and teamwork in the course.

Background

This questionnaire[1] was designed in connection with on-going research into the evaluation of nondirective teaching. This calls for measuring the degree of directiveness of various courses; hence the reason for developing this particular instrument.

---

[1]Figure 10.2 and 10.3 are from Thomas Boydell, *Experiential Learning*. Manchester, England: Manchester Monographs, Manchester University Department of Education, 1976, pp. 78-81. Reprinted by permission of the publisher.

Terms such as *nondirective, participative,* and *learner-centered* have been used by numerous authorities to describe courses with certain features in common. Although there is no generally accepted single definition of these terms, an amalgam was made of the characteristics that most people agree are associated with 'learner-centered' teaching. As a result, twelve dimensions, as outlined in the previous questionnaire, were proposed to differentiate between learner- and teacher-centered approaches.

Scoring

A forty-eight-item scale was constructed: i.e., four items per dimension. Each of the twelve dimensions has four items; two of these have a +3 score for learner-centered course, two have −3 for learner-centered. Thus, when scoring, the signs of half the responses are reversed; this gives a range on each dimension from − 12 (instructor-centered) to +12 (learner-centered).

The twelve dimensions and the associated items are as shown in Figure 10.3. (Scores on those items marked * are reversed.)

Interpreting the Data

One way to use the data is to consider two sets or clusters of scores:

A. The *control* cluster; the sum of average scores on dimensions 1–5 (goals, homogeneity, sequencing, control, evaluation). The range here is from −60 to +60.

B. The *climate* cluster; the sum of average scores on dimensions 7–10 (instructor-learner relationships, group climate, instructor, feelings). Range is from −48 to +48.

Plotted as shown in Figure 10.5, this gives four hypothetical classes of courses:

1. *Friendly learner-centered*: learners set their own goals; good, warm, supportive feelings and climate.

2. *Friendly traditional course*: instructors set goals: climate warm, supportive.

3. *Nasty traditional course*: instructor sets goals, bad, nasty, unfriendly relationships, climates, feelings.

4. *Sour T-group*: learners set goals, bad, nasty, sour, unfriendly feelings.

Figure 10.4 shows some results of courses I have recently been involved with. By studying the data in Figure 10.4 and weighing the significance of each of the twelve dimensions and their two cluster scores, I can spot areas in which I should work to make my instructing more learner-centered.

Other Interpretations

Boydell (1976) suggests a number of other interpretations that can be developed in using this questionnaire.

Earlier in this article I promised further ideas on how to correct a situation in which your scores indicate that you are instructor-centered in the feelings area. Here are my thoughts:

1. You have to express your feelings first. You have to set the tone of what's acceptable. If you don't express your emotional reactions, personal values, and feelings, then learners won't either because the *climate* is wrong.

2. You have to get in touch with (a) your own and (b) their emotions, values, and feelings. For this "getting in touch," you have to first, spot them, second, accept them, and third, react to them accurately. I realize this is a tough task but it can be done without having your programs/courses become sensitivity sessions.

3. The third thing you can do is create an open, trusting environment. I wish you luck with this because I can't tell you how to do it.

4. You have to be prepared to sacrifice class time and, initially, course content to discuss (a) emotional reactions and emotional outbursts that are present in all classrooms, if you can sense them; (b) personal values; and (c) feelings associated with the course content. Sacrifice of course time is only initial because as your reactions to the class's feelings improve you'll discover that more learning occurs in the same time as before. You will have reduced the amount of student emotional blockage present in your learning environments.

Postscript

Richard Roque, the course director with the Staff Development Branch, Public Service Commission, has suggested two modifications to this instrument:

First, change the wording on the scale to:

+3 True

+2 Most of the time true

+1 Sometimes true

−1 Sometimes false

−2 Most of the time false

−3 False

Dimension Title	Instructor-Centered	Learner-Centered	Item Numbers
1. Goals	Goals set by the instructor in advance to meet needs that he has identified.	Goals set by the learners, with assistance by the trainer, to meet the learner's diverse needs as they evolve.	5, 10*, 25*, 31
2. Homogeneity	All learners go through the same learning experiences; at any one time all learners attend same sessions, do the same things.	Wide variety of activities; at any one time, various learners will be doing different things to suit their own needs at that point in time.	3*, 13*, 22, 43
3. Sequencing	The sequencing, or order in which things are taught, is fixed in advance by the instructor according to his preferences and programming planning techniques.	The sequencing is very flexible; it is not determined in advance, but according to felt needs of learners. Similar items may be learned in different sequence by different learners.	11, 24, 30*, 40*
4. Control	Decisions made by the instructor, who maintains control over the course.	Decisions made by learners or jointly by the instructor and learners. Hence, joint control over the course.	12*, 21, 29, 34*
5. Evaluation	Instructor evaluates course in terms of extent to which instructor's goals are met.	Instructor evaluates course in terms of extent to which learners feel their goals are met.	7, 16*, 26, 32*
6. Methods	Relatively few teaching-learning methods used. Methods are selected by the instructor according to his preferences or ideas.	Wide variety of teaching-learning methods are selected by the learners according to their individually preferred methods and learning styles.	6, 15, 20*, 37*

Figure 10.3. The 12 Dimensions and Their Associated Items

Dimension Title	Instructor-Centered	Learner-Centered	Item Numbers
7. Instructor-learner relationships	Distant, closed, formal relationship.	Close, open, personal relationships.	8, 41*, 45, 47*
8. Group	Not trusting, people relatively distant from each other.	Trusting, supportive, close, deep relationships.	2, 23*, 46*, 48
9. Instructor	Instructor is seen in role, rather than as person.	Instructor is seen as a person, rather than a role.	18, 36 39*, 42*
10. Feelings	Generally not considered legitimate for people to express feelings about each other, the learning process, or the content of the course.	Full expression of feelings permitted and encouraged.	9*, 19, 28*, 38
11. Expository versus Discovery Approach	Expository approach to teaching. Information and ideas presented to learners by instructor.	Discovery approach to learning. Situation and resources provided for learners to generate, experience, and discover ideas for themselves.	1, 14* 33, 44*
12. Certainty	Positivism; ideas presented as though definite, authoritative, 'the right answer.'	Relativism; emphasis on the fact that there are no right answers, that each person's opinion is valid.	4*, 17, 27*, 35

Figure 10.3. (Continued)

SOME CURRENT RESULTS

Course 1 — Instructional Techniques:
a one-week, in-house residential course.

Course 2 — Instructional Techniques:
a three-day, public, nonresidential course.

Course 3 — Instructional Techniques:
a three-day, public, nonresidential course.

Course 4 — Introductory Management:
the first three days of a two-week, public, nonresidential course.

Course 5 — Introductory Management:
the first three days of a two-week, public, nonresidential course.

Course 6 — Problem-Solving Decision Making:
the first two days' content of a two-week, nonresidential Materials Management course.

Course Number	1	2	3	4	5	6
Control Cluster	+10.7	+15.8	+12.2	+ 4.9	+10.8	−12.2
Climate Cluster	+16.2	+24.6	+24.8	+10.6	+18.0	+13.9
1. Goals	+1.6	+4.0	+3.8	+2.3	+4.1	−3.2
2. Homogeneity	+0.8	−0.2	−1.8	−6.0	−2.4	−5.4
3. Sequencing	+3.9	+8.0	+5.8	+3.4	+2.8	−4.6
4. Control	+4.9	+3.1	+4.4	+5.2	+4.3	−0.7
5. Evaluation	+1.6	+4.3	0	0	+2.0	+1.7
6. Methods	+1.6	+4.3	+3.0	+3.5	+2.9	+1.2
7. Instructor-Learner Relationship	+9.1	+6.7	+5.8	+7.9	+7.8	+8.0
8. Group	+8.8	+10.6	+10.6	+8.0	+7.8	+10.9
9. Instructor	−1.1	+1.3	+2.8	−2.6	+1.2	−1.6
10. Feelings	−0.6	+6.0	+5.6	−2.7	+1.2	−3.4
11. Expository vs. Discovery Approach	+1.4	+4.3	+4.8	+0.4	+0.7	−0.6
12. Certainty	+2.1	+5.3	+5.0	−1.7	−2.2	−4.0

Figure 10.4.

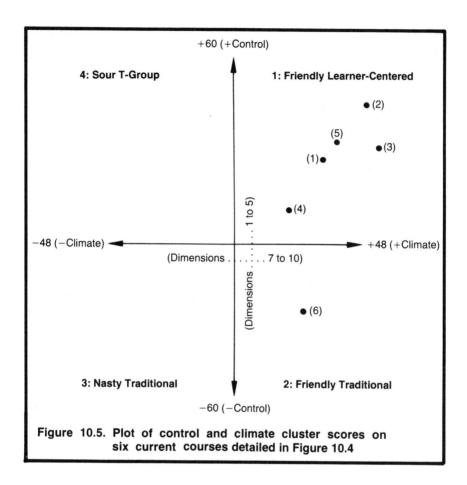

Figure 10.5. Plot of control and climate cluster scores on six current courses detailed in Figure 10.4

Second, put this scale on each page of the instrument so that the student doesn't have to keep referring back to the first page to remember the rating scale.

REFERENCES AND READINGS

Rogers C. *Freedom to learn: A view of what education might become.* Columbus, OH: Charles E. Merrill, 1969.

Romey, W. D. *Risk-Trust-Love: Learning in a humane environment.* Columbus, OH: Charles E. Merrill, 1972.

11

How to Work with Small Groups

Most of us, as trainers, have used small groups in our training efforts. Our classes may form groups to do a number of different types of things such as problem solving, case study, discussing or exploring a situation, answering a specific question, model building, developing ideas for further study, and even preparation of projects. We use groups for practically everything.

Groups are used because the students learn best when they are actively involved in the learning process, and small groups provide involvement most effectively. I doubt if many of us ever questioned this. I know I didn't. I took it on faith. Although it never was really proved in the training I was doing, it always seemed to be the right thing to do. Now I know that using small groups is right because I recently stumbled on some research done during World War II by social psychologist Kurt Lewin.

Lewin's Experiment

Lewin was concerned with training homemakers to increase the consumption of three rather unpopular but plentiful meats: beef hearts, sweetbreads, and kidneys. To reach this objective, Lewin felt it was necessary to change homemakers' attitudes toward these meats.

To accomplish his objective, Lewin set up an experiment using two groups of similar homemakers. Group One members attended a lecture that presented an enthusiastic picture of the flavor of these meats, their value to health and the benefit that would accrue to the war effort if they were more widely used. Group Two members took part in discussion groups in which the same points were made and, in addition, the members were induced to come to a group decision to serve the three meats.

Although the lecture in Group One was passive, the group discussion caused the homemakers in Group Two to become actively involved in the learning process. Both groups decided to try and use these meats. The groups even went so far as to try and think of ways to overcome the prejudice of their families against the meats. The training time for the lecture and the group discussion was the same.

Experiments' Results

A follow-up study was conducted to find out how many of the homemakers actually served the less popular meats. The results speak for themselves. Of the women who attended the lecture only 3 percent served the meats, whereas 32 percent of the group discussion members served them.

Similar experiments were done with milk, cod liver oil, and orange juice (see Figure 11.1 for the results). In all cases the group-discussion approach achieved better results or a higher rate of learning and hence changes in behavior and attitude.

	INCREASED USE	
	Lecture	Group discussion
Milk	16%	51%
Cod liver oil	53%	89%
Orange juice	57%	100%

Figure 11.1

In summing up these experiments, Lewin concluded it is usually easier to change the attitudes and behaviors of people in small groups.

In using groups, the following advantages are apparent:

1. Lectures create passive listening, and groups create active listing.

2. In small groups there is a higher level of onus on each individual.

3. Small groups prompt nontalkers to feel freer and, when they do speak, less threatened by being wrong in front of large numbers of people; this leads to:

4. A greater level of self-commitment to what has been said, hence a higher probability of following up the idea with action.

5. In lectures, any individual student is easily ignored, but in groups this is much less likely to happen.

6. Surveys of students indicate that students prefer small-group learning activities to lectures. This significantly adds to the learning accomplished per unit time.

7. Individual tutorial type of learning is more closely approached in small groups than in lectures and it is generally accepted that greater learning occurs under such conditions.

Since groups do enhance the learning process, let's consider things that increase their effectiveness such as seating arrangements, group sizes, and teacher group interactions.

Group Seating Arrangements

What happens when you tell a class to form groups? The groups form readily enough, but they don't adjust their seating arrangement. They almost always sit in a straight line, rather than forming a tight circle. Even when told to form circles, they don't do it well; often all they do is form into a half-moon shape. Something seems to affect students when it comes to moving chairs. Probably a student wants to stay at his own place at the table rather than move away from it because of a need to feel secure—like Linus being inseparable from his security blanket in *Peanuts*.

Another problem of group formation is use of tables. To work effectively in a group, the last thing we need is a table between group members. The table, although serving as a writing and working surface, also serves to (a) set up sides and (b) add one more barrier to communications. Tables reduce group effectiveness.

Groups are best formed by telling the students to move back from the table and form a tight circle. The best group formation is one in which the members' knees are touching. This ensures that the group members are facing each other and are close enough together to have easy communications within the activity. This tight group formation also increases group cohesiveness and effectiveness.

Group Size

All instructors have asked themselves many times: "What is the right group size?" Figure 11.2 will summarize my experience in this area.

Teacher-Group Interaction

Teacher-group interaction refers to the role the instructor takes as related to the group process itself. There are six ways that the teacher-group interaction can be considered, they are:

1. Task-group.
2. Discussion group.
3. Brainstorming group.

GROUP SIZE	COMMENTS
2 only	Not really a group because there are not enough members. A pair or dyad, yes. Suitable for a one-to-one situation only.
3	The barest minimum that forms a group. Useable, but limited in its capacity to generate ideas and develop thoughts. Not enough people to be effective in most situations.
4	Reasonably effective
5 and 6	This is the size that, for most courses, proves most effective. Best results are usually achieved from groups this size.
7	Reasonably effective but, in my opinion, starting to get a bit large.
8 and 9	The group structure starts to break down in groups this large. Subgroups or splinter discussions often occur in these groups. Although results are still satisfactory, the time to get these results is often longer.
10 plus	Very unsatisfactory unless you want to illustrate the problems of groups. Using eight or more people can be effective for creating situations in which group participants get in each other's way and negatively affect group achievements.

Figure 11.2

4. Tutorial group.

5. Explorer group.

6. Discovery group.

1. Task-group. This type of group is established to accomplish a specific effort, such as building a list of points, doing a particular project or task in competition with other groups, developing a solution to a case study, or some type of effort centered around a specific objective.

In this type of group structure, the teacher's role is totally outside the group. He listens in unobtrusively and periodically to be sure the group members understood the task assigned to them. The teacher's main role in this type of group activity is to introduce the task clearly to the groups, making sure the members all have understood the situation. Also he ensures that the resources needed by the groups are readily available, and he provides feedback to the groups as required. Figure 11.3 illustrates the task-group-teacher relationship.

2. Discussion group. Discussion groups differ from task groups only in their orientation toward discussion rather than task. Discussion groups are used to give the students a free and uninhibited opportunity to discuss a topic of importance and usually occur at the end of group tasks when a free flow of feelings and reactions has been generated by the task performed.

The teacher's role in this type of group is two-fold. First, to realize that the students want to discuss the situation and, consequently, not to impose his structure on them. He should let it occur spontaneously. Second, to use his judgment concerning when to cut off the discussion group. The only guide to the judgment is the discussion itself. The discussion usually is lively in the beginning when all participants are intensely involved. However, as the discussion continues, an ever increasing number of people drop out. At an appropriate point, the instructor should step in and end the discussion.

The key to this type of group is its spontaneousness and informality. Figure 11.4 illustrates this type of group.

3. Brainstorming group. This is usually a larger group (six to twelve students) and rarely used by trainers. To be used effectively, one should first train the students in brainstorming techniques. Then brainstorming groups can be used effectively. For more information on this subject, consult Alex Osborn's books, which are available in most libraries.

4. Tutorial group. There are two distinct types of tutorial groups, both of which involve the instructor.

In Type 1, the group leader or instructor presents material directly to all members of the group simultaneously. Most of us probably react negatively to this approach because it resembles the lecture format, which we are trying to avoid by using small groups. The reason for including it in this discussion, besides ensuring that all possibilities are covered, is to highlight the fact that it is sometimes advisable to use this form to get certain specific information across.

If we lecture to a large group or class, we often can't be sure our information did get across to all the students. Using this form of tutorial group we can take a more personal approach and deal more effectively with our students. This arrangement, (see Figure 11.5) allows us to present the material positively yet in a manner that will allow the students to interact with questions and comments.

The Type 2 tutorial group is not really a group situation as such. In this setting (see Figure 11.6), the group is working on a task and the instructor works with various individuals alone. Normally, one doesn't consider this as a separate way that a teacher and group can interact.

This type of tutorial interaction can come about in three ways. First, a student may ask for help voluntarily. Second, the teacher may spot a person needing help or straying off the task. Third, the teacher may set up a task that specifically requires each student to work alone and need, at various points, help from the instructor.

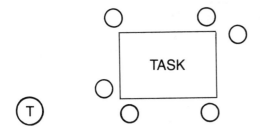

Figure 11.3. Task-group-teacher relationship

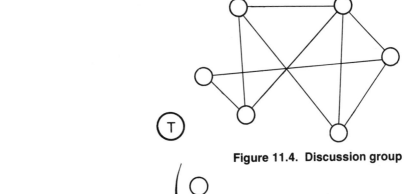

Figure 11.4. Discussion group

Figure 11.5. Tutorial group — Type 1

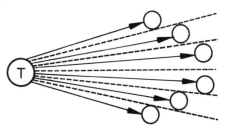

Figure 11.6. Tutorial group — Type 2

5. *Explorer group.* The purpose of this type of group activity is to develop students' skill in asking questions that lead to a suitable exploration of the situation at hand. In this form, the teacher is central. Students ask questions of the instructor as they progress through the material under investigation. This investigation is divided into three stages.

Stage 1 consists of the students asking the instructor questions about the situation. In other words, the students are analyzing the situation to ensure that they have an accurate picture of what they are trying to do. Stage 2 also is a questioning period. Here, students search for the facts relevant to the situation at hand. Obviously the teacher is central in stages 1 and 2. In stage 3, the teacher should take a passive stance because it is in this stage that the students formulate and test various solutions to the situation as they see it.

This type of group activity can be used with verbal case studies, films, problem situations, and anytime when students must search out further information to help reach a valid solution. Figure 11.7 illustrates this arrangement. Figure 11.8 shows the teacher divorced from the group though readily available to answer questions posed by the group. Either arrangement is suitable, although the divorced arrangement usually leads to better questions being asked. It's disadvantage is that it restricts the flow of questions and often causes key points, that should have been discussed, to be ignored.

6. *Discovery group.* The discovery group is just that—it discovers. Figure 11.9 shows that the instructor is part of the group and the group's findings represent discovery for him also. This type of group usually focuses on a problem that can take the form of "What do we do to . . .?" The instructor's role at the start is that of a challenger. He responds to student comments with statements such as: "Prove it," "Why that?" "Are you sure?" "Define it," and "What do you mean?" In later stages, after the facts have been established, the instructor's role shifts to passive support.

The purpose of this passive-support stance is to permit the group to come to its own solution and its own commitment to action. Hopefully, by taking this position, a deeper group sense of purpose develops and the quality of results achieved will be better than would occur if the instructor had dominated the situation.

Most instructors find this the hardest type of group activity to manage. Usually, the reason for this is that we want to propose what we consider to be a good solution. The rule must be that all solutions come from the group and not from the instructor; the teacher is passive. He can support individual students but only with the purpose of ensuring that the whole group hears a particular point the student has made. The instructor supports listening, not student ideas or thoughts.

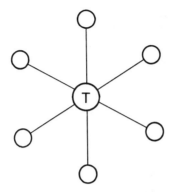

Figure 11.7. Explorer group — teacher central

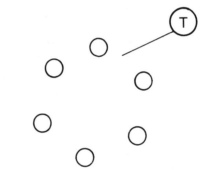

Figure 11.8. Explorer group — teacher divorced

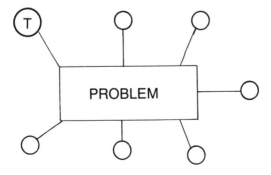

Figure 11.9. Discovery group

Take-up

Take-up, sharing the results of group activities, is best accomplished by going from group to group. This doesn't mean having group one report, and then group two, and so on. Never have one group report and the rest listen. All that this accomplishes is a repetition of answers and the mental dropping out of the people.

To avoid this mental dropping out, have each group present *only one point* at a time. After group one has made its first point, then go to group two for a second point and so on. This technique prevents people from dropping out mentally as a new point is made with each group. The group members also have to check whether or not they have the point and if they do, they must eliminate it from future possible answers.

Using this point-by-point take-up (processing) will lead to discussion among groups to verify the meaning of a group's point. To increase this activity between groups, you can do two things. First, you can take a polling of the groups to see which groups have the point. Second, you can tell the class as a whole that no point will be accepted unless all groups have it or agree that the point is valid.

Doing this increases the processing time as well as increasing the learning. When using this latter technique, you will find that many points on which there is agreement in all groups are quickly passed over to allow more time to be spent considering and discussing the new points brought out by certain groups.

Groups *do* actively involve students in the learning process. They can, if handled improperly, also lead to noninvolvement. The ideas and thoughts offered here should help improve individual involvement in group activities.

12

Small Groups in Action

Small groups are very popular and very valuable as a way of dealing with many training situations. However, they can sometimes be difficult to set up and work with properly. What follows is a number of tips I've gleaned over the years. They are separated, for reading ease, into seven areas: (1) Presenting tasks to groups, (2) Group seating, (3) Task time, (4) Answering questions and helping groups, (5) Teacher's role in observing groups, (6) Group noise-level patterns, and (7) Serial take-ups (processing) of group work.

2. Presenting Tasks

Have you ever given a class elaborate and specific instructions, only to finish and be bombarded with questions, or have some students sit and look at you numbly? Or, worse still, start working furiously at the wrong task? If you have, then the chances are that your instructions were either too elaborate or not specific enough—maybe both. Most people are not mind readers, nor do they have photographic memories. Instructions need to be clear, concise, and to-the-point.

If your setting-up instructions are more than one sentence long, *display them* on an overhead projector, a flip chart page, a chalkboard, or on anything that will make them visible, readable, and available for reference. Make sure the instructions can be easily read from all parts of the classroom, and then *shut up*. Don't give in to the temptation to read them aloud. People read at various speeds, and if you read aloud two lines behind or one line ahead of your students, you may confuse them. Having given the class time to read the instructions, you can start off with very little verbal instruction—"Go ahead" or "Start now" are two extreme examples. At this point, if there are any questions at least they won't be "What'd you say?"

2. Group Seating

Groups rarely, if ever, seat themselves properly. The participants usually sit in a straight line or, at best, form a kind of arch. Both of these seating arrangements reduce the group's ability to communicate within itself. Naturally, you want your students to form a circle. So, what happens when you suggest they do? They form a circle as large as they can; they space themselves out, increasing the communications distance. To avoid this phenomenon, I tell my classes to form circles and play "kneesies," i.e., get close enough to touch knees. This is accepted as a great idea, especially if the group is made up of both sexes. (More information on groups can be found in an earlier article in this series, 11. "How to Work with Small Groups.")

3. Task Time

Let's explore a couple of situations:

Situation A. Instructor to class: "You have twenty minutes to do this." The class goes to work on the task. Twenty minutes later, the class is still working productively and efficiently on the task.

The instructor's dilemma is whether to stop the task or let it continue because the group's productive?

Escape from the dilemma; let the group continue with its task.

You can't always let groups continue with a task past the allotted time, but if the group work is productive, and effective, *and* incomplete, the instructor is strongly tempted to let the group effort continue. Most instructors weigh the situation and cut the processing time to let the groups continue. I think it's better to let the group continue. Stopping the group introduces the risk of having resentful students and a less enthusiastically received or less meaningful processing. So, for Situation A, most instructors let it continue.

Situation B. Instructor to class: "You have twenty minutes to do this."

The class goes to work on the task and, ten minutes later, obviously has done it. In fact, the students have reached the stage where an experienced instructor realizes that the groups probably will wander away from the task to gossip.

The instructor's dilemma: do I stop the exercise, having announced a twenty minute time? This really isn't a dilemma; all instructors take advantage of this situation to gain ten minutes.

The result of exploring these two situations is that one decides that giving a time limit for most exercises is meaningless. As a rule of thumb: don't give a group a specific period of time for an exercise unless you mean it.

Some group tasks are exact in time. OK, then use a time limit and stick to it. Students *sometimes* do ask how long they have. My current reply takes the form of "As long as you need. I figure it should take you about twenty minutes."

4. Answering Questions

Often when a task or exercise is presented to a class, the teacher is so inundated with questions that one wonders if the group work will ever get started. The cause of this often is the teacher's attitude. His attitude in presenting the task invites questions, giving the impression that the class is bound to need help. There is nothing wrong with a helping attitude but let's put it in the right place.

First, be businesslike. Get the task going, then be helpful to the groups *if* they need it. Approaching a group exercise in a get-at-it format does sometimes lead to questions. If your answer is a point you forgot to tell the class, by all means broadcast the answer, but if the point is specific and unique to a group, go to the group and answer it privately.

One of the dangers in going to a group that has asked a question is to become trapped by the group. It can keep you answering questions for ages. Don't stay with a group. Try and answer its question and then move on to other groups. Providing complete answers usually isn't a good idea. Remember, part of the process is to get the group members to learn to think and solve problems for themselves. They'll call you back if they really need help.

5. Observing Groups

Trainers who are observing group activities sometimes seem like people who read over one's shoulder on the bus: annoying and distracting. Since this is not the function of a trainer, try to reduce the distraction as much as possible while still being aware of what is happening in your classroom. Some suggestions for reducing this disturbing influence follow:

a. Stay at the front of the class in your usual area and listen carefully. You needn't hear the whole conversation to know what a group is doing. Listen for key words and watch expressions. They will tell you what's going on. The technique here is the same you'd use if you were sitting in a corner at a noisy party and trying to listen to a conversation across the room. It can be done. We seem to be able to screen out extraneous noise and listen only to those things we want to hear.

b. Instead of monitoring a group from behind, wander in front where the people can see you and listen from there. This will still disturb group members, but it's better than observing them from behind their backs.

c. Pretend to be doing something else. Look out of a window, look at a picture on the wall, read your notes—anything that will make you look unconcerned and still allow you to eavesdrop.

d. Really do something else. Study your lesson plan; prepare for take-up (processing the results of the groups' work), get ready for the next part of the lesson. In other words, don't observe the groups, trust them. If you have used the particular group activity before and it went properly, you don't need to observe it now. It will go the same way, usually. If it wanders off path, either you will sense it or the students will call for help. Even new group activities don't always need observing, although sometimes it pays to be a little more watchful.

6. Noise-Level Patterns

The noise-level pattern of most group activities tells you when the group has finished its task. Figure 12.1 shows a noise pattern for a typical classroom group activity. Stage 1 is the start-up noise level, which quickly reaches a peak and plateaus briefly. During this period the group sorts out what is to be done, voices readily available answers, and sometimes tries to decide how to approach the task. In Stage 2 the groups are usually wondering what to say now. They're really collecting their thoughts to go on with the task. Don't interrupt them because this thought period is essential to allow them to complete the task. This stage is characterized by a sudden decrease in noise and the gradual rebuilding of the noise level again. Sometimes activities that are fairly easy may not go through this stage at all. The ease of the task allows the group to charge right into Stage 3 without pausing to think.

Stage 3 is the main working stage. The noise level fluctuates but it is high overall, although usually less boisterous than Stage 1. This third stage has a varying length depending on the task. It is many times longer than the first two stages combined.

Stage 4 occurs when the groups finish the task. It is characterized by a sharp drop in noise level. However, the room never becomes silent because some group may still be finishing up or people start to chat. Past the point when most groups have finished their activity, the chatting level will start to rise. This chatting can and often does rise to the noise level of Stage 3. Listening will tell you whether the groups are just chatting. Often, more laughter occurs here too. If all else fails, you can

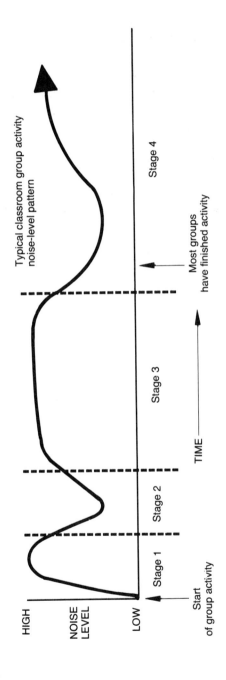

Figure 12.1

probably see by their posture that the participants are relaxed and have stopped working on the tasks.

7. Serial Take-up (Processing)

Have you ever been in a learning situation in which groups were used and this happened: The teacher had the first group give its report and you listened; then group two followed as did groups three, four, and so on and finally it was your group's turn? If this has happened to you, you probably started with "Most of what we had to say has been covered." That line can be avoided with a serial take-up, which simply is asking each group in turn to give one point or idea they came up with. You can continue this around the room until all points have been exhausted.

Part

Classroom
Interaction

13

Handling Classroom Problems

People have asked about particular problems in the classroom and this column is an attempt to answer some of their questions. The format I am following is taken from the "Co-facilitating Inventory" by J. W. Pfeiffer and J. E. Jones (Jones and Pfeiffer, 1975). The answers are necessarily my own and if readers have suggestions, I'd be glad to hear from them.

The questions (in italics) are from Pfeiffer and Jones and the answers are mine.

INTERVENTION STYLE

1. *When starting the group I usually . . .*

Ask the class to form groups and present an overhead projector visual saying:

Decide what questions you want to ask me about:

A. Your concerns in coming to this seminar

B. Our sessions together

C. Me

Please feel free to ask any question you feel is important.

I then give the groups up to ten minutes to formulate their questions. The take-up (processing) of the questions is done serially. I answer one question from a group and move on to the next group, and so on around the room. (See "How to Begin," for more detail.)

2. *When someone talks too much, I usually . . .*

Use one of the following techniques, which are ordered in the sequence I use:

A. Do not positively reward his answers even when they are correct.

B. Avoid looking at or having eye contact with the person.

89

C. Ignore his contributions in favor of someone else's.

D. Cut off his answers, calling on another student to answer.

E. Reward, nonverbally, his efforts to keep quiet when others are talking. This one is vital to getting cooperation.

F. Reward him, nonverbally, when he has restrained himself from talking and let someone else speak first.

G. Thank him for his efforts letting him know that I know that he could give right answers and that I will call on him when I need help.

H. I also use nonverbal cues to reduce the talker's verbosity. These include:

(1) A finger to my mouth making a silent sh-sh-sh-sh motion and looking directly at him.

(2) Eye winks letting him know that I'm aware he wants to speak but is restraining himself.

(3) A facial expression showing my lips clamped tightly together.

(4) A hand raised like a policeman stopping traffic suggesting "hold on, don't talk" by gently adding a dampening-down, pulsing motion.

(5) Displaying a scowl and frown.

(6) A gentle pat on the shoulder (if it's possible) in a friendly way of thanks when he's quiet and allows others to talk.

3. *When the group is silent, I usually . . .*

Let the members think out the issue at hand. I extend the silence until they break it.

If the group is silent and not interacting with the course content as my experience indicates it should, I confront the group with this difference. I am still developing the techniques for this confrontation. They include:

A. The key premise is *I am at fault, I have failed them*. It is easy to say they are at fault because they are different. No, the fault is mine because somehow I have missed their needs.

B. I present to the class this feeling I have of failing the group.

C. I put aside my lesson plans, telling the students I'm doing this because the plans are only more of the same thing we have been doing, and I get them to realize I am prepared to deviate totally from my plan and the course's content as specified.

D. I carefully word my ending question to the group to get them to express their reactions and feelings that support the feelings I have. A sample question is "I'm sure some of you have had similar reactions, too; can we share them in order to find out what I've done, so I won't do it again?"

E. I accept their verbalization and say "I'm sure a number of you are satisfied and haven't felt like we're failing." Because I try to reflect exactly what the class said to me here, this last statement will vary with the situation. I watch the speaker to see if he reacts to my rephrasing. If I haven't rephrased correctly, his face will show a frown, puzzlement, or some negative reaction. If he reacts negatively, I get a rephrasing by him of what he said. If I've been accurate in my reflection, I continue with "but I know some of you must feel I've missed you." I then wait.

G. I continue this effort until we get out the issues at hand.

H. I work with the group to share effectively their position and my own and to determine what path we should take from there.

I. Last, if one of the course objectives deals with any of the following items, I use the parallel of the discussion I've had with the class to explore how the situation went. Items that trigger me to include this last point are: conflict, confrontation techniques, dealing with problem situations, problem employees, understanding people, and employee-boss relationships.

In this sequence I've taken the blame because if I blame the group members, they will react against me for attacking them or, more likely, they won't react at all. Remember, this is done to get a group that should be interacting more with you to do so. Attacking the members only backs them away further. Blaming yourself allows them an easier way to express their dissatisfactions. We can criticize others more easily than we can criticize ourselves, although we also are basically reluctant to criticize others. Given an opportunity to do so in a meaningful, helpful way, we will come forward and express our positions. That's the premise on which the above outline was built.

4. *When an individual is silent for a long period of time, I usually*

. . . Let the person remain silent until he or she wants to speak. I treat this type of person as if he or she has a gigantic hangover. If you've ever had a ringing head after a grand party and then gone to a meeting, the last thing you want is to be asked a lot of questions. If I get the feeling that I may have said something to turn this person off, I speak to the individual privately during breaks in the class to check out the situation.

The truly silent person—one who has talked only once or twice during the seminar—I leave alone. I do keep an eye on such people to pick up the occasions when they have things to say, and I stop all other talking to hear what the silent person has to say.

5. *When someone cries, I usually . . .*

Offer comfort if it is wanted. If individuals wish to be alone with their tears then I try to let them work it out by themselves. I always introspect to try and figure out whether I may have caused the sorrow so that, if necessary, I can change my future classroom behaviors to reduce student anxieties.

6. *When people come in late, I usually...*

Ignore them totally. I try diligently to start on time. People shouldn't be rewarded with attention for lateness. Waiting for them and acknowledging them when they are late are both forms of attention and positive rewards for lateness. Waiting and acknowledging also are both negative rewards to those who were on time. Therefore, I ignore the late students to the best of my ability. I don't even try to tell them what we are doing. Let them suffer and flounder. The first opportunity I have when I won't be disturbing the rest of the class, I approach the latecomers privately. I make no mention of the lateness, indicating nonverbally that I can accept their lateness because they are responsible adults and wouldn't have been late if they could have avoided it. I'm friendly and understanding in this contact bringing them up-to-date with what the class has done and is doing.

7. *When someone introduces outside information about family or friends, I usually...*

Let it run its course. Often real learning can be developed from what's said. Also, tangents to the program are allowed because they serve as breaks and rests for all. I do try, however, to steer the program back on course at the first opportunity. I'm task oriented.

8. *When group members are excessively polite and unwilling to confront each other, I usually...*

React nonverbally with disgust while trying to continue with a program that should establish an atmosphere in which being real is safe. If the politeness and unwillingness to confront each other and the issues continue, I may use the confrontation technique as outlined in item 3.

9. *When there is conflict in the group, I usually...*

Work with the group to develop and explore the issues. I mediate. I try to get the opposing sides to see each other's position, to have a true sharing of the issue. I also try to get them to learn how to deal with conflict. I get them to introspect on what went on in the conflict and its resolution in order to learn personal methods for effectively dealing with conflict.

10. *When there is a group attack on one individual, I usually...*

Weigh the issue at hand and also weigh the person being attacked for defensiveness and ability to withstand the attack. I then do one of the following:

A. Side with the individual being attacked.

B. Side with the class.

C. Stop the attack and point out to the class its irrationality.

D. Remain aloof from the issue but follow it carefully because my intervention may be necessary as the situation changes.

E. Stop the whole issue if it is meaningless or way off the seminar content.

11. *When the group members discuss sexual feelings about each other or about me, I usually . . .*

I've never had this to cope with, so I don't know what I would do.

12. *If there is physical violence, I usually . . .*

Stop it cold. I use all the power that being a facilitator gives me to *stamp* on the situation. I end it as abruptly and fast as humanly possible. Physical violence is a way of dealing with personal problems that I abhor. It should only be used as a last resort in situations of extreme duress. These shouldn't happen in a learning environment in which we are trying to learn to handle ourselves better.

REFERENCES AND READINGS

Pfeiffer, J. W., & Jones, J. E. Co-facilitating inventory. In J. E. Jones & J. W. Pfeiffer (Eds.), *The 1975 annual handbook for group facilitators*. La Jolla, CA: University Associates, 1975, 225.

14

Instructors and Dependent Classes

Consider the following learning situation to see if it describes a familiar scene to you. A class concentrates on the instructor until the instructor steps out of the room, then nothing happens—"learning" stops. When the instructor is present the class's needs are being supplied. The students concentrate on the ideas and concepts being developed. They do what they are asked to do. When discussion develops it isn't uncommon to hear the students voicing the instructor's position. In these discussions they often disregard or do not even hear or listen to each other.

If this describes any classroom you are familiar with, that classroom is in trouble. Learning is only marginally occurring, although it may seem like a lot is being learned. The class is dependent on the instructor, and dependent classes don't learn effectively.

Consider Figure 14.1 in relation to instructing and learning. Can you see the two different boxes in this diagram?

Instructors must see the hidden as well as the obvious in every situation. In this article we are going to be looking at one of the hidden dimensions of instructing. Examine Figure 14.1 for a minute. You can see it as a box with AB being the nearest edge or with CD being the nearest edge, as shown in Figure 14.2. If you look hard at Figure 14.1, you can see the two boxes, but you will find that you can't see both of them at the same time. You have to change your point of view to do this. The total of the lines (words) remains the same, but the message is quite different depending on the point of view you take. The same is true of instructing.

A look at our own classrooms can reveal that much of what we do creates classes that are dependent on us as instructors. A dependent class's culture seems to be such that an external object, an instructor, exists whose function is to supply the needs of the group.

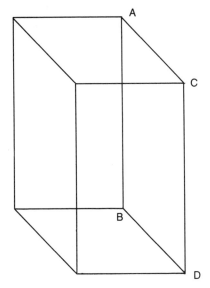

Figure 14.1

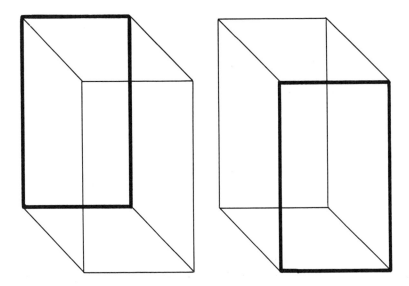

Figure 14.2. Two different positions of the box are revealed by the darkened lines

It is the instructor on whom the immature class depends for nourishment, material, and spiritual protection. The dependent group has as an integral part of its structure a belief in the omniscience and omnipotence of one member of the group—the instructor. This dependency works against deep personal learning that could be applied back on the job.

It is the nature of the dependent group to first concentrate on establishing the idea of instructor and student as firmly as it can. It is common to see a group insisting that the instructor is the only person to be regarded, and at the same time showing by its behavior that it doesn't believe the instructor knows his job.

With its elevation of the instructor, the dependent group makes difficulties for those who really want to work (learn). People who want to say something significant do so in a group environment that causes them to appear to be rivals to the instructor. It is felt that benefit comes from the leader alone and not from the group. Group members feel they are learning only when they are listening to the instructor. When someone else speaks, the instructor can't—and the students feel cheated or deprived of the instructor's "wisdom." The group fails to comprehend and recognize the values inherent in itself. There is an inability on the part of the students in the group to believe that they can possibly learn anything of value from each other. "The leader knows all the answers."

Most of us have experienced the type of situation in which the instructor keeps us dependent on him. It can be very annoying to want to work at the course's objective and have to be dependent on the instructor's pace and inputs. The instructor has to change the dependent nature of the classroom to a work environment.

Consider the effect of a pause that follows an instructor's input. What happens in dependent classes is a silence that is more than a pause for thought. It is a tribute of silence to the instructor's input. The silence also (a) serves as an expression of determination to deny to the leader the material he requires to run the class and thereby preserves the class's dependence on the instructor and (b) serves as an expression of worshipful devotion to the leader for his, and only his, astute inputs.

If a group wishes to prevent development the simplest way to do so is to allow itself to be dependent.

Changing Group Dependence

Because of our training, when a group makes demands of us as instructors we tend to give the answers. This works against us. By giving in, we have increased the group's dependence on us and, consequently, reduced its productivity and ability to work. The moment we instructors give in to our impulses to make inputs we increase the class's emotional dependency upon us. We are being influenced by the class's dependence on us instead of breaking it down and developing self-reliance.

The group is being influenced most by the component of the instruction that is responding to its dependency need, while little influence is achieved by the message intended by the instructor. This also partly explains why so little is learned from instructor inputs.

In responding precisely to the group's request for help, we err, yet not to do so is an error also. This is a true human dilemma. In giving in to the group's request for help we decrease learning and defeat the primary purpose of instructing.

In conclusion: the only way to break class dependence is to assign clear tasks and require the class to work on them. Firmness in delivering task assignments and encouragement of input from the group members are essential elements if real learning is to take place.

15

Coping with Instructional Issues

This article consists of a number of questions on differing instructional situations. Each question is followed by responses and by typical comments that might be made to the response. To make it easier to review the questions, we have printed them in bold type.

Question 1: What can you do if a person who behaves like a joker/comedian or is troublesome volunteers to be one of the people involved in a special class activity?

Response: When the troublesome type volunteers, accept him and continue to fill your other openings requiring helpers. If you make the natural response and reject the troublesome one after asking for volunteers, the others may fear a similar personal rejection and not volunteer to help. After you have all your volunteers you can go back and confront your character concerning his usual disruptive behavior.

Comment: You can't confront him publicly unless you have had the class for a long time and have developed tremendous rapport with it.

Response: True, so confront him privately. In most instances like this, you are passing out instruction sheets, reading notes or materials of some kind, and usually you would be giving the participants some time to study them. During this study period, approach the individual and get him to agree to be serious during this part of class in order to help everyone. Then, to avoid the impression that he is being singled out for special treatment, spend a few seconds with each of the participants in turn. You can say something as simple as "Any questions?" Since no one knows what you have said to the others, no one feels that anyone was treated differently.

Question 2: How can you keep track of time in a classroom with no wallclock without calling attention to it, which looking at a wrist watch always does?

Response: Buy a wall clock.

Comment: That's not possible in all situations, especially if you instruct in numerous classrooms.

Response: Another solution is to place your watch on the table in front of you. There are some disadvantages to this. First, every time you glance at the table, all the students become time conscious because they think you're looking at your watch. Second, a watch on the table is hard to avoid handling. Most instructors who do this move the watch or play with it. The watch can also become so covered with papers that you can't find out what time it is without calling attention to the problem.

Of course, you can always conceal the watch behind something on your desk as long as the something doesn't become a barricade between you and the class. Sometimes, just the simple act of placing the watch in an unusual place is enough to tell the class you are overly time conscious. Most of the time, however, you can solve this problem by reading students' watches. Most men's watches are big enough to be seen from some distance and usually there will be at least one watch showing. The problem here is that you have to learn to read watches that are upside down or sideways. You can practice this at social functions until it's almost second nature.

Question 3: What do you do in a class where you have two groups finished and one group still working?

Response: Give the finished group some extra work.

Comment: Then you're punishing performance that you want to encourage, i.e. working hard, fast, and diligently on assigned group activities.

Response: Go to the group still working and ask it how much more time is needed (not how much longer it wants). Then tell the other groups how long their wait will be and reward them for their effort by letting them get an early/extra coffee, take a stretch break, or review the work they have done. The reward consists of *freedom to do what they like* with the time available. Of course, if you feel that they have finished early because they sluffed over the task, then don't reward them; don't even pay them any attention. Sitting doing nothing can be punishing and can be used in a subtle way to tell that group it should have worked harder on the group task.

Question 4: What do you do if a class activity is running much longer than planned?

Response: Circumstances affect this question. If class time is just about over, then firmly cut off the activity and wrap up the lesson as you'd planned.

Comment: That isn't fair to the students, all of whom are working hard on this activity.

Response: Even if the class is working productively, if you just let it go on until dismissal time, I think your people will feel cheated and unsure of their results. I think you have to break in and at least have time left to confirm their answers. After all, you are the expert and they need to know whether or not they are correct.

Comment: What if the activity runs long in the middle or beginning of class?

Response: Let it go on. This of course means you've assessed the situation and feel that the students' activity is valid and learning is taking place. Also, letting it go on is safe, as long as they are interested and working, you are assured of their attention. By shifting to take-up (processing) or moving to another topic, you risk having the class find the new situation dull, irrelevant, or even valueless. You also could lose your students if they are still mentally involved in the last topic.

Comment: OK, but letting it run on means that other activities you had planned may not get enough time or, even worse, some may have to be dropped.

Response: You've just said that dropping a topic is worse than not having enough time to do a topic fully. You've got that wrong. Dealing with a topic in a compressed fashion or just briefly is worse. It's like starting to paint a house and never finishing it; it looks worse half done. Besides, half a job can't adequately equip the students; it can leave them frustrated though.

Comment: But you can't just drop topics. Students expect them, organizations want them, and the instructor has to do them.

Response: Right, so this possibility has to be built into the design of the course. Priorities should be decided before you begin, and all high priority subjects placed at the start of the course so that if you wind up dropping something—it will be on the low-priority end of the scale.

Question 5: What do you do if your class expresses a split in interests, i.e., doing two different things at the same time?

Response: Split the class, giving each section the different tasks that relate to their expressed interests. This probably means you will have to come up with a task that is not instructor-centered for one of the splinter groups.

Comments: It could happen that you don't have a non-instructor-centered task for either group.

Response: That should never happen. Consider the two directions chosen by the class, pick the direction you understand best and feel most comfortable with, and think up a question for this area. State the question to the group in such a way that it asks for a list of points as an answer. Don't worry about not having any answers yourself. You asked the question—they have to answer it. Just make sure the question is difficult enough to require consideration and an answer of more than one point.

Having done this, you are free to go to the other group and explore with it what it wants to work on. You can either stay and work with this group or you can formulate a task question for it also. Now you have both groups working and you have some time to consider taking up the two groups. You may use this time to develop answers of your own. You could have each group present its findings to the other and permit discussion, or you could present your own findings for comparison.

Question 6: What if a class exercises its right to disagree with you and disagrees solidly?

Response: That's a tough situation. I think the first thing you have to do is listen carefully to what the class is saying—listen to its answer and *why* it has come up with it. Maybe you can redirect the group's thinking with a question, and just maybe it is right. If you can redirect it, the problem's solved; but if it is right, the problem is compounded.

Comment: I've already built a lesson plan that includes a fair bit of commitment to my own answers and I expect the class to go my way.

Response: Obviously you have some reasons for the answers you have. You could present them to the class and, if this is a clear-cut situation, the class should see it your way. If this is an opinion type of situation, I'm afraid you're in deep trouble. If you force your own answer on the class, you had better remember the words of Robert Burns: "A man convinced against his will, is of the same opinion still." By forcing, you'll probably alienate the class and you won't really convince it anyway. If you accept its answer, you have blown your lesson plan. This brings us to the main problem here: if you have given the class the opportunity to come up with its own answer—and there is the possibility of differing answers—your lesson plan should have taken that into account. Since it didn't, you'll either have to spend time defending your own position, force an acceptance of your position, or throw out your lesson plan and accept the class's answer. Try your best to redirect the class's thinking and, if that fails, accept its answer and adjust your lesson plan.

Question 7: What if a planned lesson falls flat and the class knows it, and you still have over an hour planned for that lesson?

Response: The first thing to do, hard as it may be, is admit it. Students support instructors who admit they are in trouble. An example of this occurred when I took over an on-going weekly course from another instructor. I went in with my lesson all planned and started the class, only to be informed that it had done that same lesson three weeks before. I revealed my problem and took a few minutes to think up something else for us to do. The class response was terrific; I had its total support.

Comment: That's all right if you can come up with something else to do, but what if you can't?

Response: Admit to the class that it's not working. If you can let it go early, do so and re-work your lesson for next time. If you can't, explain what you were trying to do and ask for the group's thoughts. In the process of reworking your lesson, you'll probably get much of the material across and you will get some valuable insights into the group's feelings on the subject and your lesson.

16

Why You Should Eliminate the Negative

If you teach or train fairly regularly, it is almost a certainty that within the last month you taught something that you didn't want to teach. How did you do that? It's easy; you taught what I would call the negative lesson. Examples of a negative lesson could include: "Problems in opening a sale," "What not to do in designing a building," "Things that make public speeches dull and boring." All of these lessons teach the negative; they don't teach what was supposed to be taught.

The school system was supposed to teach me to read, write, spell, love history, and a number of other things. What it taught me was that I couldn't read, that I couldn't write, that I couldn't spell, and that I hated history.

Is it possible that we trainers do this to our trainees? I think we do. Take for example a person who is afraid of mechanical equipment. Many workers *know* even before a lesson is taught that they can't run a particular machine: "It's too complicated," "It's noisy," "It requires mechanical ability," "I've never done this type of thing." This kind of trainee can become *convinced* that he can't learn how to run the machine. If you, as the trainer, start the lesson by telling the trainee that anyone can run this machine or that it doesn't require mechanical ability to run it, the trainee will reject your words. In fact, no matter what you say, he will reject it.

A parallel to this rejection is trying to teach math to someone who says he can't do math. No matter what you say by way of encouragement, the learner will not accept it.

So why not show the trainee how easy it is? What do you think the learner sees? He sees knobs, levers, dials, clamps, figures, hands, feet, pulleys, wheels, and thingamajigs all in operation at once. He learns that he was right; he now *knows he can't do* the job. He has seen living proof of that.

103

So let's break down the task into small, easily learned steps. Let's explain each step adequately. Let's have the trainee try each step *after* we have presented it. Again he sees knobs, levers, etc. all going at once. Again he learns he can't possibly do the task. When forced to practice the step he tries to remember the adequate explanation. He fumbles. He looks dazed. He tries gallantly, usually with corrections, and finally stumbles through the step.

The last paragraph may seem like an exaggeration. If isn't, if seen from the point of view of the learner who dreads mechanical things such as VTR's, movie projectors, and other mechanical gadgets. It is all too real, especially the last part of that paragraph. The learner sees his fumbles through a magnifying glass. He really feels dazed and he hears your gentle, helpful corrections as gigantic criticisms of the unbelievable inadequacy he thinks he is displaying. In reality, he probably does not display any more inadequacy to you, the trainer, than the last trainee; but to himself, look out!

Positively Negative

I have just described one form of a negative lesson. The way out of it certainly isn't through more explanation and more demonstration. These two methods only add to the learner's feeling of inadequacy. The more you explain and demonstrate, the more this "mechanically inept" learner becomes truly inept.

Well, what happens to other "more normal" learners in this type of situation? Do they also learn they can't do the task? The answer from my experience is a qualified yes. Qualified, in that some of the learners are so keen to learn certain things that they grasp absolutely everything there is to grasp in the learning situation. Their keenness knows no bounds. Their minds jump ahead in the lesson. They are the first to try the task. They ask questions. They dominate the lesson and really learn.

Oh, for every class to be composed of this type of learner! Most classes aren't. Most have the "normal" learner who reacts to the explanation and demonstration somewhat like the "mechanically inept" learner. Maybe the normal learner doesn't react to quite the same extreme, but he does react in a similar fashion.

Before explaining how we can get out of this kind of problem situation, an example from real life might help. In the April 19, 1971 issue of the *Toronto Globe and Mail*, Joyce Hall wrote of her experiences while learning to become a teacher. She said, "The more we read, talked, and thought about education, the more our fear increased until we were paralyzed at the words: 'In a few weeks, when you are out teaching . . .'"

Here we have an example of fears increasing and a paralysis developing. In fact, the teachers are teaching what they don't want to teach.

Overcoming this reverse teaching is simple, but we trainers avoid the solution because we usually feel it's too hard for the student. The simple solution is: let the student do the task *without* any explanation or demonstration. That's right, don't tell or show; just put the students right into the task. This is not to say that you do nothing. You certainly do have a teaching task but it is radically different. Your task is to manage the student's learning experience. Note: you're not teaching; you're not managing the classroom; you're <u>managing the students' learning experience.</u>

Probably at this point, if you are like most people I've discussed this with, you're saying "Show me" or "Yes, but it won't work in my area." The fact that you are sceptical about this approach is a good sign. However, let's explore an example of this type of learning situation.

The best example I can think of, that would relate to most trainers, involves teaching an individual or a group with no previous experience with VTR, to run a $4000 video-tape recording unit.

Picture the situation as follows: all the required equipment is piled in the middle of the floor—tape deck, tripod, microphone, camera, zoom lens, television set, video tapes, takeup reel, cords, and more cords. In fact, unknown to the students, a few extra cords and things have been thrown into the pile, just to add extra challenge to the situation. You tell the students that they are to assemble the equipment, run it, record a picture with sound, and play it back to be sure they have done the task to their satisfaction. You also tell them that it is not possible to damage the equipment.

Fear Reducer

If you think that the students can damage the equipment, don't forget that the students, too, have this reaction. Ask them why you can say that the equipment cannot possibly be damaged. Their response is that the trainer or teacher will be there to prevent them from damaging the equipment *if* they do something wrong.

This, then, to a certain extent relieves their fear of damaging the equipment. Besides, if they do damage it now, it won't be their fault; it will be the teacher's. Naturally, at this stage it has to be the teacher's fault: he hasn't taught them to avoid damaging the equipment.

With a bit of coaxing the students will go at the problem and assemble and record. Meanwhile, the teacher positions himself so that he can always see what's going on. This positioning allows him to stop the students at strategic points to explore such things as "What happens if the camera is turned on bright lights?" and "What happens to the tape if you go from rewind to play?" Also, by positioning himself in order to effectively see what is going on, he can reward students as they do things correctly, and he can reinforce students who begin to do correct things but appear to be wondering if they should try out what they are thinking. He can say "Why don't you go ahead and try that?," "That certainly appears worth exploring," or "What do you think would happen if you did that?," and then reinforce their response.

The assumption has been made that by managing the student's learning experience as previously outlined, the teacher has caused learning. Experience shows that this assumption is correct. Although initially horrified at the thought of running the equipment, the students were able to run it smoothly and correctly after this lesson. In one case, a student who had experienced this lesson and then had no practice on the equipment for six months, assembled and ran (without any further instruction) a completely different make of VTR. When asked if he wanted help before using the different VTR, he said that since he had done the last one himself, why shouldn't he be able to do the same with the new one? His answer means that besides learning how to run one type of VTR, he also had learned how to run different VTR's.

Let me give further examples of this type of learning. Consider the value of not going to great depths of telling and showing in teaching someone to write reports, drive a car, install a cost-improvement program, or even to swim. No one really learns any of these just by listening to a teacher. When most classes start, everyone knows that the teacher can do the task, and at the end of the class, strangely enough, the teacher is still the only one who has done the task. The students have been forgotten in the teacher's lesson.

How to manage the classroom so that the students are not forgotten is outlined in the VTR example. The main steps in teaching this type of lesson are:

1. Set up the situation before the students arrive;
2. Reduce the students' anxiety level by putting them right into the task;
3. Position yourself to be able to see the learning situation and the students' behavior;
4. Use positive reinforcement
   a. For things done right;
   b. To encourage students to try out new behaviors they feel tentative about;

5. Use questioning and developmental techniques, as previously illustrated, to develop *student ideas* not teacher ideas;

6. Lecture and teach when requested by the students but restrict the lecture length to thirty seconds by shifting to questions as early as possible;

7. This step overrides and is imbedded in all the other steps, i.e., let the students do the task or experience the learning. *Remember: the teacher can already do what the lesson is teaching; it's the students who must do and act before really successful lessons can occur.*

17

The Positive Versus the Negative

As one gains more and more experience in the training field, the subtleties of training endeavors become more and more complex. This article demonstrates how experience creates subtle complexity.

Let's look at a typical lesson from three points of view: first, the original uncomplicated lesson; second, the way it affects a student, which starts to increase the subtle complexity; and third, at the way the lesson could have been given by making use of the information that is available in the classroom.

THE ORIGINAL LESSON

This lesson comes at about the middle point of a course designed to improve the students' skills in writing reports. The students have brought in reports that they have written since the previous class. The class is divided into groups of three students. Each triad is instructed to exchange reports. Then each person circles items that need improving on the reports of the other two group members.

After each report has been scrutinized and changes have been suggested by the other two group members, the report is returned to the person who wrote it. When everyone in the class is once again in possession of his own report, the class is instructed to rewrite the reports and correct the errors. Throughout the whole lesson the students are encouraged to discuss, compare, and question each other about the editing.

Looking at the lesson, we can see that it has the following features:

1. It develops each student's editing ability;
2. It improves each student's ability to rewrite his own material;

3. It allows each student to compare his editing with another person's editing;

4. It indicates where improvement really is needed because two people might mark the same spot for improvement;

5. The edited report is promptly returned to the person who originally wrote it; and

6. He can easily get immediate feedback from the other group members in rewriting his report.

A reasonable lesson? Yes. Similar to those any of us have taught? Probably, yes. Any glaring or apparent reason for changing it? No, not on the surface anyway. It is working well. Students are gradually writing better reports, and that is the purpose of the course. But wait. Let's look at this lesson to see how it affects a student.

EFFECT ON THE STUDENT

On the surface the lesson looks good, but it isn't good at all. The lesson is a student's and especially an instructor's nightmare. The problems are well hidden but they are there, buried in the subtler points involved in instructing.

There are at least five or six problems in this lesson. All of them are in the effect the lesson has on each student when his report is returned. See if you can list them before reading further. This will help develop your ability to spot similar problems in your own class activities.

The first problem occurs with the suggested improvements: the circled items. In many cases the number of marked spots completely overwhelms the student author. He becomes demoralized by what he sees.

This leads to a second problem: he loses confidence in his ability to write.

Which in turn develops a third problem: he learns something he has always suspected—that he can't write. The recommended changes just serve as proof to convince him that he was right in thinking he couldn't write. We want the students to learn that they can write and here is a lesson that is developing them in just the opposite direction. In other words, *we are not teaching them to write, not even that they may be able to write, but that they can't write*.

The fourth problem is that no one likes to have others point out where he needs improvement. We would rather discover our own faults. When others point out where we should improve, we tend to reject their comments.

This rejection brings on problem five. The students become defensive about the work they've done. They build up reasons to justify what they did. They don't really hear the other editor's point of view; they only hear their own reasons. In a way, they stop learning. They become strong defenders of the position they have established and must justify it at all costs. Naturally the editors react, substantiating their recommendations. Although the result is not a violent pitched battle, it is a subtle quiet discussion with both sides failing to hear or learn from each other. What is being learned is how to react negatively to editing.

The sixth problem is almost as bad as problem three in which the student learned he couldn't write. The whole process of this lesson in report writing is negative. It focuses exclusively on improvements needed. Never once does the lesson focus on the capabilities each student has. The lesson design is such that anything good or anything well written gets lost in the shuffle to find needed improvements.

This latter point, the negativeness of the lesson, is true of many lesson designs. We instructors build a lesson with total disregard of the student's need to use *in a positive way* behaviors he already has when he enters the course. If we do design the lesson to bring out the students' behaviors, we then respond more negatively to these behaviors than we think we do. In some courses I have been involved with, I did research on the teachers' negative and positive behavior patterns. All the teachers felt they behaved more positively toward the students than negatively. In actual practice all were more negative than positive or their use of negative and positive behaviors was very close to equal.

Think back to your own lesson plans; they are probably more negatively oriented than positively oriented. They may contain reminders to "watch for" and "not to do" such-and-such. Few of us plan solidly to develop and expand the *good* things the students do.

If your list of problems with this lesson included that the teacher should have done the editing or marking, you are possibly wondering why we didn't include it in our list. The first and most obvious reason is that it is the students who should do the work, not the teacher. Think of all the teachers you've heard talk about the marking they have to do. Then think of the opportunity that the students have been deprived of.

Another reason we didn't suggest at the outset that the teacher should mark the reports is that many of the six problems already mentioned would still occur. Students would still feel that certain points weren't wrong. No one likes another person, even his teacher, to point out where he should improve.

An issue of critical importance in relation to the negative-positive lesson design is this question: does marking have negative or positive implications? The only possible answer is that marking has completely negative connotations. The whole concept of marking implies the finding of errors and deducting them from total perfection. Marking schemes fail to be positive in all respects.

ANOTHER APPROACH

We have dropped some pretty strong clues concerning how the original report writing lesson should be changed. You will have deduced that we feel it should be changed from a negative lesson to a positive lesson. The change should retain the basic concept that the students will edit each others' reports. The objective of the lesson, improved student ability to write reports, is to remain intact. The question for you to consider now is how you would change the report writing lesson to a positive approach. Take a few moments to design the change from negative to positive, remembering that the basic concepts of the original lesson should be generally retained.

The Change

Within the context of the lesson, the change from negative to positive is not an easy change—the key question being how you can make the editing positive. In the end that turns out to be simple enough—you edit for the highlights or significant things and when you find them you circle them. Result, a positive approach to a usually negative lesson.

The effect in the classroom is just as significant. The problems vanish. No longer is the student overwhelmed by a mass of circles on his work. He is revitalized, not demoralized, by what he sees. He gains confidence. He learns he can write, that there are good parts to what he writes, although no one has ever found them before.

The highlights of the report are accepted and the student searches for the reasons why others feel they are highlights. He listens and hears their reasons as well as his own. In fact, he consolidates, internalizes, and reinforces his own strong writing skills, increasing the likelihood of his using them again.

A Further Positive Change

After having had the small groups of three discussions that naturally occur when the reports are returned to their original writers, you then can have the students break into groups again. These small groups are to pick the best highlight or two from each of their reports and prepare to present them meaningfully to the rest of the class. In other words, they must extol the key features and benefits of the highlights they have found.

This further positive development of the lesson helps speed the learning that occurs. Through the highlight presentations, the students learn good techniques that fellow students have used. This means that the next time they write they can draw from a larger repertoire of skills.

Dealing with Errors

Under this positive approach, we have said nothing about the glaring errors or faults in the reports. Nowhere has there been any attempt to deal with these negative aspects of the students' writing. The reasons for this are many, as indicated under the heading, Effect on the Student.

Other reasons for not dealing with the errors or faults are tied into the technology of dealing with the lesson positively. Circling the highlights obviously indicates that the parts not circled are not as good. Each student writer will arrive at his own conclusions concerning the uncircled writing and strive to improve these points himself. If he feels that certain points should have been circled, he may ask the editors why they were not. Hopefully, *he will listen and absorb their comments better when he has initiated the request for negative feedback.*

SUMMARY

Avoid the negative lesson. Use student behaviors in a positive way. Highlight the good points of the students' behavior. Always structure the lesson to find the things the student does right: highlight the right things, encouraging and developing them further.

All of us prefer to be right. We especially like to have our good ideas and concepts pointed out. We want to be right; in fact, we strive to be right. Yet research constantly shows that we don't reward people as often as we think we do. To overcome this problem, we must start redesigning our lessons to emphasize and capitalize on the recognition of the positive attributes in our students.

18

How to Use Questions Effectively

Everyone in the training field today is after participation, discussion, or an interchange of ideas. Toward this end, games, simulations, role plays, cases, and in-baskets have been tried. All of these activities result in participation if they are used properly, but what happens before or after? More often than not, the instructor lectures.

To avoid long structured monologues, the trainer can simply use questions. In fact, he can recede into the background almost completely if he uses the right questions. Here, we'll take a look at how to get to the happy state where students take over the discussion of a topic.

TYPES OF QUESTIONS

Basically, there are two types of questions, *open* or *closed*.

Closed Questions: a question that can be answered adequately in a few words, for example:

1. *Identification-type question (closed)*
   - "What kind of machine is this?"
   - "Who is responsible for controlling the flow of goods and materials?"
2. *Selection-type question (closed)*
   - "How many of you feel that closed questions are better than open questions?"
   - "Who is right, the controller or the sales supervisor?"

Who, what, how

Marit Stengels was co-author of this column.

3. *Yes/No-type question (closed)*   *Yes or no*

- "Does preparing a lesson come before setting objectives?"
- "Is the first step in problem solving to get the facts?"

Naturally, for purposes of encouraging or developing participation, these questions all fall short.

Open Question: a question that requires more than a few words for an adequate answer, for example:

1. *Leading (subjective) question (open)*
   - "Why do you think the controller was right?"
   - "What do you think?"
   - "Who should lead the group and why?"
2. *Objective question (open)*
   - "Why was the controller right?"
   - "What factors are necessary in a good training situation?"
3. *Problem question (open)*
   - "What course of action should the controller take now?"
   - "How quickly should you implement these steps in your job enrichment program?"

Obviously, the open questions will stimulate participation. This means they must have a number of characteristics that make them good questions. A comparison of closed versus open questions resulted in the following list.

Characteristics of Good Questions

- The answers are more than one word;
- The answers are not obvious;
- The question is concisely worded;
- The question is easily understood;
- Use of "Why, What, When, Where, Who, and How (The five W's and How) appear in all open questions;
- Each question requires thought before answering;
- Each question relates to the lesson being taught (this is not obvious when the questions are out of context as they are here);
- Finally, the questions are prepared in advance.

Acquiring an understanding of the types of questions and the characteristics of a good question is only part of what is necessary to succeed in obtaining class participation through questions. Success comes from following the six steps as illustrated in Figure 18.1.

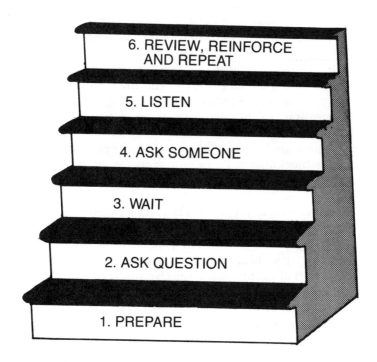

Figure 18.1. Steps to take in making maximum use of questions

SIX STEPS IN USING QUESTIONS

1. Prepare

You must stimulate students in order to gain their participation. This requires planning in advance. *Prepare*, but make it appear spontaneous enough to stimulate further interchange and discussion.

Start the class with a specific question that you have prepared in advance. The wording is critical. Look at your question and try answering it from the student's point of view. Look for answers, not on the basis of how you'd give them, but what answers your students might give.

In preparing your question, weigh the psychological aspects. Does the question create mental blocks in the students, causing them to go off on irrelevant tangents? Does it lead to erroneous mental procedures, causing the students to arrive at wrong (or even right) answers because of fallacious thinking stimulated by a poorly-worded question?

In preparing your question, the level of challenge has to be considered. Do you make the questions so easy that everyone can answer them, or do you prepare blockbusters that will stop everyone? Usually, a middle-of-the-road approach is taken, which leads to some people taking part but the vast majority just sitting there. This problem can be overcome by dropping the blockbuster. The silent lack of answers that follows will get the people sitting there thinking, particularly if you repeat the question. In this way, you've got everyone thinking and, ostensibly, with you.

The easy question has its place, too, as a change of pace or as a build-up to the blockbuster. Proper interspersement of hard and easy questions is important and must be planned in advance of the seminar or session.

It is important, too, to prepare for the atmosphere in the classroom. Students won't automatically start talking. The tone is set by the instructor. Students can sense that they aren't to talk, discuss, or ask questions. And they know, too, when they can. Setting a spontaneous atmosphere is part of your preparation. *Usually, the first step in setting the atmosphere is realizing that your main function is to start the session and to sum it up.*

Then, you must decide whether the task can be done in the time available. If it can't, cut the content to what can be covered. Students can sense when the instructor is concerned about time and they will stop discussion and leave it to the course leader to finish because they know he can do it.

Finally, the class needs a stake in what's happening. This is done by providing an informal, relaxed atmosphere, a feeling of freedom, and the assurance that you know they can do it. All this requires a tremendous commitment on the part of the instructor. A commitment to keep quiet, not to talk, not to provide easy answers to questions, and not to visibly lead.

The commitment boils down to creating a situation in which *the students can reach the lesson objective without the instructor.*

Points to Consider

- The phrasing of the question;
- The answer that will be elicited;

- The level of challenge of the question;
- The development of atmosphere.

2. *Ask the Question*

The second step is to *ask the question*. Many training sessions begin with "If you have any questions please ask them," and then the person goes on with his presentation. It's no wonder participation doesn't develop. The emphasis has been reversed.

Students don't start the discussion; the course leader starts it. Students aren't prepared to ask questions. The instructor is. Students often don't know what the topic is, while the instructor does. Consider it for a moment. Preparing questions isn't easy. Yet instructors invariably place the onus on their students to come up with questions. Students must prepare these questions, remember them, and at the same time, listen to the course leader lecturing. That's a task that's impossible to achieve, even for the brightest student.

If participation is the goal, it's the instructor who must ask the question; it is his responsibility, not the students'. To illustrate this point, try starting a lesson by asking "What are we going to work on in this session?" That question will stir up some real participation. Students will dig into the course outline or whatever went with the course to find the topic.

3. *Wait*

At this point, the third step of questioning comes into play: *wait* for the answer. That may seem obvious but, in fact, it isn't. The average instructor will wait between three and five seconds for an answer.

The brevity of this wait is caused by two factors. First, the wait seems ten times as long as it really is. And second, the tension of silence weighs more heavily on the leader than on the students.

Consider the situation: the student must digest the question, realize that an answer is expected, (something he doesn't initially expect), consider the possible answers, formulate the answer into words, and then consider the correctness of his response. By the time he has gone through the "What if I'm wrong?" stage, he will have decided not to give his answer or more likely, he will have forgotten the question. At about this point, the course leader has become so uptight about the lack of answers that he gives the answer instead of repeating the question.

Repeating the question can break the silence, but it may not help. Maybe no one will speak up. This can mean two things: the question should be rephrased or everyone is afraid to break the ice by speaking out.

4. Ask Someone by Name

Step four breaks the ice. *Ask someone by name*. This is a simple thing to do. But knowing who to ask is far from obvious. In the initial stages of the development of the class, ask those who appear to have the right answer. One way to recognize this is by the expression on the student's face or by his apparent physical enthusiasm. Another way is to watch for a slight raise of the hand, finger, or pen. This half-raised hand is a modification of the arm-raising behavior we were taught in school. Watch for it closely as it always signifies someone who has something to say or ask, but is reluctant to declare himself wholeheartedly.

Once you have the uninhibited individuals talking, shift to the more timid people in the class. Here again, use names and, if necessary, silence the more vocal students. An hour of this obviates the emphasis on *who* answers questions. Those who want to speak, to a point, will. In a successful session, the class will spontaneously come up with a flood of responses to any question. This may happen to such an extent that it's a problem, e.g., what do you do when five good answers all come at once? If only one answer is accepted and written on the board, then the other four are ignored.

5. Listen to All Answers

Step five—*listening*—saves us when we are offered too many answers. All answers can be listened to, talked about, and considered. It isn't necessary to write answers on the board. This approach gives students vital reinforcement for responding. An attitude of "Why bother answering, he won't notice it anyway" is prevented.

Dealing with five answers at one time may be confusing. But it is better than taking one answer and ignoring the others. The instructor must listen to and follow up all questions or answers. If he does not, the review becomes an instructor's monologue.

The instructor must hear everything that is said and must remember who said what, so that if problems develop in the discussion, he can enter in and ask a question such as "What was it you said, Bill?" or "Bill said, (repeating Bill's statement) . . . What do *you* think?"

The instructor must also gauge from the student response what his next question to the class should be. Many people use the excuse that it takes longer to cover the same ground if you use planned questions. This isn't necessarily so. By being carefully aware of the group's reactions and responses, the instructor can adjust his questions to take this specific group's progress into account.

By careful listening, the instructor can slip the next question into the discussion, leading the group on to further development of the lesson. A combination on the part of the instructor of asking the right questions and being acutely aware of all responses leads to progress toward the session's objective.

6. Review, Reinforce, Repeat

Step six is the 3R step: *review, reinforce, and repeat*. Naturally, it depends on the instructor's listening to this point. Here, further repetition can be developed. In the previous steps in questioning, the major points of the lesson were brought out but have not been put on the board, overhead projector, or flip chart until now. In the review this can be done with the help of questions.

The leader can ask, "What are the major points?" and then listen. If some major points are missed, it is good to call on those who gave them in the original discussion.

An interesting aspect of the participation/discussion method is that once a student has said something, he *never* forgets it. Concentrated listening makes it possible to draw out the points that tend to be overlooked. Another benefit here is that the student *realizes* you were listening to *his* answers, and he's encouraged to take a more active part in future sessions.

OTHER TIPS

When a question comes from the floor, the instructor should bounce it back for others to answer. Saying, "What do the rest of you think?" may work, but rewording the question is usually necessary. It's even better to have the questioner ask the others what they think.

This bounce technique of having a questioning student ask other students has three benefits:

1. It takes the emphasis off the instructor;
2. It encourages everyone to listen more closely to everything;
3. It develops the participation even further and eventually leads to a total de-emphasis of the instructor. Students quickly learn to ask questions, and to question each others' statements.

Any Questions?

Watch out for the phrase that many instructors use, "Have you any questions?" This is usually followed by the instructor looking at his notes to find out where he is in his presentation. What "Have you any questions?" means is "I don't know where I am in the lesson so give me a moment to find out." This may seem like a harsh generalization but if you doubt it, just watch other instructors. Your chances of seeing this happen are good.

To stimulate participation, use the chalkboard and overhead projector to record answers. Also, putting the question in front of the group in written form helps immensely because it gives the discussion a focal point.

Interruptions Welcome

Once participation develops, students tend to interrupt the instructor. As an instructor, the key here is to stop whatever you're saying, even if it is a key point, and involve the interruptor. *Never* finish what you are saying if you are interrupted. Let them interrupt. What the students have to say has to be more important. Why?—because what the student *says*, and only that, relates closely to *him*.

To Stimulate Discussion

- Get students to repeat their statements for other students.
- Have students ask other students the meaning of what they said.
- Ask one to repeat what another has said. If he can't, have him ask the original speaker to repeat his statement.
- Never center out a student unless he is right—then, get his help in teaching the rest.
- Use positive reinforcement to stimulate discussion. Reinforce right answers.
- Start the lesson with a general question with many possible answers. Everyone should have some answer for it.
- Use a batting-order approach if you have too much participation. Students soon catch on and ask to be placed on the list.
- Ask people to write down their questions if they can't be discussed at the time. Be sure to get back to them later.
- Structure for total participation.

SUMMARY

Questions are a major function in getting total class involvement. Other methods include cases, role plays, in-baskets, games, and simulations; and even student panels help to develop total student involvement.

Student participation is never easy. The instructor must have faith in the concept and have the will to develop participation. Otherwise, the inevitable result will be more lectures and more speeches, courtesy of the instructor.

19

Questions, Answers, and Socrates

Since our last feature on question-and-answer technique, we have learned a great deal more about the method. And it was our students who taught us.

What can a student teach an experienced instructor? We learned to begin a lesson with a question that is probing and challenging. We learned how to pace the lesson more effectively. And we even learned how to handle the bright student who knows it all.

OPENING QUESTION

How do you start a session based on questions? Do *you* start with a question? Most trainers don't; most of us tend to talk to or at the students. We tell them what the topic is. We tell them what we are going to do based on *our* objective. We tell them how we are going to reach our objective; that we are going to ask them questions and will expect them to respond. We tell them something about the subject so that they will have a basis on which to respond to our questions. And we tell them, and we tell them, and *finally*, we get around to asking them a question.

Much of this preamble appears to be necessary, especially the topic and the objective. But is it really essential? Doesn't a question such as *"What things should you check in making a vehicle circle safety check, before driving off in your car?"* give your students a topic and an objective? And doesn't it effectively demonstrate the method by which you expect the students to reach this objective?

How about using a question such as *"What things are necessary in a good training objective?"* as an opener for an instructor training session

---

Marit Stengels was co-author of this column.

on objectives? Doesn't the second example cover the same ground as the first one?

Can we possibly start lessons with a question? Can we start without *telling* the student *our* topic, *our* objective, and without *explaining* to them what we expect from them? The answer is a definite yes.

Do students respond? Again, yes.

How do they respond? It varies with the question you ask and the specific group you are working with. Let's take an example of what we've found to be a good opening question and see what makes it effective:

How can an instructor get real participation in his classroom?

We've learned that the parameters of this opening question—

- open the session on topic;
- are such that all students have the ability and opportunity to answer;
- invite many potentially correct answers;
- challenge students.

Questions That Challenge

Basically, there are three different types of challenging question:

1. *Convergent:* a question that brings together facts to form a fact or theory;
2. *Divergent:* a question that evokes interpretation, explanation, and translation;
3. *Evaluative:* a question that requires the student to make certain judgments about the facts presented. When the student is confronted with an evaluative question, he can respond by exploring and analyzing within the parameter of facts set out by your question.

The types of *challenging* question as set out above don't seem too complicated. If this is so, why don't teachers make better use of challenging questions? There are a number of facts that cause this situation:

1. It's unrewarding to the teacher; students find challenging questions difficult to answer; the teacher faces long stretches of silence, while students try to work out an answer to the challenging question; many teachers would rather fill this silence by answering their own questions instead of waiting for the class to do so;

2. Frequently the teacher has no answer to a challenging question; because the teacher doesn't have the answer, he's afraid to ask the question and expose the fact that he doesn't "know it all";

3. Challenging questions require much thought and preparation on the part of the teacher; many teachers feel they don't have enough time to insert them in the preparation of a session;

4. Asking a challenging question requires an understanding of the student thinking process and, often, we aren't too sure of this process ourselves.

What happens to the class if teachers stick to asking questions that have *one specific answer in the mind of the teacher*? For instance, if the teacher wants his student to answer with the word *tracks*:

Instructor: What do tanks run on?
Student: Roads.
Instructor: What else?
Student: Fields.
Instructor: Yes, but what do they run on, on roads and fields?
Student: Gas.
Instructor: Let's try it another way, what do athletes train on?
Student: Steaks.
Instructor: Yes, but what do they run their races on?
Student: Spikes.
Instructor: Well, what do cattle make across fields?
Student: Paths.
Instructor: Hmm! What do tigers make in the jungle?
Student: Tigresses.
Instructor: Come on now!
Student *(finally)*: Tracks.
Instructor: Right! The tracks of any tank can be destroyed by this grenade.

Socrates has often been credited for using the question-and-answer techniques. The following is an excerpt from one of the dialogues of Plato, *Meno* 70A-71E (See Figure 19.1).

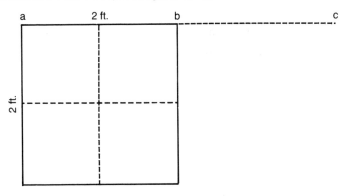

Figure 19.1

Socrates: Is this a four-cornered space having all these lines equal, all four?

Boy: Surely.

Socrates: And these across the middle, are they not equal too?

Boy: Yes.

Socrates: Such a space might be larger or smaller?

Boy: Oh yes.

Socrates: Then if this side is two feet long and this two, how many feet would the whole be? Or look at it this way: if it were two feet this way, and only one the other, would not the space be once two feet?

Boy: Yes.

Socrates: But as it is two feet this way also, isn't it twice two feet?

Boy: Yes, so it is.

Socrates: So the space is twice two feet?

Boy: Yes.

Socrates: Then how many are twice two feet? Count and tell me.

How would you evaluate Socrates's technique in posing *challenging* questions?

Who does most of the talking? Socrates. Who does most of the work? Socrates himself. What does the student do most? He listens and answers yes-and-no questions. Will the student later be able to go through the same logic process without Socrates' assistance? Not very likely. Even Socrates himself doesn't think so. According to B. F. Skinner (*The Technology of Teaching*, 1968), Socrates was a believer in the frequency theory, e.g. make the student *memorize* facts through the repetition process.

Socrates asks few challenging questions and does most of the work in getting the answers to the questions he *does* ask.

Learning occurs only when students work hard (participate) in arriving at answers to challenging questions. We've developed an axiom based on this fact:

1. the harder the instructor works, the less learning occurs;

2. the harder the student works, the more the student learns.

20

Questions and Answers, Part 2

In the preceding article, we said that a session using the question-and-answer technique should open with a question that—

- opens the session on topic;
- all students have the ability and opportunity to answer;
- invites many potentially correct answers;
- challenges students.

From there, we went on to discuss the characteristics of *questions that challenge*, giving the three basic types of challenging questions as we see them:

- Convergent,
- Divergent,
- Evaluative.

In discussing the types of questions that challenge, we get into the problems of both pacing the session and of handling the bright student in the class.

The simplest way to examine this situation is through Figures 20.1 to 20.4.

Figure 20.1 could be representative of any instructional situation. *A* represents the starting point of the session; e.g. the students' abilities and prior knowledge, the instructor's capabilities, and the resources available to the students and the instructor. *B* represents the instructional objective of the session. The straight line between *A* and *B* represents the most direct route to the objective.

Marit Stengels was co-author of this column.

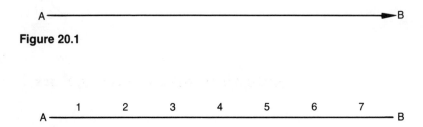

Figure 20.1

Figure 20.2

In trying to use question-and-answer technique, many instructors make the mistake of asking the first question in such a way that the answer only puts them at point 1 in Figure 20.2. They follow up with a second question for which the answer is only at point 2. By the time point 7 is reached on a one-by-one in-turn basis, the students have a highly justified complaint that the session is boring and does not take their abilities into account.

Instead, the instructor should open with a question that can potentially place the class at point 4 or 5.

Supposing you, as the instructor, ask a question that should place you at point 4 along the line. Instead of getting the full answer you anticipated, which would put you at point 4, you're likely to get an answer that would put you—

A. in front of point 4;

b. behind point 4;

C. above point 4;

D. below point 4;

E. not even remotely related to point 4.

Figure 20.3 illustrates these types of answers. Answer A and B respond in greater and lesser depth respectively than your individual question meant to evoke. Answers C, D, and E represent responses that are off the topic to varying degrees.

This diversity of possible answers, as illustrated in Figure 20.3, is one of the main reasons why, after the first question, the teacher often abandons the questioning technique. He shouldn't, because it is at this point that he can get the class to think further about the problem under consideration. Significant learning can occur at this point. How can you handle these diverse answers? You can use the answer you have received to form another question. If you do this you are probing the class.

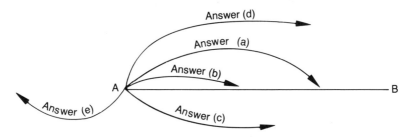

Figure 20.3

Probing

The five different ways of using a probing question are:

1. to *clarify* an answer;
2. to *justify* an answer;
3. to *refocus* an answer;
4. to *expand* an answer;
5. to *redirect* the answer.

You can *clarify* one student's answer by getting another student to state more clearly what was said. This clarifying probe will probably take the form, "What did he mean by . . .?" and include a summation of what was originally said. This repetition of the original answer is necessary because often students don't hear what other students say. By restating what was said, you don't have an extended and embarrassing silence from a group of students who didn't hear the answer.

Getting a student—or better still, the rest of the class—to *justify* an answer is easy. Just ask, "Why?" or "Why that?" Then the students will consider the original question and the answer given in order to get at the reasons behind the answer. In other words by asking "Why?" about an answer, you are increasing the class's critical awareness.

With *refocusing*, you are working on the problems illustrated by answers C, D, and E in Figure 20.3. In all of these three cases, the students involved have somehow missed the main thread of the original question. The reasons for missing the thread range from the student's failure to listen, to the more probable reason that you, the teacher, asked the wrong question. Sometimes you can use the students' answers in these cases and loop the answer back into the direction you are going. At other times you have to refocus your thinking completely to see how students could possibly answer your well-prepared question so far off the topic. With successful reorientation of yourself in relation to the students, you should have no problem coming up with the proper question that will refocus the class back on the track.

Expanding an answer is easy. Just look puzzled and keep quiet. Either the person who gave the answer or another student will talk further on the point just made. Of course you can always say, "What do the rest of you think?" or "Could someone expand on that?" You should use this type of probing question in the following situations:

1. The class looks puzzled and needs more information to understand the answer that was given; or

2. You, the trainer, don't understand the answer. If you use expansion-type probing questions when you don't understand a student's answer, you will often find that an answer you thought was wrong is right. How's this? Well, the students always give answers related to their frames of reference and only rarely do their frames of reference coincide with your own.

Finally, *redirecting* the answer means you *get other students involved* with your original question. For some reason, a right answer given means most of us trainers move on to the next question. But we shouldn't, because only one person gave the answer. Use the class, the whole class. Redirect your question and work it until all students have grasped the point being made.

Handling Bright Students

In Figure 20.3, answer A could be from a bright student. What do you do? It is possible that the rest of the class hasn't made the mental jumps your bright student has made. How can you ensure that the rest of the class moves up to the same point your bright student is at; and at the same time how do you maintain the bright student's high level of participation?

First, in terms of handling your bright student you can do the following:

• Reward him by letting him out early. Unfortunately this is a negative action in terms of the rest of the class. It implies the class is a bad place to be and that those not let out early are being punished.

• Let the bright student know that he knows (e.g., reinforce him) and then ignore him.

• Ask the bright student to teach the rest of the class to arrive at the same answers he has. This is highly reinforcing to the bright student but unfortunately there's a problem: the students don't want the instructor to abdict his job—they want the instructor to teach the lesson. This can be handled as the situation arises: break up the class into informal groups and ask the students to help each other.

- A fourth way of handling a bright student's answer—or, for that matter, any answer—is to use the probing technique discussed earlier.

When you ask a question that puts the whole class at point 4 (Figure 20.4), but a bright student gives a response that is at point 6, you can loop back to point 5, (and if necessary, to point 4) to ensure that the whole class has learned to this point.

Figure 20.4

With both extremes of bright and slow students in any class, the question of pace can be a thorny one. However, you can use the following suggestions in general:

- The questions you pose should elicit student answers that eventually lead to a breakdown in the questioning and the development of an on-the-topic, in-depth, class discussion of the point being developed.

- If you're building a number of potential answers from which to develop a concept, the pace should be fast. List all the answers given by the students and focus on the ones you want in the next step.

- When you're developing concepts, go slowly, giving students time to think. Use lists of quickly compiled answers to focus on those that are relevant to your objective and have students develop the concepts you are after.

Question-and-answer technique can be a highly effective means of initiating students into necessarily participatory learning. Perhaps one of the biggest drawbacks to using questions is that they have an intrinsically aversive nature to them.

Suppose that an instructor asks you, "What are the possible consequences of uncontrolled, snowballing pollution?" Your first reaction at an almost subconscious level is likely to be, "Oh! oh! He knows something and now he's testing me to see if I know. If I don't give him the right answer, he'll have made me look ignorant. Maybe, if I look at the floor he'll think I'm not listening and ask someone else."

Undoubtedly, disclosure (responding to questions) is threatening to an individual. This can be overcome by reinforcement: encourage students to answer and dont' put them down for incorrect answers. If an incorrect answer is given, don't reinforce the answer itself, but reinforce the responding student for the simple act of *answering*.

21

Memorizing Versus Understanding

This article is based on three premises about instructing. These are: (1) that learning is desired, (2) that retention is desired, and (3) that the most effective and instructional technique is desired.

To set the stage for exploring the way to find the right lesson format to achieve the results we want, I'm first going to outline an experiment from the field of learning research (Katona, 1940). Then I'll add my own experiences in adult education and hopefully draw some conclusions about lesson formats.

LEARNING RESEARCH

To keep the research on learning and retention within bounds, only two types of learning process will be outlined here: memorizing and understanding.

Three learning groups were set up by Katona: the understanding group of nine people, the memorizing group of nine people, and a control group of four people. Figure 21.1 outlines the card tricks used. Figure 21.2 outlines how each group was instructed. Figure 21.3 outlines the results of the experiment.

RESULTS EXPLAINED

The general summary of results in Figure 21.3 reveals that the memorizing group had a slight advantage in the pure memory tests, but the understanding group had *considerable* advantage in the tests in which variations of the learning material were presented. Trick A, which was included in the learning period of both groups, was solved somewhat better by the memorizing group than by the understanding group and the same holds true of Trick B, which was taught to the memorizing

Trick A

The trick consists of taking eight ordinary playing cards in your hand and saying to the audience: "Watch. I take the top card and place it on the table. It is a red card. Then I take the next card and put it at the bottom of the deck without determining what it is. I place the third card on the table. It is a black card. The following card, of undetermined color, I put below the others; while the next card, which is red, I put on the table."

The procedure of alternately placing one card on the table and one at the bottom of the deck is continued until all the cards in the deck were placed on the table. The cards appeared on the table in this order: red, black, red, black, and so forth.

Trick B

Same trick as above only eight spades, ace through 8 were used. They wound up on the table in assembling order, 1,2,3 etc., through alternately placing one on the table and one on the bottom of the deck.

Trick variations

There are many variations of this trick. First, it is possible to vary the number of cards used; for example 4, 13, 52, or any number for that matter. Second, the trick can be varied by putting two or three cards instead of one card at the bottom of the deck each time after a card is placed on the table. Third, a simple variation consists of starting the trick by placing one or two cards at the bottom of the deck before turning up the first card.

Figure 21.1[1]

Memorizing group

Time of learning period—4 minutes. In this period the members of the group repeated aloud the arrangements required to solve Trick A and Trick B. No explanation of how or why the order of cards was arrived at was given.

Understanding group

Time of learning period—4 minutes. In this period, the members of the group listened alternatively to the explanation of how the cards are assembled to allow Trick A to be performed. Note: they did not memorize the order but learned to understand how the order was arrived at. Trick B was not shown to this group.

Control group

Received no instructions.

Figure 21.2. The instructing procedures

---

[1]Adapted from George Katona, *Organizing and Memorizing: Studies in the Psychology of Learning & Teaching*, pp. 34-45. Copyright 1940 by Columbia University Press. Adapted by permission of the publisher.

	Understanding group		Memorizing group		Control group	
	Correct	Failed	Correct	Failed	Correct	Failed
Task 1: Trick A	6	3	8	1	0	4
Task 2: Easy variation of Trick A	6	3	1	8	1	3
Task 3: Difficult variation of Trick A	4	5	2	7	0	4
Task 4: Trick A with material B	6	3	5	4	1	3
Task 5: Trick B	6	3	7	2	0	4
Task 6: New easy task	9	0	7	2	3	1

Figure 21.3. Results of the experiment[2]

group but not to the understanding group. On the other hand, the results obtained with Tasks 2, 3, 4, and 6 indicate the understanding group as a whole was able to apply its knowledge to variations of the practiced task, while the memorizing group was not. The results of the control group indicate the degree of difficulty in solving the tasks without any instruction. From this we can see that the pure memorizing process causes learners excessive difficulties when they have to solve variations of what they have learned.

Katona goes on to draw the following preliminary results of his experiment.

Length of Instructing Time

In memorizing, the time required for learning depends on the number of repetitions. Learning takes longer for a substantial amount of material than for a small amount. On the other hand, learning by understanding is independent of the amount of material, since the understanding of a trick with a few cards is sufficient to ensure knowledge of the trick with a very large number of cards. Therefore memorizing is a quicker method of learning only when a small amount of material is involved.

For a large amount, and for more complex material, meaningful learning is much easier and much more acceptable than memorizing. In addition, it must be kept in mind, as proved by many old experiments, that in memorizing a considerable amount of over-learning (repetitions beyond the point of first mastery) is required to ensure retention after a long interval. Thus, even

---

[2]Ibid., p. 39.

with comparatively simple materials, memorizing is often not a quicker method of learning than understanding if retention over a long period of time is desired. (p. 44)[3]

Performance Time

When, in tests, the subjects were asked to perform a task which they had learned in the training period, the members of the memorizing group completed their work quicker than the members of the understanding group. Memorizing may therefore have some advantages over understanding if for any reason it is necessary that reproduction time be very short. (p. 44)[4]

Applications

Memorizing permitted transfer of training from one material to the other to a very limited extent only. When the tests consisted of tasks different from those which were practiced, the memorizers often were at a complete loss, while most subjects who learned by understanding succeeded easily. Often it is no more difficult for meaningful learners to deal with variations of the material and to apply a principle than to deal with the practiced material. (p. 45)[5]

Retention

After an interval of one week or more, retention resulting from meaningful learning was better, and after memorizing forgetting occurred sooner. These results were obtained even with short and simple material. (pp. 44-45)[6]

Figure 21.4 summarizes these research results.

Using memorizing	Using understanding
Shorter retention.	Longer retention.
Longer learning time (as amount to be learned increases).	Shorter learning time (as amount to be learned increases).
Less task adaptability.	More task adaptability.
Fast performance of memorized tasks.	Slow performance on tasks.

Figure 21.4. Summary of research results

---

[3]Ibid., p. 44.

[4]Ibid., p. 44.

[5]Ibid., p. 45.

[6]Ibid., pp. 44-45.

EFFECT OF RESEARCH

How does this information affect choosing a lesson format? It affects it tremendously. Let us consider a task that is used often, has a short cycle or has few steps involved, and has no variations possible. Retention can develop from the repetition of the few steps involved. Understanding is not needed because there are no variations involved in this task. In essence, this is a "monkey see, monkey do" situation and very suitable to the memorization type of teaching outlined at the bottom of the list in Figure 21.5.

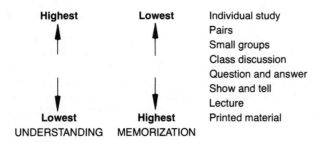

Figure 21.5. Relationship of memorization/understanding to eight instructional techniques

Now consider the opposite type of task: one that has low use (it is used on a random or infrequent basis), has a long cycle or has many steps involved, and an infinite number of possible variations. This kind of learning situation has a lot of problems built into it for the instructor. Because of the infrequent use, we need long retention of what was taught. The variation means we need to develop the students' ability to adapt what they learn to other situations. Looking at Figure 21.4, we find that the retention and adaptability needs of this learning situation indicate a need to use the understanding type of learning. This means we need to teach the material using individual study if we refer to Figure 21.5.

Individualizing Learning Material

Overcoming the problem of individualizing this complex learning material is simple, but it requires a lot of testing of learning materials on the part of the instructor. The simple solution is this: *make the student aware of where to find the information needed to accomplish the task and have him use it to solve problems and tasks that are progressively more difficult.* In other words, teach the students to use reference material to find out what they are to do. Then have them apply what they have read. This teaches the student to interpret reference materials. And if there is a misinterpretation, the instructor is able to correct it. If reading material on the task isn't available, the same solution still applies. You structure the situation so that the student can solve progressively more complex problems using whatever knowledge is available (it may be already in his head).

Contrast the above with what is usually done: a lecture that is quickly forgotten, and a student that is in a beginning situation the first time he has to try the task but without the benefit of an instructor to provide feedback. The whole point of this type of instruction is that the instructor *is available* if he is needed.

WHICH METHOD IS FASTEST?

Which is fastest? Memorizing? Understanding? Neither. The fastest way depends on what is being taught. Material learned by memorizing is rapidly forgotten if it is not used frequently. I suspect that in most cases a lecture is forgotten in two or three days. So, if you need retention, remember: *as the frequency of use decreases, the amount of understanding a student has must increase.*

22

How to Make Case Studies Come Alive

Case studies can be deadly dull especially for the student. They should be dynamic. The student should find them lively, exciting, and anything but insipid.

The reasons why case studies often fail are many, ranging from poor research and foggy writing, to badly administered cases. Let's look at group size and seating arrangements, and then delve into methods of taking up (i.e., sharing and processing) group findings after the group has discussed a particular case.

Group Size

A group of four or five participants is generally best, although other sizes can serve specific purposes. A group of three can be used when the case material leads to a role-play situation in which two can play the roles and the third serves as observer. Groups of more than five can illustrate the problem of control. The larger the group, the harder it is for it to work effectively. Usually, large groups working on a case tend to break up into smaller groups; this leads to coordinating problems and less group unanimity in the findings. The four-or-five member group can avoid these problems and proceed quickly and effectively with group work on the case.

Seating Arrangements

Have you ever watched a class breaking up into groups to solve or discuss a case? Unless they are experienced, students tend to sit in a

---

Marit Stengels was co-author of this column.

way that restricts the group's functioning ability. Figure 22.1 illustrates a few seating arrangements groups can take.

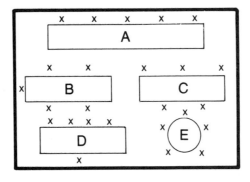

Figure 22.1. Seating arrangements

Arrangement E, the circle, allows each person to see everyone else. It permits a tighter arrangement of the group and greater group involvement. Rarely do groups take the optimum arrangement illustrated in E. The major reason for this is that most classrooms have either desk-type seats or chairs and tables—not small round coffee tables. The usual arrangement results in the students being inhibited by the furniture. They won't push the desks away, nor will they disregard the table, move back, and form a circle.

You, as the instructor, must act by *asking* the members which seating arrangement in Figure 22.1 will lead to the best group problem-solving performance. And, when they say E (which they will) ask them why. On the other hand, if you *tell* them to form in a circle, you will discover that you are reducing the class participation. You are indirectly saying, "You people don't know enough to arrange your seating properly." They may conclude that if they can't even arrange their seating without direction, then how are they supposed to solve the case?

Taking Up Group Findings

You have probably been at seminars in which the extremely good case is discussed heatedly by small groups and then the whole session fizzles when the groups meet to share or take up, the results of their discussions.

Why? Because most instructors do it the wrong way. They either reveal the textbook solution to all the groups at the end of the small group activity or, even worse, they have each group in turn report its findings as shown in Figure 22.2. Imagine having eight or nine groups all report their findings on the same case. Group 1 reports. Then Group 2 tells you its findings have some similarity to those of Group 1. Then Groups 3 and 4 add theirs, usually qualified by "much of what we have to report was covered by Groups 1 and 2." Groups 5, 6, 7, and 8 stand to report and say, "All our findings have already been covered." If that isn't disastrous, we don't know what is.

Having eight groups in one class is an extreme. Most classes have only about four or five small groups, so the problem isn't as bad. But it is still there.

Another problem is: what do the groups do while the others are reporting? They listen. How effectively do they listen? Nichols' (1957) research indicates that immediate recall of a ten-minute talk is 25 percent of what was said. Note that he measured *immediate* recall. What about half an hour later, or a week later, or longer? Something should be done to improve the passive class's involvement. The ideal would be to have all the groups interacting together as illustrated in Figure 22.3. How you can accomplish this will be explained after we've coped with one more problem.

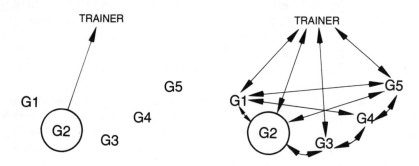

Figure 22.2   **Figure 22.3**

Usually, the other groups have no stake in the group's report because everyone knows that the trainer will sum up the findings in the end anyway. If you are willing to accept the findings of the class as a whole, you can get everyone listening, participating, interacting, and having a stake in the outcome.

When the groups report their findings, accept only *one* point from each group in turn and refrain from posting it as part of the case's solution unless the other groups agree to accept it.

To do this, limit the first group to one thought or point and ask the other groups if they have that answer. If they do, post it on the chalkboard or flip chart. Then ask Group 2 for another point, and so on.

Usually by the second or third point, if not the first, there is no agreement. When this happens, all the trainer does is say, "What do the rest of you say?" or "Well, I guess we can't post that" (in such a way as to say "Are you sure it shouldn't be posted?" or "Reporting Group, you had better defend your position because the point is valid"). If this is done properly, everyone is involved, arguments between groups develop, communication problems are solved, greater understanding of the case develops, and, most important of all, everyone has a stake in the solution of the case.

Use of Competition

You can improve the processing of cases by using competitive activities, such as the following:

- Have the small groups role play as management consultant organizations that are bidding to work with the company in the case;
- Establish a board of judges (one judge from each group) in another room; the board hears the report from the chairman of each group and chooses the best solution suggested;
- Have the entire class choose the best solution to the case, which requires the kind of exchange shown in Figure 22.3 (if the trainer can keep out of the discussion).

Cases aren't the only way of having meaningful group discussions. Questions often serve just as well. For example, consider the group learning that occurs when this question is given to a small group: "Using the resources you have (experience, previous training, etc.), prepare to present:

(a) what you, as a group, feel are the functions of a manager;

(b) how each function is used in doing your jobs."

The discussions of this question are taken up, a point from each group at a time, and when the members are agreeing or disagreeing as to whether or not a point should be posted, the group temperature rises with the discussion. The last time we used it, it was next to impossible to complete the activity within the two-hour limit.

REFERENCES AND READINGS

Nichols, R. G., & Stevens, L. A. *Are You Listening*. New York: McGraw-Hill, 1957.

Zoll, A. A. *Dynamic Management Education* (2nd ed.). Reading, MA: Addison-Wesley, 1969.

23

What to Do About Handouts

Recently we received a letter from an instructor requesting advice. The problem was outlined as follows: "I am now with the . . . . School of Radiography. The commission has directed us to use precise notes (each student receives a copy) on every heading, sub-heading etc. that is in our 120-page syllabus. Naturally this requires a lot of work but this is not the problem. What has me stumped is how to use these notes to best advantage."

Before looking at possible solutions to this problem, it is necessary to examine some of the facts governing class handouts.

Fact 1: Even in the most effective and dynamic course, students feel cheated unless they receive handouts. Students want them.

Fact 2: Most handouts are never read. Long experience has shown that while students are very careful to collect their handouts, a large percentage of them file them away and never look at them again.

These facts immediately raise a number of questions:

A. Is there an alternative action to giving out handouts?

or, barring that,

B. How can you get students to read them?

In this column, we are going to concern ourselves with B: *how to get students to read handouts.*

There are a large number of variables affecting the fate of such material:

- The nature of the handout itself;

Marit Stengels was co-author of this column.

- The timing, e.g., *when* the student receives it,
- What the student is expected to do with it once he receives it.
- How do you as an instructor follow-up on the handout and the actions the students are to take with it?

Let's take a look at a couple of examples.

HANDOUT 1: A fifteen-page recap of the day's session on scheduling is handed out at the end of the class. It is implied that students are meant to read this handout but no follow-up action on the part of the instructor is scheduled.

This is one handout that is not too likely to get read. Would telling students that they are to be *tested* on the contents at the next session induce greater readership? To some extent, yes. But it's hardly valid to do so. In the first place, if the session has gone successfully, you won't need to test students because you'll already be aware of what they have and haven't learned. And if the session has not been so successful, announcing a test on the handout is merely using it as a crutch for poor teaching.

A more significant objection is that threatening students with a test in order to get them to read material is not far removed from coercion, and there are more effective and direct ways to accomplish the same objective.

What would have happened if this handout had been given out at the beginning of the class or during it? It is likely that the result would have been disruptive. Unless you had planned that students would work with the handout during the session, you would have to cope with students paying more attention to the handout rather than to the activity in progress.

HANDOUT 2: This is a three-page handout in objectives. The first page contains various examples of acceptable and non-acceptable objectives. The second page directs the students to come up with specific types of objectives. The third page asks a number of questions designed to evoke the basic criteria for objectives. The material is given out after an introduction by the instructor at the beginning of the session. The session activity revolves around the content of the objective.

Immediately we can see that:

- This handout must be read by all students participating in the session;
- No artificial coercion is necessary;
- The students' desire for a handout is satisfied;
- The handout is meaningful in terms of the activity of the class.

From this example we can evolve the basic criteria for handouts that are meaningful, and at the same time satisfy the following student needs and administration requirements:

- The handout must be pertinent to the session;
- The handout must be an integral part of the session activity;
- The handout must be such that the student is expected to work with it.

Preparing such handouts may be more difficult and time consuming than preparing summaries or supplementary facts. You have to find a way to get students involved and working with the material. But the extra time spent is more than justified; e.g., you can spend two hours preparing a reading handout (with no follow-up) that only 20 percent of your class might read, or you can spend an extra hour preparing one that everyone must read in order to participate. The benefits of spending that extra hour are pretty clear.

Chiefly, you try to adjust the material in the handout and plan your session in such a way that the student *must* get involved with the material in it in order to participate in the session.

An overworked, but nevertheless valid, example of this is the use of case studies followed by a set of questions that the students must answer. This makes it necessary for them to read the case before going on to the questions. Or your handout might simply be a series of questions that students must answer in the course of a session. Thus, in your handout, you're giving them the questions instead of the answers. The answers they formulate themselves, with your help, in group discussions.

Handouts are generally most effective if they're given out at the beginning of the session and used as an integral part of the session activity. When this simply is not possible and you must give them out at the end of the session, design the material in such a way that the student is expected to take some overt actions with it (in this case, simple reading not being overt enough). Then schedule a follow-up on these actions. It is extremely important to let the student know that he can expect this follow-up.

Example: You have just completed a session on Herzberg's theory that money is a hygiene factor rather than a motivator. Your handout is a recap of Herzberg's theory. Ask your class to investigate the attitudes of other prominent industrial psychologists toward this theory and to come prepared to discuss it at the following session. Or you might ask each student to find out how the people he works with feel about this theory.

Meaningful Notes Result

If you prepare handouts that are truly a vital part of a course, students should have, at the end of the course, a set of personalized notes that are far more meaningful than "reading" handouts, which few people look at.

Using handouts in the way suggested here gives you an opportunity to improve your effectiveness as an instructor.

24

On Name Tags and Why They Matter

Remembering and using people's names helps improve your training. Think of the effect that hearing *your* name has on *you*. You look up, move toward the speaker, and feel good inside—all because your name was used. These same effects apply to students. They, too, respond positively to the use of their names.

Name tags are essential. They add a personal touch to training sessions. They make the participation more meaningful because the students' names can easily be used by both the teacher and the other students. In this article I will outline a collection of ideas I have found helpful in making and using student name tags.

Making Name Tags

This may seem like a section you should skip if you *know* how to make name tags. Well, don't—because this section contains a number of valuable tips.

Tip 1: Make the name tags yourself. Never let the students print their names on the cards. The reasons for this are: (a) they print their names too small to be read at any significant distance, such as across the classroom, and (b) you, the instructor lose the opportunity to write the students' names. Why is that an opportunity? Simply stated: by writing the students names on the tags, you have a chance to start relating and memorizing them.

Tip 2: Make the name tags as the students enter the class. Waiting until all students are present, or until the starting time for the class, is unnecessary. Making the name tags as the students enter does require that you arrive early to greet them as they arrive—not too much of a hardship for most instructors. If you need an early morning coffee, ask one of the early bird students to get it for you, if he is going to get one for himself (somebody will offer, you can bet). By making the name tags early, you also give the students a chance to learn each others' names.

Tip 3: Put only first names on the tags. This allows you to use *large* letters. The advantages of this are obvious. You can read the names easily, other students can read them easily too and, probably most important, you don't use the last names, company divisions, or any of the other information often put on name tags. If you are like me, you just use the students' first name—period. If you feel that other information would be helpful, have the students print it on the tag under the first name. A corollary is to use a person's nickname, if he has one.

Tip 4: Use a felt pen with a very broad marking surface. Whatever you do, don't use the felt pen you usually write with. The nib isn't broad enough to be seen at a reasonable distance. Another "don't" is the use of red for making name tags. It's harder to see than almost all the other major colors. Use black, dark blue, or green pens, because they are easily read from a distance.

Tip 5: Write the students' names on both sides of the tags. This may seem like wasted effort, but there are several reasons for doing it. If the name tag happens to become turned around or if the student places his name toward himself, you can still see it; students sitting on the same side of the table can still see the other names; and you may, at some point in your lesson, find yourself at the sides or at the back of the room and, if this happens, you can still see the names.

Tip 6: Use every opportunity to memorize peoples' names at the start of the class. Structure your classes so that you have a group activity near the beginning. This will allow you mentally to connect faces to the names. Also, in the period before class starts, where you are making the name tags as the students enter, use the time between student arrivals to talk with the early birds. While doing this, use names as often as possible.

Tip 7: Suggestions for what to do when you arrive at a class and there are no name tags. First, don't panic. Make name tags out of ordinary paper. But paper name tags won't stand up. Even cardboard ones sometimes sag or fall. What you can do is nip the corners, as shown in Figure 24.1. Take a sheet of paper and try it—it works.

Tip 8: Use name tags for communicating ideas, as shown in Figure 24.2. Note that the top third is printed upside down. This comes out right when the card is folded properly. In printing this, be sure to indent the company name or logo about one inch from the side of the card. This will leave enough room to allow you to nip the corner of the card so that it will stand better.

Tip 9: Ideas for placement of name tags in classrooms. If there are no tables or little room for them on the students' desks, this problem can be solved in any number of ways. Place the name tags on the floor in front of each student; they can still be seen easily. If the ceiling is relatively low, you can hang the name tags from the ceiling, using a putty type of substance. Get the type of name tag that can be either pinned or stuck on clothes. In making these tags, don't have them typed; print them using a felt pen, as shown in Figure 24.3. I have used a relatively long name deliberately to show that it can be done.

Tip 10: Name tags should be skewed when placed in front of students. Usually, name tags are placed squarely in front of students. This is fine as long as you are facing the student directly. Figure 24.4 contrasts a usual and a skewed arrangement of name tags for students sitting on the sides of a U shape. Note how the name tags can be read easier by both the teacher and the students.

Tip 11: When everyone knows all the students' names, remove the name tags from the class. This doesn't mean remove the name tags when you know all the students' names. Make sure they know each others names before you take the tags away.

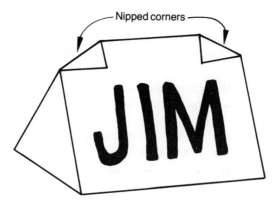

Figure 24.1. An easy way to strengthen name tags made from paper

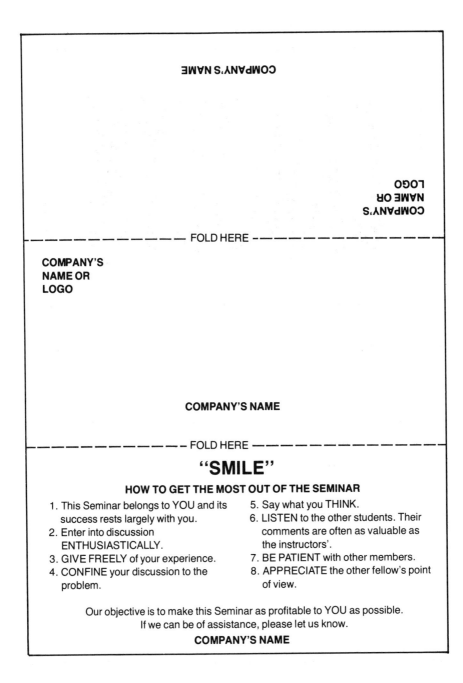

COMPANY'S NAME

COMPANY'S
NAME OR
LOGO

—————————— FOLD HERE ——————————————

COMPANY'S
NAME OR
LOGO

COMPANY'S NAME

—————————— FOLD HERE ——————————————

"SMILE"

HOW TO GET THE MOST OUT OF THE SEMINAR

1. This Seminar belongs to YOU and its success rests largely with you.
2. Enter into discussion ENTHUSIASTICALLY.
3. GIVE FREELY of your experience.
4. CONFINE your discussion to the problem.
5. Say what you THINK.
6. LISTEN to the other students. Their comments are often as valuable as the instructors'.
7. BE PATIENT with other members.
8. APPRECIATE the other fellow's point of view.

Our objective is to make this Seminar as profitable to YOU as possible. If we can be of assistance, please let us know.

COMPANY'S NAME

Figure 24.2. One way to gain extra mileage from name tags

Figure 24.3. A full-size example

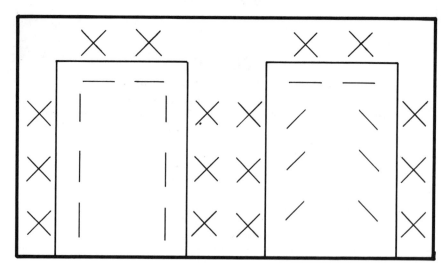

Figure 24.4. Skewed arrangement of name tags (right) makes them easier for the instructor to see than the more usual placement (left)

Part

Audio-Visual
Aids and Resources

25

What Aids to Use, and When

I recently received the letter that follows. While reading it, ask yourself these questions: How would *you* answer it? Are slides more effective than films? Is this really a question of stills versus motion pictures or is there some other issue in question? Are the points mentioned in the letter valid?

Here it is:

We would very much appreciate your opinion concerning the relative merits of motion picture training films as compared to projected still pictures. Not being a commercial producer of either motion or still pictures, you are in an ideal position to weigh the pros and cons objectively.

The value of visual aids in training is of course fully appreciated but we want to determine which of the two types mentioned is of greater value, and why.

For example, it is obviously much more economical to use projected still pictures (slides and transparent and opaque projections). This type of aid has unlimited flexibility—permitting additions, deletions, and sequence rearrangement at any time to tailor a presentation to the background, abilities, interests, and responsibilities of any audience, or as time dictates. It also permits any presentation to be kept completely up to date to meet changing conditions and new knowledge. Duplicate sets can be made much more economically.

Other advantages of still projections would appear to be the ability both to leave any picture on the screen as long as desired and to rescreen the same picture quickly and easily for review or discussion of specific points in the presentation. But what about the relative merits of the two media for audience retention? Is one type more effective than the other?

It has been stated that although sound tracks can be very effective in some ways by taking over the teaching function, a sound track tends to reduce the instructor's responsibility for thorough preparation and to place his personality and experience in the background.

The capital investment in a motion picture is extremely high, and when it or any part of it becomes outdated, replacement is equally costly.

Although motion pictures are undoubtedly very popular for instructional purposes, it is possible that in reality they are a status symbol because in comparison to still pictures, they seem more sophisticated to the group using them.

It would appear that the advantages of projected still pictures outweigh those of motion pictures both economically and in flexibility. But from a purely educational viewpoint, which is more effective?

Can one give categorical answers to the questions this writer poses? Unfortunately, no—because these questions give rise to a great many others that need to be answered first.

It would be wholly untrue to say that either medium is more effective, *per se*, than the other. The effectiveness of any medium depends, not on its intrinsic merits, but on a number of very basic factors—not to mention the quality of concept and execution. It's the need that determines the *ideal* choice, which is then subject to budget parameters. It is the quality of the course design, together with the relevance and quality of supporting aids, that determines their effectiveness.

Here are some of the effectiveness factors:

- What kind of information, knowledge, ideas, or skills are to be imparted to whom?
- How many people do you plan to reach at any one time?
- In what location?
- Under what circumstances?
- Will the course be administered by a trainer, a supervisor, self-instruction, or a mix of these?
- What provision is there for *immediate* reinforcement of learning on the job or through hands-on simulation?
- How often does the information need to be updated?
- What resources—cash, equipment, graphic skills, personnel—are available to you for purchase, lease, hire, production, and presentation at the receiving end?
- What suitable material is available off the shelf, and in what media? Is it valid in its entirety or would it be more effective to use segments, integrating them into your own programs—possibly converting them onto other media?
- Is it practical—even preferable—to produce your own aids (or have them custom produced if the budget permits), bearing in mind that retention as well as subsequent application may receive

an assist through the audio-visual participation of people known personally to your audience in places and situations that they can readily identify?

The action of motion pictures does have an undisputed edge for certain situations, such as the facility for slow motion and single-frame projection when the training need calls for this kind of flexibility. Can you match this effectiveness through progressive slides, filmstrips, or overhead projectuals? Only thorough analysis of the message you want to convey can give you the answer.

Tabulated matter, such as statistics, charts, graphs, and the like, provides an example of material that can be presented effectively through skills of one kind or another, and that can come to life through imaginative use of the medium, such as progressive overlays on overhead projectuals, or working model transparencies. Their significance may be delivered more effectively on film—particularly through animation—but at a price.

One route to the choice of media is to ask another basic question: Will it work? The simplest presentation is an outright liability, even if it is absolutely free, if it doesn't have the required effect and produce the required results. Cost must be related to the probability of success. So another question presents itself: What is it worth, in dollars, to achieve the sought-after learning objective?

Our correspondent mentions the side effect of sound tracks preempting "the instructor's responsibility for thorough preparation." This need not be so. One solution is to transfer film segments onto video tape just to reinforce specific points or to promote debate, while the program as a whole remains essentially the instructor's own work. In fact, this technique calls for more preparation than for less and, in the process of researching suitable material, exposes the instructor to new inputs from other people.

On the subject of costs, the options are wide open as far as either stills, films, or video tape are concerned. Slide-making kits are on the market at very low cost. Overhead projectuals are more a matter of adequate planning and preparation plus time spent in making them properly than of cash outlay. Super 8 is finally making the grade in industry, business, and government for low-budget film making, and new developments in Super 8 cartridge projectors increase simplicity of use in the field. Even video tape, about which much has been written, is now a relatively inexpensive as well as very flexible tool.

Bearing in mind our correspondent's involvement in safety training, consider the potential for shooting poor in-plant safety practices as they occur, either on film or video tape. After screening them, the trainer can select segments to build into a safety program, present them, and then complete the loop by having the people concerned correct faulty procedures. Then he can film the new practices and show the before-and-after films or tapes. It would be difficult to equal this kind of involvement (with retention *and* application, which unfortunately do not always go together) through stills.

Either way, it pays to build as much learning material as possible around the actual job to be done by the people who will be doing it. Remember that the things they are working with—whether they are machine tools, statistics, forms of procedure, or whatever—are teaching aids too.

We tend, too easily, to fall into the trap of thinking of teaching aids in terms of something projected on a screen or of sound waves from a speaker, and we give a nod of recognition toward flipcharts, flannelboards, and chalkboards. Anything the student uses in the learning process, from pen and paper to a simulated casualty in a safety class to equipment he is required to operate, is an actual or potential teaching aid. We don't necessarily *have* to use electricity just because it's there.

Here is another thought on in-house preparation of audio-visual presentations of any kind: *do you know what resources are already available within your organization*? We know of many companies where individual departments are completely unaware of the audio-visual resources (or their compatibility status) that other departments have and that could be used. How about a central and readily available inventory of what is available and where? We acknowledge difficulties in the implementation of this due to an understandable paternalism on the part of some departments towards their own equipment, but maybe a greater measure of cooperation is possible.

To revert to the original questions, the most effective medium depends on what you need to achieve, what has to be learned by whom, and the resources available to you. To start with a media decision, then try to develop a course to fit, is to fall into a dangerous trap in which you will have plenty of company. If the course design is sound, the choice of supporting media will virtually suggest itself. That is putting the priorities where they belong.

26

On Using the Overhead Projector

What changes would you make in the training situation shown here? You should be able to name at least seven errors.

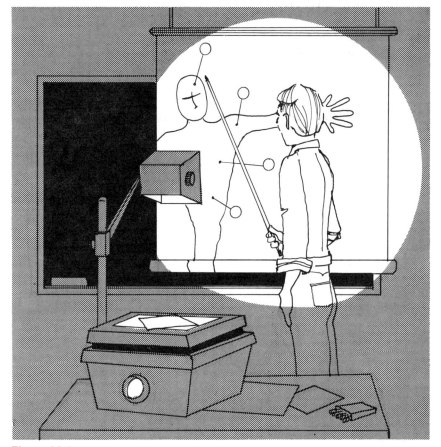

Figure 26.1

Change 1. Stop, think, and adjust. Don't just use an overhead projector where it sits. *Decide* that if you are going to teach using an overhead projector (OPH), you are going to use it correctly. *Decide* in your own mind that you want to be a professional trainer, not a fumbler. *Decide* to take a moment or two before you start the class to set up the OHP properly. For example the visual should be in focus on the screen.

An idea that may prove helpful to you in adjusting the projector's focus in front of a class, when you don't want them to see your visuals, is to put one on upside down and backwards and then adjust the focus. It preserves your lesson and yet assures you a sharp image.

Change 2. Turn the instructor around so that he faces the class. When using an OHP, the instructor should always be facing the class—not the screen.

Change 3. Get rid of the pointer. It is a lethal weapon. Many students remember themselves or others being rapped with this teaching tool.

Figure 26.2 is a swizzle stick and is offered as a substitute for the pointer. Next time you are in proximity to one, save it and put it with your overhead projector pens. As a pointer, it works like a charm.

Figure 26.2

Change 4. Move the instructor so that he doesn't block the image on the screen by standing in front of it.

Change 5. Move the instructor so that when he turns to face the class, he isn't staring straight into the light from the projector.

Change 6. Put the visuals squarely on the stage of the projector. This will eliminate much of the tilt and the keystone effect. (Keystoning is the narrowing of the image on the screen at its base). I feel that eliminating the keystone effect is important only after everything else is perfect. A small degree of keystoning does not distract an audience nearly as much as do pointers, crooked images, blocking of the screen, and so on.

Change 7. Move the OHP. The projector, as shown, is sitting on the table directly in the line of vision of about a third of the students. Students can't see through projectors. Place the projector low. Tables are always too high except in large, high-ceilinged convention halls. My definition of low is that the stage of the OHP should be less than two and a half feet off the floor. Chairs appear to work well if you are trying to keep the projector down low.

Change 8. Raise the screen. This one is hard to catch in Figure 26.1, but the screen is not as high as it could be. Why this concern about height? Like Change 7, it has a bearing on the students' line of vision. The lower the screen, the higher the image level, and the risk of obstruction diminishes accordingly. Because these factors have proved to be so true for me, I always jam my screens up to the ceilings—and even into the ceilings if I am lucky enough to be in a room with movable ceiling tiles.

In conjunction with this, I always do my best to fill the screen without overlapping the edges, which often means moving the projector a number of times in order to arrive at the optimum size.

Change 9. Move the projector so that the image is centered on the screen. Failure to do this adds to the generally sloppy appearance in Figure 26.1. Center what you have to show neatly on the screen, keeping the image as high as possible.

Change 10. Revise the layout so that the chalkboard can be used too. The screen can be to the side of the board and the projector, placed low enough so that it won't block the students' vision. Also, the screen should be right up at the ceiling.

Sometimes, on entering a classroom, you will find that the screen is recessed into the ceiling and comes down in front of the chalkboard. I suggest not using this screen; it takes away from the dynamics you achieve by shifting from the OHP to the board. Ask for a mobile screen. Most places have them. Explain that you like to use both a chalkboard and a OHP together, and you will usually be provided with what you need.

Change 11. Make things easy for yourself. Go back and look at the position of the OHP in Figure 26.1; it is at the back edge of the table. If the instructor wants to write on the projector, he has to stretch right across the whole table to do it. Why not move the projector to the edge of the table closest to where you have to stand when you write on it? But we have already indicated that standing by the projector isn't such a good idea because you may block out some portion of the image. The answer is to sit at it while you are using it. When you are through with the OHP, you can shut it off and stand up again, continuing with your lesson.

Sitting at the projector offers a number of advantages: it just happens to be the right height if you have set up the OHP as previously suggested; it's informal and promotes the kind of class atmosphere many of us are striving to achieve; sitting and then standing changes the dynamics of your lesson. You move, yet you move purposefully.

Finally, by sitting you give the students a new point on which to focus their attention. We all know how dull it is to have to watch the same area and the same thing continuously.

When setting up the OHP, a table isn't necessary. Another chair can serve just as well. The visuals can be placed on the seat of the chair while the instructor's lesson plan is taped to the inside back where he can see it with ease. Admittedly, there is less surface area on a chair than a table, and that is why taping the plan to the back helps. If one chair doesn't provide enough space, just add more chairs to the configuration.

The chair being used as the projector stand can be turned so that the back is in a different position—to the side rather than facing the class. This is to allow any visual on the projector's stage to be moved up, toward the class and hence higher on the screen. If the instructor wants the image on the bottom of his visual to be seen easily, he can do it by moving the visual straight ahead. If the back of the chair had been facing the class, this wouldn't have been possible. The back would have been in the way.

Change 12. The last change is to become more concerned about the student than the content. In Figure 26.1, the instructor is primarily concerned with his lesson and its content—not the students or viewers.

27

How to Make Effective Use of Films

Films are used frequently in training situations but often they leave little or none of the desired effects on the trainees or course participants. It isn't enough to schedule a film for a particular training session, show it, and sum up with a short discussion period at the end. Generally, this amounts to a waste of time for all concerned.

To come up with a good training session using a film, you almost have to go through these five stages:

1. Find a suitable film; one that fits with your objectives for a particular session;
2. Screen the film a number of times so that you are completely familiar with it;
3. Decide how you're going to use this film and plan a session around it;
4. Conduct the session;
5. Adjust the lesson plan in terms of class feedback.

TYPES OF FILM

There are four general types of film available. We've assigned them names for identification purposes:

1. The Didactic Film

This kind of film depicts straight facts, starting out by telling what it will show, then showing it, and concluding with a logical summary of what it has shown.

Marit Stengels was co-author of this column.

Didactic films, like peas, are plentiful. Some examples of such films are *Writing Letters that Get Results, Second Effort, Listen Please,* and *Styles of Leadership*.

2. Point of View Film

As its name implies, this type of film takes a particular stand on a situation or subject and uses the film to build support for this idea. The idea is of course summed up and reinforced at the end of the film.

The point of view film also is in great supply. Some examples: any one of the films in the Gellerman Series; also, *The Inner Man Steps Out,* NFB's *Everybody's Prejudiced,* and *What on Earth*.

3. Attitude-shaping Film

This type of film takes a preconceived idea and does one of two things with it. It either solidifies or alters this idea in the viewers' minds. How this is done can be explained best through the example.

The film is called *Glass*. What images does such a title conjure in your mind? This little European film with no soundtrack shows the contrasting pictures of an automated glass factory, harsh and impersonal, and a skilled craftsman at his meticulous work of shaping glass. At the end of the film, the viewer feels strongly allied with the craftsman against all the cold, crude machines. Another example is *Why Men Create*. A classic example is Ontario's Expo 67 film. There aren't many successful attitude-shaping films around.

4. Open-ended Film

An open-ended is really a case study on film. The problem is built up but not solved. The answers must come from the viewers.

This type of film is relatively scarce. The case study portions of some of the AMA films fall into this category. (These case studies are in the AMA series on Basic Principles of Supervisory Management and Developing Supervisory Leadership Skills). Two other examples: *The Engineering of Agreement,* which has three cases illustrating the ideas presented in the first part of the film; and the NFB film, *The Purse*.

THE IDEAL TRAINING FILM

The ideal training film is the one that most readily facilitates class discussion and argument on points to be covered and learned. In other words, the film that generates the most trainee participation is the best, provided of course, that the participation is related to the lesson's objective. This generally means an *open-ended* film, and few of these are available. Does that mean you're restricted to second best? Not at all!

Did you ever stop to think how versatile your projector is? If it's in proper working order, it can of course do the obvious job of showing a film at the right speed with the sound track coming through clearly. Most projectors can also be used to:

- show a picture with *no sound*;
- project *sound only*, with no picture;
- *show stop-action* at a particular frame;
- run a film *backwards*;
- *shut off* completely at any point in a film.

Running a film backwards isn't going to do much for the cause of training. However, you can take a film from either the didactic or point-of-view categories and shut the projector off before the point of resolution in the film. This way, you've created your own open-ended film.

It takes some planning and work on your part but it can be done successfully with available films as described in the following three examples.

The Trouble with Archie

Shown as it is, without projectionist alternations, *The Trouble with Archie* is of the didactic type.

Archie is a hot-headed fellow who goes around the shop playing dangerous practical jokes on people and using his fists to drive his points of view home. The film is essentially about constructive discipline on the job and how to handle problems like Archie.

In a training session on discipline, this film is shown in segments. The projector is stopped the first time at the precise moment the boss catches Archie playing a practical joke. The instructor solicits group discussion by asking questions, such as "If you were Archie's boss, what would you do now? Would you fire Archie?" After a group discussion that takes from ten to fifteen minutes, the film is continued. Archie is given a reprieve and a warning by his boss. At his second blow-up, the film is stopped again and the class is asked to discuss how they would now discipline Archie. Through this discussion about the film, the various points of effective discipline are covered.

At the end of this discussion, the group usually wants to see the ending of the film to see if they were "right." More about this later.

Styles of Leadership

Styles of Leadership can be used after introducing McGregor's Theory X and Theory Y propositions concerning the nature of man, power, and management.

Projected straight, it's just another didactic film. It teaches four leadership styles that might be colloquially described as:

1. the Tell style
2. the Sell style
3. the Consult style
4. the Join style

This movie needs a careful introduction because of the way it is shown to the class. The class is told to watch and analyze the way the men in each of the four episodes are going to act; in other words, the class is expected to verbalize each particular style of leadership. And just before the film is run, the class is told that it will be run *silently*.

The purpose of this is to get the class to exert maximum visual concentration on the film in its effort to do analyses. It also forces a cognizance of some aspects of nonverbal communication.

When the first episode of the film has been shown, the projector is shut off. Although there is an explanation immediately following each episode, the explanation is not shown to the class at this point.

Instead, as soon as the projector is shut off, one class member is appointed recorder, and the rest of the class discusses and tries to analyze the leadership style in this episode.

When the discussion is completed, the next episode is shown and its explanation is skipped. After a group discussion of the second episode, the next two episodes are treated the same way.

After the class comments about the four styles of leadership have been recorded, a discussion follows, based on such questions as "Which type of superior would you prefer?" and "Why?"

At the end of this discussion, most of the participants are anxious to see the *whole* film *with sound* to see if they were "right."

This is an excellent opportunity to help them see that there are few absolutes in this game and even though their analyses might differ somewhat from the film's explanation, both are right and relevant.

The participants feel so insecure about their analyzing abilities that it is necessary after the first and second episodes to give them much reinforcement for being on the right track. They usually gain confidence by the third and fourth segments.

The National Management Test

To quote the distributor's fact sheet on this film, "The format of *The National Managerial Test* is patterned after the various tests seen on national television. A narrator introduces a typical management problem. The audience is then asked to watch a short episode and make a decision regarding an important aspect of the scene. This decision can be made with the help of multiple choice questions included in the film. There are ten questions covering things like delegation, communication and overcoming resistance to change."

The film provides the answers for each of the questions but the trainer who needs an open-ended film can turn off the projector as soon as the multiple choice question is presented and then have the class discuss the questions and come up with the answers. To avoid burning the film by holding a single frame too long, the multiple choice questions can be prepared in advance for display on a chalkboard or for an overhead projector.

Film Sources
- **Buy them**
- **Rent them**
- **Borrow them** from:
  Public libraries*
  Private industrial and business libraries*
  Film producers
  National Film Board
  TV stations
  Book publishers
  Service distributors (distribute industrial films without charge)*

*no charge
The films mentioned in this column are ones that we have used. They are not necessarily representative of all available films suitable for training purposes.

Figure 27.1. Film sources

PLANNING A FILM ADAPTATION

When you've found the film that fits your needs, you have to familiarize yourself with it completely. If, as in *Styles of Leadership*, you are going to show only part of it, you have to time those parts that you won't be showing so that you can delete them with a minimum amount of fuss in the class.

How you introduce the film to your class is important. The introduction must take the film out of the realm of entertainment and challenge the class to watch with concentration. If a film is to be successful, the class must be involved with it from the first frame.

One of our readers, Shirley Purvis from the BC Institute of Technology, introduces films by telling class members that they will be required to prepare discussion questions immediately following the film. After the film, these questions may be used in one of two ways. The instructor can collect the questions and have the class discuss them, or the class may be broken into groups, with the members of each group discussing the questions they had prepared.

After Your First Showing

When you find a film and adapt it for open-ended classroom use, take advantage of the feedback from your class to improve the whole session. In this way, you'll find yourself developing some very successful training sessions using readily available films.

28

A Review of Available Films

Films are supposed to help us, but they don't always. This article, which is based primarily on an idea of Evan Altshuler, Ontario Ministry of Health, provides you with some criteria Altshuler and I use in judging films.

Criteria for Judging Films

The accompanying list of films was compiled using the following criteria:

A. The film has relevance to either management development or organizational development. (A few noteworthy films on selling are included, thanks to some added input to this article by Ross Smith of George Brown College.) We realize this criterion makes literally hundreds of films relevant but it was the first criterion we used.

B. The second criterion was that the film had to be useful as a means of either starting or crystallizing a group discussion, demonstration, or lecturette. This means that the film has the potential, or has been deliberately designed, to be stopped at various points to allow for comments or interaction among the students. This criterion eliminated a large number of films that fit criterion A but could not be used to trigger student involvement in the learning process.

C. The film had to be fairly contemporary and the content had to be imaginative and stimulating. This criterion resulted in a number of excellent films being discarded because of dating. The styles of clothing, cars, and background for the films proved to be a distraction. Some

---

Evan Altshuler, Ontario Ministry of Health, was co-author of this column.

RATING	TITLE	SOURCE
***	Anatomy of a Group	Indiana University
***	Appraising Subordinates — Myths and Realities	Omega Films (Made in Australia)
***	Are You Listening	Henry Strauss Assoc.
*	Behaviour Game (The)	Barclay's Bank (London)
*	Berlo, Effective Communication Series: Film 5 "Communicating Management's Point of View"	BNA Films
*	Bob Knowlton Story	Roundtable Films
***	Breaking the Delegation Barrier	Roundtable Films
*	Case of the Missing Magnets (The)	BNA Films
***	Customer and You (The)	Rank
*	Dispute	British Productivity Council
***	Eye of the Supervisor	National Educational Media
***	Glasser — On Discipline	Media 5: Film Distributors
*	Grid O.D.	University of California
***	How Good is a Good Guy?	Roundtable Films
***	Human Considerations in Management	University of California
*	Human Nature and Organizational Realities	BNA Films
*	Information Explosion	Dynamic Film Institute
*	Information Processing	Psychological Films
***	Is it Always Right to be Right?	Roundtable Films
***	Listen Please	BNA Films
***	Making Human Resources Productive	Gellerman Series
***	Management by Participation	Gellerman Series
*	Maslow and Self Actualization	Psychological Films
***	Matter of Method (A)	Rank Audio Visual

Figure 28.1.

RATING	TITLE	SOURCE
***	Meeting in Progress	Roundtable Films
***	More Than Words	Henry Strauss Assoc.
*	Motivation Through Job Enrichment	BNA Films
*	Patterns of Management	Sterling Institute
***	Pay for Performance	Gellerman Series
*	Personality Conflict	McGraw-Hill Films
*	Rumor	Columbia University
***	Sharing the Leadership	Indiana University
***	Small World of John J. Pennyfather	Rental only in Toronto through International Tele-Film Enterprises
***	Something to Work For	Roundtable Films
***	Staff Meeting	Institute for Development of Educational Activities
*	Stephen Banner — Supervisor	National Film Board
*	Styles of Leadership	Roundtable Films
*	Supervisor: Motivating Through Insight	National Educational Media
*	Talk Back	Rank
***	That's Not My Job	Roundtable Films
*	Trouble With Archie	BNA Films
*	Understanding Human Motivation	BNA Films
*	Ways of Dealing With Conflict in Organizations	University of California
***	Who Did What to Whom? (Robert Mager)	Research Press
***	Who Killed the Sale?	Rank
***	Why Man Creates	Kaiser Aluminum and Chemical
*	Writing Letters that Get Results	Roundtable Films
***	You're Coming Along Fine (Performance Appraisal)	Roundtable Films

were just like watching a 1930s film on television. Eliminated also were the films that were dull, plodding, and had little to say.

D. The film had to be realistic, practically oriented, or at least bridge the practical with theory. This criterion still causes us some trouble as we look over our list of films because we fear some people may see a number of films as highly theoretical. How an instructor uses a film determines whether it becomes practical or remains conceptual or philosophical. In fact, despite the ideal criteria we've given for choosing a film, any or even all of these recommended films can fall flat if they aren't used properly.

Guidelines for Using Films

For the purposes of this article, we do not intend to tell you how to use each film. However, the following guidelines may prove helpful.

1. Avoid showing any film without first previewing it.

2. Avoid showing a film that doesn't have a practical task associated with the showing. Students should have an assignment or be given a question to *immediately* apply the major issue or ideas in the film. Otherwise, don't show the film.

3. A number of films should be shown only in part. Don't hesitate to stop a film after showing only a part of it. Although the end may be important to the producer of the film, it may be unimportant to you and could even destroy an effort to create learning.

In one case, Ross Smith uses two projectors in one training session. The reason for this is that he shows only seven minutes of a twenty-eight minute film, has a group activity, and then on the other projector shows a film case study that requires the students to apply the ideas and thoughts they have just developed.

4. As a corollary to the last idea, don't be afraid to stop a film *anywhere*, have a class discussion, and then turn the projector back on and show the rest of the film. This technique can be highly reinforcing if the discussion evokes from the student points that are made later in the film.

5. A film sequence of longer than fifteen minutes duration is usually too long to permit the students to learn the content of the film. The reason for this is that many films have so much in them that it is difficult to retain all their content. You must provide some means to allow the students to digest the content.

6. Films should be shown between 9:30 A.M. and 11:00 A.M. and between 2:30 P.M. and 4:00 P.M. Outside of these hours people are not as receptive to learning and are more inclined to fall asleep in a darkened room.

Developing the Film List

In developing the list of films, a number of important considerations occurred to us. We have not made any evaluation of the possible application of these films. Some of them can be used only in government while others are only suitable for industry. Nor have we indicated the topics of the films. This has been done deliberately. We want to avoid having someone order one of those films without having seen it first.

We do recommend *any* film on the list. Obviously, you will have to structure its use. This recommendation doesn't mean other films aren't good. We may have missed some good films.

Interpreting the Ranking

Deciding on how to rank the films for this article caused the most trouble for Evan Altshuler, Ross Smith, and myself. Originally, we were going to use a four-star ranking system: one star for acceptable, two stars for very acceptable, three stars for highly acceptable, and four stars for most acceptable.

Having decided on the four-star system, we then realized that the whole system would be misinterpreted easily, because one star in a four-star system usually means the film isn't too good. For this reason we decided to scrap the star system, leaving about fifty films for the prospective user to sort through, all of which were more than worth seeing. However, this procedure tended to be a bit hard on everyone's time and energy, so we have used a two-tiered star system to make it easier for one to see the films we feel shouldn't be missed. *One star* means that the film is more than acceptable; *three stars* means the film has, at least in our opinion, some highlights that, hopefully, others will also see.

Conclusion

No description of the films is provided because: (1) it would take too much space in this magazine; (2) film catalogues are available that *do* describe these films; and (3) we feel one should investigate, or preferably preview, any film before purchase.[1]

---

[1]For an up-to-date and thorough listing of films, see D. L. Smith, "Human Relations Films for Group Facilitators," in J. W. Pfeiffer & J. E. Jones (Eds.), *The 1978 Annual Handbook for Group Facilitators*, La Jolla, CA: University Associates, 1978. Smith describes the content of some seventy-five films and includes the production date, screening time, color, price, and the address and phone number of the distributor. Also listed are resource addresses for major university film collections, videotapes, audiotapes, and catalogs.—ED.

29

Books You Should Not Be Without

A trainer's library is a highly personal thing, carefully built up over years of work and change, greatly influenced by his own personal philosophy and designed to meet his own specific needs. No two trainers will or should have identical book collections. However, some books are basic for all trainers and some may have been missed, so this list may give you some titles that might be missing from your shelf.

I have divided the list into four parts:

The first section, "Musts" for All Trainers, lists books I feel are crucial. These are generally either "state-of-the-art" books, designed to improve one's training skills, or resource texts for simulations and other activities.

The second section, Not Quite "Musts," are books I feel should be included in this list, but they aren't nearly as critical as the books in the first section.

The third section, Other Books, is just a list of books I've found helpful over the years and look back on with fond memories.

The fourth section, Periodicals, has been carefully culled over the years to contain just those training journals that, as an industrial trainer, I find most useful. It contains only one magazine from the area of education, and that one regularly has industrial training applicability.

BOOK LISTS

"Musts" for All Trainers

The Mager Library contains six books by Robert F. Mager; all of them are available from Fearon Publishers, Belmont, California. These books are excellent in content, easily read, and primed with practical examples. If you have missed any of the following books, you will find it well worth your time to read them:

Mager, R. F. *Developing Attitude Toward Learning,* 1968

Mager, R. F. *Goal Analysis,* 1972

Mager, R. F. *Measuring Instructional Intent,* 1973

Mager, R. F. *Preparing Instructional Objectives* (2nd ed.), 1975

Mager, R. F., & Beach, K. M., Jr. *Developing Vocational Instruction,* 1967.

Mager, R. F., & Pipe, P. *Analyzing Performance Problems; or You Really Oughta Wanna,* 1970.

Managing With People: A Manager's Handbook of Organization Development, by J. K. Fordyce & R. Weil, was published in 1971 by Addition-Wesley, Reading, MA.

This book makes sense of a lot of the techniques and verbiage in the mysterious area of organization development. It is loaded with tips, ideas, charts, and models that can help anyone working anywhere on organization development. Also included are four case studies that outline, with comments, the steps involved.

The Pfeiffer and Jones Series in Human Relations Training is published by University Associates, La Jolla, CA.

A better and larger source of training materials will be a long time coming. The *Handbooks* contain activities for experience-based learning. The *Annuals* are yearly compilations of new materials, including simulations and other structured experiences, questionnaire-type instruments, some excellent articles pertinent to human relations training, and important resources.

Pfeiffer, J. W., & Jones, J. E. (Eds.) *The Annual Handbook for Group Facilitators.* 1972, 1973, 1974, 1975, 1976, 1977, 1978.

Pfeiffer, J. W., & Jones, J. E. (Eds.) *A Handbook of Structured Experiences for Human Relations Training,* Volumes I, II, III, IV, V, VI. 1974, 1975, 1977.

Pfeiffer, J. W., & Jones, J. E. (Eds.) *Reference Guide to Handbooks and Annuals* (2nd ed.). 1977.

The Rational Manager, by C. H. Kepner & B. B. Tregoe, was published in 1965 by McGraw-Hill, New York.

As far as I am concerned, this is the only approach to problem solving. Once you have digested and thoroughly absorbed the systematic approach to problem solving in this book, you will be well on your road to grasping some of the most basic principles involved in doing in-plant training consultation work.

Role of the Teacher in the Classroom, by E. J. Amidon & N. A. Flanders, was published by the Association for Productive Teaching, 1040 Plymouth Building, Minneapolis, MI. 55402.

This is loaded with information on how to evaluate your own teaching behavior in the classroom and that of others. Anyone using the system advocated in this booklet can tell just what went on in the classroom by analyzing the live classroom or a tape recording of the lesson.

Freedom to Learn: A View of What Education Might Become, by Carl R. Rogers, was published in 1969 by Charles E. Merrill, Columbus, OH.

This book stresses participation and student involvement, and goes beyond them to the core of the learning situation. It deals with the student-teacher relationship and with developing and designing student-centered, student-initiated, student-directed learning situations.

Group Techniques for Program Planning: A Guide to Nominal Groups and Delphi Processes, by Andre L. Delbecq, Andrew H. van de Ven, & David H. Gustafson, was published in 1975 by Scott, Foresman, Glenview, IL.

The authors call this book a guide to nominal groups and Delphi processes. Don't let that bother you if the terms are unfamiliar; they are simply labels for two different techniques for helping groups to reach consensus and make affective decisions. This book is best described as a practitioner's handbook. The contents are so well developed that you will find you can use either technique in many of the training situations in which you find yourself.

People at Work, by Dave Francis & Mike Woodcock, was published in 1975 by University Associates, La Jolla, CA.

Books on organization development (OD) come off printing presses every day. I don't even try to read them all because so many seem to cover the same ground. They theorize on organizational change; but few really provide the guts or working framework an OD trainer needs. *People at Work* is different. It is a manual, a guide; in fact I'd say it is a bible on how to implement an OD effort. It gets right down to the business of helping you make your own organization more effective.

Management of Organizational Behavior: Utilizing Human Resources (3rd ed.), by Paul Hersey & Kenneth H. Blanchard, was published in 1977 by Prentice-Hall, Englewood Cliffs, NJ.

I wish I had read this book the first time I picked it up. It changed a number of the things I said and did in teaching the management sciences. I found the book an excellent summary of the work done by management behavioral psychologists. The book sharpened some of the things the psychologists were saying, and it put a focus on a whole new area I like to refer to as situational management. Three years after reading this work I still refer to it regularly.

Not Quite "Musts"

Designing Training and Development Systems, by W. R. Tracey, was published in 1971 by AMACOM and distributed by Prentice-Hall, Englewood Cliffs, NJ.

This book develops a systems approach to the training function. It is an in-depth study of the functions a trainer should follow in designing, developing, and implementing an organizational training plan. This work manual should allow you to develop your own in-plant training system.

Effective Management Selection: The Analysis of Behavior by Simulation Techniques, by C. L. Jaffee, was published in 1971 by Addison-Wesley, Reading, MA.

This manual outlines a course or assessment-center type of program. It is sufficiently detailed for the reader to easily grasp how the activities fit together and are used. The roles of observers and lead instructor are clearly spelled out and are definitely practical. A kit based on the book is also available from Addison-Wesley or, if you are already using simulations and in-baskets in your programs, you can readily rebuild this selection program to suit your own needs.

Technology of Teaching, by B. F. Skinner, was published in 1968 by Appleton-Century-Crofts, New York.

Skinner deals with three theories of teaching: (1) we learn by doing; (2) we learn from example; and (3) we learn by trial and error. The book is a platform from which one can gain a real grasp of how to teach by using a response-reinforcement mechanism. The first chapter is the key to this book and is always refreshing to reread.

Teaching as a Subversive Activity, by N. Postman & C. Weingartner, was published in 1969 by Delacorte Press, New York.

The authors can shake-up many of the basic concepts of education held by even the most progressive reader. For example, it is rationally and validly suggested that teachers: declare a five-year moratorium on the use of all textbooks, be prohibited from asking any question to which they already know the answer, be required to take a test prepared by students on what the students know.

Communication of Innovations, by Everett M. Rogers & F. Floyd Shoemaker, was published in 1971 by The Free Press, New York.

It is impossible to do this book justice in two or three sentences. Because of its far-reaching implications, it should be required reading for everyone.

Organizational Psychology, an Experiential Approach (1972) and *A Book of Readings* (1974), by D. A. Kolb, J. M. Rubin, & J. M. McIntyre, were published by Prentice-Hall, Englewood Cliffs, NJ.

If two of the topics listed in these books interest you, then they are worth the money: organizational socialism, learning and problem solving, organizational decision making, motivation and organizational climate, achievement motivation, the dynamics of power and affiliation motivation, decision making in groups, interpersonal perception, interpersonal communication, leadership, intergroup relations, organizational structure and communications, personal growth and career development, helping and consulting, and finally, planned change and organization development.

Dynamic Management Education, by Allen A. Zoll, was published in 1969 by Addison-Wesley, Reading, MA.

This is another handbook, but it covers some of the more specialized areas of training in an excellent and informative manner. It is indispensable to the active trainer who is about to use the case method, role play, the in-basket, or any of a number of other training approaches.

The Role Play Technique: A Handbook for Management and Leadership Practice, by Norman R. F. Maier, Allen R. Solem & Ayesha A. Maier, was published in 1975 by University Associates, La Jolla, CA.

Here are twenty role plays for management and leadership training, and you are at liberty to use them provided you give credit to the source. If you would like a manual detailing how to use a particular role play, what to expect from it, and how to process the role play, this handbook is for you.

Interpersonal Conflict Resolution, by Alan C. Filley, was published in 1975 by Scott Foresman, Glenview, IL.

This is the most authoritative and informative work I have found in my reading on conflict. This book is so effective that I wound up believing a win-win result in a conflict situation is possible ninety-nine times out of a hundred. I leave you to read the book to find out how this is possible.

Explorations in Managing, by Allen A. Zoll, was published in 1974 by Addison-Wesley, Reading, MA.

This is designed not as a management text but as a student activity book. It contains personal-exploration activities, in-baskets, an action maze for managing change that is outstanding, questionnaires, forms to fill out, cases, role plays, and some excellent readings, although the readings make up only a small part of the total.

Behavior Analysis in Training, by Neil Rackham & Terry Morgan, was published by McGraw-Hill, New York.

This book deals with the broad area of developing interpersonal skills for supervisors, managers—or, in fact, anyone. It explains how to: measure and research appropriate interactive skills, evaluate people's interactive behaviors, and design behavior-analysis instruments. It also tells how to provide feedback to people on their personal behavior patterns, while keeping personal dissonance factors at a minimum.

Other Books

Adult's Learning Projects, Research in Education No. 1. A. Tough. Ontario Institute for Studies in Education, Publication Sales, 252 Bloor St., W. Toronto, Canada.

Analysis of Behavior. B. F. Skinner. McGraw-Hill, New York.

Are You Listening. R. Nichols & L. A. Stevens. McGraw-Hill, New York.

Born to Win. M. James & D. Jongeward. Addison-Wesley, Reading, MA.

Changing Classroom Behavior: A Manual for Precision Teaching. M. L. Meacham & A. E. Wiesen. T. Y. Crowell, New York.

Creating More Meaningful Work. F. Foulkes. American Management Association (out of print).

Creative Growth Games. E. Raudsepp & G. P. Hough. Harcourt Brace Jovanovich, New York.

Designing Instruction. P. A. Friesen. Friesen, Kay & Associates, P.O. Box 11005, Ottawa 6, Ontario, Canada.

Evaluation of Management Training. P. Warr, M. Bird, & N. Rackham. Gower Press, Great Britain.

Good Memory–Good Student: A Guide to Remembering What You Learn. H. Lorayne. Thomas Nelson, New York.

The Guide to Simulations/Games for Education and Training. D. W. Zuckerman & R. E. Horn. Information Resources, P. O. Box 417, Lexington, MA 02173.

How to Get Control of Your Time & Your Life. A. Lakein. McKay, New York.

How to Read a Person Like a Book. G. I. Nierenburg & H. Calero. Prentice-Hall, Englewood Cliffs, NJ.

I'm OK–You're OK. T. A. Harris. Harper & Row, New York.

Industrial Skills. W. D. Seymour. Sir Isaac Pitman, Toronto, Canada.

Industrial Training for Manual Operations. W. D. Seymour, Sir Isaac Pitman, Toronto, Canada.

Management Development: Design, Evaluation & Implementation. R. J. House. Bureau of Industrial Relations, Graduate School of Business Administration, University of Michigan, Ann Arbor, MI.

Management of Work: A Workbook. Q. E. Broudwell, Jr. Addison-Wesley, Reading, MA.

Managing Change. J. S. Morgan. McGraw-Hill, New York.

The Modern Practice of Adult Education. M. S. Knowles. Association Press, New York.

New Patterns of Management: R. Likert. McGraw-Hill, New York.

The Practice of Creativity. G. M. Prince. Harper & Row, New York.

Programmed Learning–a Practicum. D. Brethower & D. G. Markle. Ann Arbor Publishing, Ann Arbor, MI.

Safety Training for Supervisors. J. E. Gardner. Addison-Wesley, Reading, MA.

Say What You Mean. R. Flesch. Harper & Row, New York.

Small-Group Instruction: Theory and Practice. J. A. Olmstead. Human Resources Research Organization, Alexandria, VA.

Taking Your Meetings Out of the Doldrums. E. Schindler-Rainman & R. Lippitt, in collaboration with J. Cole. University Associates, La Jolla, CA.

Training and Developing Handbook (2nd ed.). American Society for Training & Development. McGraw-Hill, New York.

Training for Results. M. W. Warren. Addison-Wesley, Reading, MA.

Understanding People: Models and Concepts. W. C. Boshear & K. G. Albrecht. University Associates, La Jolla, CA.

Periodicals

The Business Quarterly. The University of Western Ontario School of Business Administration, London, Ontario, Canada. Management-oriented and largely theoretical; an excellent source of recent developments in the theory of managing people.

California Management Review. Graduate School of Business Administration, University of California, Berkeley, CA 94720.

Canadian Training Methods. Chesswood House Publishing, 542 Mt. Pleasant Rd., Suite 301, Toronto, Canada.

Educational Technology. Educational Technology Publication, 140 Sylvan Avenue, Englewood Cliffs, NJ 07632. Slanted at both teachers and industrial trainers; a good source of audiovisual information.

Group & Organization Studies: The International Journal for Group Facilitators. University Associates, 7596 Eads Ave., La Jolla, CA 92037. Offers both practical and theoretical articles, and regular features (such as interviews, abstracts, instrument and book reviews) to keep you up-to-date on significant developments in applied behavioral science.

Harvard Business Review. Graduate School of Business Administration, Harvard University, (subscriptions, HBR Subscription Department, 108 Tenth Ave., Des Moines, IA 50305). Covers a broad spectrum of business activities and has many excellent articles about training, management, and motivation; emphasis on new theory.

Human Resource Management. Office of Publications, Graduate School of Business Administration, University of Michigan, Ann Arbor, MI 48104.

Industrial & Commercial Training. Wellens Publishing, John Wellens Limited, Guilsborough, Northampton, NN6 8PY. Not a widely known publication in North America, but this has not stopped it from being one of the best training publications available anywhere. If you are planning to get any new periodicals, this is the one to get.

Psychology Today. P.O. Box 2990, Boulder, CO 80302.

Training and Development Journal. American Society for Training and Development, 517 North Segoe Road, P.O. Box 5307, Madison, WI 53705. An excellent source of facts and ideas for trainers.

Training in Business and Industry. 731 Hennepin Ave., Minneapolis, MN 55403. Practical and theoretical articles about training.

Summary

In writing this article, I stumbled on something that really slowed me down. I found myself re-reading and discovering some books that are old friends. Maybe you, too, would enjoy taking a few hours thumbing through some of the books you have in your library. By the way, if you find some titles you feel I should have included, please drop me a postcard at *Canadian Training Methods*. I always like to hear about good books related to training.

Part

5

Evaluation and Costs

30

Thoughts on Evaluation

Most post-course evaluations shouldn't be done.

I realize the shock value of the opening statement; however, it does not say "evaluation should not be done," but that most of them shouldn't. In the remainder of this article, I hope to back up my first statement and suggest improvements.

How Do You Evaluate?

Below, I have listed different types of post-course evaluations. Which type do you use most? Commit yourself to an answer by circling either A, B, C, or D as the one you use most often:

A. At the end of the course/workshop/session, the students are asked to give their immediate reaction to the program by filling in a questionnaire or evaluation form. Also included is asking for their reactions verbally.

B. Between the two weeks and the year following the program *you* do a formal follow-up to the program. This follow-up can be by questionnaires, memos, or face-to-face interviews, but it is planned and not a chance happening.

C. Both A and B are used most of the time.

D. You do not evaluate, so neither A nor B applies.

Interpreting Your Answers

The following interpretation of your circled answers can give you a perspective to use in reading the rest of this article.

D: If you circled D because you don't believe in evaluation as it is done today, then the rest of this article will probably serve to strengthen some of your thoughts. If you circled D because you have never considered using evaluation, you should do some reading on evaluation. A short reading list is provided at the close.

C or B: You will find while reading this article, that many of the thoughts expressed will be in agreement with yours. In fact, you probably have arrived at many of them on your own.

A: You are certainly not alone in circling A. Most trainers will fit into this category. The remainder of this article is written for you. You will find that, in some places, it challenges some of the premises you accept. The purpose of what follows is to challenge you to change your methods of evaluation.

A Typical Evaluation

The evaluation form in Figure 30.1 is typical of the end-of-course evaluation most of us use. My reactions today are quite different from those I had a few years ago when I first wrote it. Now I see it as having a split objective of (1) finding out whether the students learned, and (2) how the student felt or reacted to the session. Although I felt that both objectives were valid then; today, only the first objective appears to be valid.

The reasons why I feel that evaluation of a student's reaction to a session is not valid are as follows:

A. In any learning session, the reaction of the student to the session is less important than what is learned. Learning or changing behavior is what training is all about. The reactions of students to training are of secondary importance and should be evaluated separately, if at all.

B. Students don't give you their honest reactions on these forms. The reasons for this are infinite. Some examples from a student's point of view are (1) I don't want to hurt the instructor's feelings, (2) I can't say that, (3) I wonder what is wanted here, etc.

C. Students don't know what their reactions are. In completing a post-course evaluation, many students are not aware of their reactions and feelings because much of their development has taught them to hide and suppress their feelings. The result is further breakdown of the evaluations.

D. Students don't rate poor instructors as low as they should. Using the evaluation form shown in Figure 30.1 with a large cross section of instructors, you get a low rating of about 9 to a high rating of about 18.5 in sections F and G. The low 9 rating represents the worst instructor you have ever seen. Students won't rate an instructor lower. Why not? I'm not sure, but I think they don't want to hurt the instructor's feelings; the students feel the instructor has tried and, at least, deserves a fair rating.

There's a rule on this nonuse of low ratings. Given any evaluation rating scale, students will not use the bottom 30 percent to 40 percent of it. As an example of this, look at part A, Method of Instruction, in Figure

30.1. You can, from this rule, predict which areas students will check off. They generally check Very Effective and Quite Effective. Sometimes they check Neutral, but they rarely to never check the Not Effective area.

The high rating of 18.5 percent is reached by "good instructors." They are the showmen of the instructing world. They don't necessarily create learning or behavior changes, but they do entertain. They have tremendous stories to illustrate their lessons. Although they put on a beautiful song and dance routine, learning is secondary. Liking them, enjoying them, talking about how great they were—that's what *we* measure them on. We measure showmanship with this type of instrument.

Figure 30.2 is a graph of this teaching phenomenon. It shows that as entertainment increases, ratings increase. It also shows the range for the average instructor is 12.5 percent to 15.0 percent. It should also be noted that this graph is related to a knowledge-type lesson.

If you doubt that increasing the entertainment value of your lesson while reducing the message to be learned will increase your ratings— forget it. Students rate entertainment over learning every time. I say this because I have clients who have used these rating systems on my lessons. I have experimented by using opposite techniques with the same lesson. One was full of involvement and high content levels—and, I hope, lots of knowledge for the student; the other was less involving, lower in content but offering more stories, more entertainment. My ratings reflect not the depth of knowledge but the enjoyment factor of the lesson.

Knowledge Learning vs. Change of Behavior

In order to get behavior changes, a lesson must be structured so that the students actually are confronted with their behavior as it is and get a chance to try out the new behaviors you want them to exhibit. This is not as pleasant and entertaining as a knowledge-type lesson and the ratings will reflect this. Furthermore, the confrontation and subsequent feelings of inadequacy on the part of the students happen at the beginning of the lesson and chances to succeed come later. This too has an effect on the ratings. Nobody likes to feel deficient and if this type of lesson is short (i.e. it ends before success in the new behavior happens) then the ratings will be lower still.

Figure 30.3 takes a good instructor and shows the ratings path through various levels of a change lesson with a group of students. The lesson starts well at about 18.5 percent on the rating scale. Then, as students become more and more aware of their deficiencies and lack of skill, the class reaction to the lesson plummets sharply. The reaction

EVALUATION

A. METHOD OF INSTRUCTION

How would you rate the methods of presentation (where applicable)

	Very effective	Quite effective	Neutral	Not effective
Student participation	□	□	□	□
Use of teaching aids	□	□	□	□
Speakers' content	□	□	□	□
Reading notes (if any)	□	□	□	□
Completeness of coverage	□	□	□	□

B. PRESENTATION

In your opinion the presentation was

1. □ Elementary □ Advanced □ Just right
2. □ Fast □ Slow □ Suitably paced □ Erratic
3. □ Too detailed □ Too general □ Too theoretical □ Correct

C. SESSION CONTENT

Which information was of most value to you?

Figure 30.1. Post-course evaluation form.

Figure 30.1. (Continued)

D. REACTION TO SESSION AS A WHOLE
To what extent did you get the information you expected from this session?

☐ To great extent   ☐ To some extent   ☐ Not at all

E. PLEASE INDICATE WHY YOU FEEL SOME PARTS WERE NOT EFFECTIVE
You may check more than one box

☐ Read speech   ☐ Not adequately prepared   ☐ Boring   ☐ Strayed from subject

☐ Repeated previous work   ☐ Too formal   ☐ Repetitious   ☐ No objective stated

Other:

F. CAN YOU APPLY THE MATERIAL PRESENTED?
Mark this way

21	20	19	18	17	16	15	14	13	12	11	10	9	8	7	6	5	4	3	2	1
Very much so				To some extent				Just barely				Not too easily				Not at all				

G. RECORD YOUR OVERALL REACTION TO SESSION

21	20	19	18	17	16	15	14	13	12	11	10	9	8	7	6	5	4	3	2	1
Excellent				Good				Average				Fair				Poor				

Feel free to make any comments you may have regarding this session. Use the back of this sheet.

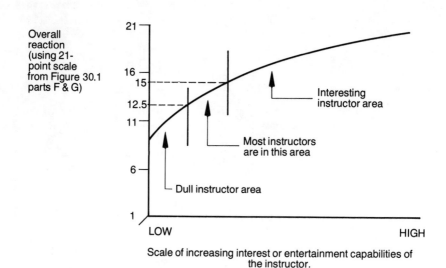

Figure 30.2. Graph of student reactions to knowledge-type lessons

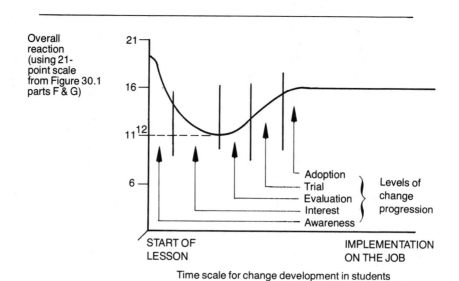

Figure 30.3. An interesting, "good," instructor developing a change in student behaviors

continues to slope slightly downward, levels off and moves steadily upwards as the students gain more success and confidence in their new behavior. This type of lesson never hits the same height as a knowledge lesson.

Conclusion

Evaluation forms measuring class reactions are useful but must always be weighed against the type of lesson taught, and it should be kept in mind that students are not always honest.

REFERENCES AND READINGS

Broadwell, M. M. Broadwell on instructor evaluation. *Training in Business Industry*, 1973, *10* (10), 25.

Fast, D. A new approach to quantifying training program effectiveness. *Training & Development Journal*, 1974, *28*(9).

House, R. J. *Management development: Design, evaluation and implementation*. Ann Arbor, MI: Bureau of Industrial Relations, University of Michigan.

Rackham, N. Recent thoughts on evaluation. *Industrial & Commercial Training*, 1973, *5*(10), 454.

Rogers, E. M. *Diffusion of innovation*. New York: Collier Macmillan.

Warr, P., Bird, M., & Rackham, N. *Evaluation of management training*. Philadelphia: Saunders.

31

The True Costs of Training

What does training cost? Most organizations and their training and development personnel just don't know. Most of them don't want to know, because the "true" costs are so high they almost always exceed by far the measurable benefits in dollars produced by the training.

In this article, I will develop the 10 Percent Rule[1] for establishing the "true" costs of training. I have taught this material a number of times, so I know the results can be frightening. Brace yourself!

TRAINING COST AREAS

What are the cost areas involved in training? Let's list them, with the notes that follow the list as clarification of the points referred to:
  1. Salary of trainee(s)
  2. Organization benefits (see note A)
  3. Replacement cost while a person is on course (see note B)
  4. Lost production
  5. Overhead (see note C)
  6. Instructor costs
  7. Course material costs
  8. Cost of classroom
  9. Course design costs
  10. Administration costs (see note D)
      (Items 6-10 may be combined under the heading of tuition or course fee—see note E).
  11. Travel and living costs.

---

[1]This is an average figure. The costs for many companies are not as high as those shown in the tables here. The point is to recognize that they do exist.

Note A. Organization Benefits

I'm listing these because we sometimes lose sight of how many there are: paid vacations, paid statutory holidays, Canada Pension Plan and Unemployment Insurance premiums, which are imposed on the employer by law (social security, unemployment insurance, state unemployment, and workmen's compensation in the United States), plus organization retirement plans, sick leave, hospitalization, and educational benefits.

There are many others, I'm sure, which vary from place to place. Most organizations know what these costs are, on top of a person's salary. They currently average about 30 percent of salary.

Note B. Replacement Costs

I've included this item because many people don't consider it as a training cost. It is, even if a replacement isn't officially made. For example, if a secretary is sent on a course, sometimes a replacement is hired—so we have an obvious replacement cost.

Often, though, no secretarial replacement is made, but the cost is still there. The person whose secretary is on course is now interrupted by phone calls and visitors. The secretary would have been able to handle a number of these. Work is delayed—or put off completely until the secretary returns. Alternatively, the person without a secretary runs around and tries to find someone with enough spare time to do the job his secretary would normally do. Are these costs? I certainly feel they are, and they can add up quickly.

Note C. Overhead

Whenever I teach costs, overhead is the hardest to deal with. First, many trainers don't know what overhead is. Second, they don't feel it is a valid cost. Third, next to nobody knows the overhead cost for a person in an organization. I find this frightening. If trainers don't know what overhead is, what right have they to be training?

If it costs more to train than the training returns to the company, the training shouldn't be done; and you cannot know what the costs are unless you know what the overhead is.

Overhead takes in the fixed costs that will not change materially as an organization varies its activities. Overhead can include the cost of the building or rent; its facilities, desks, and equipment; caretaking services; phone and other communication services; stationery and other office supplies; staff personnel such as legal staff, accounting staff, personnel departments, etc.

The factor for overhead varies from organization to organization. I've been given estimates from as low as zero (that person obviously didn't know what overhead was) to as high as twelve times a person's salary. The range for most organizations is usually between 0.75 and six times salary.

Note D. Administration Costs

By this, I mean the cost of running the training department. It includes such items as the training director's and secretarial or clerical salaries; the costs of screening and selecting students; equipment and training room costs; audio-visual supplies; costs of in-company promotion or announcement of courses.

Note E. Tuition

This combination of items is included because some programs have a tuition fee that is designed to cover the instructors, materials, class-room, design, and administration costs. Two cautions in applying this tuition figure are:

1. Although outside courses offered by universities, professional associations, or private firms carry tuition fees, these fees only cover instructor, material, classroom, and design costs. You must add the administration costs of your departments in processing, approving, and post-course evaluation.

2. Some organizations now charge tuition fees for internal courses. In those cases you must be sure that the fees are real and do cover *all course costs*. My experience indicates that most internal tuition fees are not based on the real costs of the training department, and/or the design and purchase costs of the courses are not included.

What these two points amount to is that tuition fees are in need of adjustment upward to ensure that they include *all* costs associated with the program.

ESTIMATING COSTS

Figure 31.1 provides a set of estimates for three individuals on different salaries. Some explanation of how I arrived at the salary factors may be needed for an understanding of this chart.

Benefits: The .33 represents one third of the person's weekly salary as mentioned in Note A. This salary factor was then multiplied by the weekly salary to give the figures on the benefits line.

	Salary factor	Student A	Student B	Student C
1. Salary per year		$10,000	$15,000	$20,000
Salary per week		200	300	400
2. Benefits	.33	67	100	133
3. Replacement	1.0	200	300	400
4. Lost production	1.0	200	300	400
5. Overhead	1.5	300	450	600
6,7,8,9. Tuition	—	500	500	500
10. Administration	.33	67	100	133
11. Travel	—	Nil	Nil	Nil
Total		1,534	2,050	2,566
Percentage of yearly salary		15.3%	13.7%	12.8%

Figure 31.1. Costs for a one-week training course

Replacement: A factor of 1.0 is used, based on the assumption that the salary of the replacement will be approximately equal to the salary of the trainee. For further justification of this 1.0 figure, see Note B above.

Lost production: This expense is calculated at 1.0 times the salary. This figure may be low or high but it is never zero. A person away from the job affects production, no matter how you look at it. If you think that people make up for the missed work when they return, just remember that other people experience delays in receiving the replies or help they need, so some cost is involved.

Overhead: 1.5 is probably a low figure for most organizations. Note C helps to explain this in more detail.

Administration: 0.33 is a guess because I don't know what it is for your organization.

Travel: This expense is indicated as Nil on the assumption that most training is done locally and doesn't involve travel cost. Where it is involved, it should be added.

The normal reaction to Figure 31.1 is to feel that some of the salary factors used are wrong and some of the items are not costs. I feel that *all* the items are costs of training and will be part of the expense *any* organization has attached to *all* courses. The salary factors are, I agree, debatable because they will differ from place to place and from time to time. Some will result in a higher percentage of yearly salary and others lower. You can calculate your own firm's costs by using Figure 31.2.

	Salary factor	Dollar cost
1. Salary per year		
Salary per week		
2. Benefits		
3. Replacement		
4. Lost production		
5. Overhead		
6,7,8,9. Tuition	Fixed	
10. Administration		
11. Travel	Fixed	
12. Total		
Percentage of yearly salary [Total (Item 12) divided by yearly salary (Item 1)]	. . . .	

Figure 31.2. Calculate your firm's training cost for a five-day course

I personally use 10 percent of a yearly salary when I do a cost-benefit for a client. The cost of training varying numbers of students on varying salaries, based on the 10 percent cost figure, is shown in Figure 31.3. What this 10 percent figure tells me is that this is what my client must get back in improved productivity if the course is run in his firm. Then I try to see if we can justify the cost involved by the improvements expected. I might add here that we usually find that the costs far, far outweigh the expected benefits. Whether or not to run the program is then a client's choice.

Unfortunately, I rarely can get from *any* client what improvements he expects. He doesn't know them in measurable dollar terms. Sometimes he does, when the training succeeds.

How to help a client determine the value of the proposed training is still an open and involved issue in need of more research by trainers.

Yearly salary	$10,000	$15,000	$20,000
10 percent figure	1,000	1,500	2,000
No. of students			
10	10,000	15,000	20,000
15	15,000	22,500	30,000
20	20,000	30,000	40,000
25	25,000	37,500	50,000

Figure 31.3. Cost of one-week course for varying numbers of students at various salary levels

32

Finding the Dollar Return

First, Try This Quiz

1. **What did the last course you administered, taught, or helped on cost?** (Use Figure 31.1 in the previous article to calculate this.) $. . . . .

2. **Was the last course you administered, taught, or helped on worth what it cost?** (This question may seem simple, but it's important that you answer it before going on to Question 3.)   Yes . . . . No . . . .

3. **In dollars and cents, what was the value of this course?** $. . . . .

4. **Is the dollar figure in 3 greater than the dollar figure in 1?**   Yes . . . . No . . . .

If you found the quiz disturbing, or if you couldn't answer all of it, don't worry—you are not alone. This article will attempt to shed some light on how one can calculate the value of a course.

PINNING DOWN DOLLAR BENEFITS

Suppose an office manager tells you of a problem with his staff. A job that must be done once a month is taking longer than necessary and is costing overtime every month. With training, he feels his staff could do the job in time and eliminate the overtime pay.

You figure out the cost of the problem (overtime premiums paid, cost of rework or correcting, lost sales or production, hours of plant down time or office delays). In this case, five people do four hours of overtime each, or approximately twenty hours of overtime, at an average of $5.00 an hour, for a total of $100.00 a month. This can be saved by training.

Next, you figure out the cost of the training program; let's say, it is $1,200. Obviously, this can be repaid in one year—*if* the training program is successful on a long term basis and *if* the five people involved stay that long in their jobs. However, if an average industrial turnover is expected, then the training program will almost certainly cost the company more than any benefits accrued from it.

As a general rule, if training costs are equal to or greater than half of the yearly cost of the problem, then that training probably is not economical and should be avoided.

ANOTHER APPROACH

When there is a lack of specific cost data, it probably is impossible to do a precise cost benefit analysis as just suggested, so do the following:

1. List the skill deficiencies of the employees;

2. Rank order the list from most important to least important;

3. Give each skill deficiency a weighting scale ranging from 1 for not greatly affecting to 10 for affects greatly. More than one item may have the same weighting. The least important area doesn't necessarily have a 1 weighting and neither does the most important area have to have a 10 weighting. The rule is simply to weigh the items on a scale of 1 to 10.

4. Calculate the percent of each item. Suppose you have six items in the list with weightings of 2,4,7,8,8,10; the total is 39. You convert to percentage by multiplying the weight of one item by 100 and dividing it by 39. For example, take the item with a weighting of 7: $7/39 \times 100 = 18\%$.

5. Estimate the total cost of the problem.

6. From your list, identify which items are attributable to an employee's skill deficiency and add their percentages together to get a single figure for the lack of skills involved in your training situation.

7. Now calculate the cost of skills deficiency by taking the skills deficiency percentage (item 6) and finding out what percent it is of the estimated cost (item 5). For example:

The estimated cost of a problem is $100,000 per year.

The percentage of skill deficiency involved is 24 percent.

The cost of the lack of skill is $24,000.

The other 76 percent of the problem must be ignored when comparing costs for training purposes. If you can't fix it with training, then don't count it.

When it is truly impossible to discover the cost-benefit of a particular training program, buy a copy of Robert F. Mager's book *Analyzing Performance Problems.*[1] In the meantime I will expand briefly on three questions presented by Mager:

1. Is there a performance discrepancy?
2. Is the problem important?
3. Is there a lack of skills in the person doing the job?

Is There a Performance Discrepancy?

The trick to answering this question is to be specific in identifying performances. Saying that "the job isn't done right" or "we have a lot of grievances" isn't enough. Write what is not being done right, specific incident by specific incident. That will define the discrepancy. If you prefer, write what you want done. Be specific. Then write what is being done. The difference is the performance discrepancy.

If it is impossible to define a discrepancy and the only reason for doing the training is that someone has told you to—and that someone is your boss—figure out the true cost of the program. Present your boss with the figures, and ask if he still wants the training done. If he does, you have little choice but to do it. However, in this case you might as well realize what you are doing and make sure the program is enjoyable for the participants.

For those of you who find there is a real and identifiable training need, we go on to the next step.

Is the Problem Important?

Every time that question is asked, the answer is *yes*, but think about it for a minute. What would happen if you left the problem alone? What would happen if you did nothing? If everything would remain the same, then the problem is *not* important. If something would happen, then you're probably ready to put a price tag on the training benefits. If you still can't get a return-value figure, then have a go at question three on lack of skills.

Is There a Lack of Skills in the Person Doing the Job?

Take your training situation and think of all the people doing the task who are potential trainees. Pretend that you are very wealthy and don't

---

[1]R. R. Mager & P. Pipe, *Analyzing Performance Problems; or, You Really Oughta Wanna.* Belmont, CA: Fearon, 1970.

mind giving away your money. Now offer the potential trainee $1,000,000 *if* he can perform the job function correctly, and to your satisfaction. Then allow time for the potential trainee to do the task. OK, who has the money—you or the student-to-be? If *he* has it, you do not need to train—if *you* have it, training is valid. For a summary of this, see the accompanying nine-point test in Figure 32.1.

If you apply this third approach carefully to each training issue that you can't cost out, you will find well over 75 percent of the situations wind up as non-training issues. Those that remain and are valid should then have a cost-benefit analysis done on them, which means you should now be able to apply the first two approaches outlined in this article.

CONCLUSION

If you do a real and detailed cost-benefit analysis of your training issues you should find:

1. Training will be easier to justify to management;
2. You will avoid uneconomical training;
3. Your objectives and your achievement of course results will be better;
4. Less training will be done, but what is done will have greater relevance.

---

1. Think of all the people doing the task or skill under consideration;
2. Choose an average person in that group;
3. Pretend you are wealthy;
4. Offer $100,000 to $3,000,000 to that average person;
5. Tell them they can have money . . .
6. *If* they can do the task;
7. You get money back if they can't do task;
8. Allow time to do task;
9. Who has the money, you or the worker?

Results
If the worker has the money, then training is not needed.
If you have the money, then training may be needed.

Figure 32.1. Nine-point test to determine a lack of skill

33

The Cost of Training Revisited

"The True Costs of Training" outlined comprehensively the cost items involved in training. Here, I would like to propose an expanded and slightly altered approach in making cost valuations to arrive at the true costs of training.

Figure 33.1, which is from the previous article, shows the cost items that I shall attempt to re-evaluate are lost production and re-placement costs.

Valuation of Lost Production

A profit-motivated company would employ a resource if the value of goods and/or services produced is greater than or equal (at least in the short-run) to the cost of the resource. Hence, if I have a company with three employees and my company is viable, it is because the sum of my employees' salaries, fringe benefits, and overheads is less than the total value of goods and/or services produced by them. If I send my employees for a one-week training course, my lost production would then be valued at least by the sum of the salaries, fringe benefits, and overheads, plus a foregone profit for that period of time they were absent from work. To avoid double counting my training cost items, I would include lost profit in the cost analysis in lieu of the term lost production. For a detailed outline of evaluating lost profit, see Figure 33.2. Using basic data from Figure 33.1, I would calculate my cost for a one-week training course in the manner shown.

This article is the work of Manuel I. Caramancion, Market Research Analyst in Humber College's Center for Continuous Learning. He adds further depth to my previous analysis of "The True Costs of Training." I am sure you will find his exploration of replacement and lost production costing useful in finding your true training costs.

Cost items	Salary factor	Student A	Student B	Student C
1. Salary per week		200	300	400
2. Benefits	.33	67	100	133
3. Replacement	1.0	200	300	400
4. Lost production	1.0	200	300	400
5. Overhead	1.5	300	450	600
6,7,8,9. Tuition	—	500	500	500
10. Administration	.33	67	100	133
11. Travel	—	Nil	Nil	Nil
Total		1.534	2,050	2,566

Figure 33.1. **Costs for a one-week training course**

Valuation of Replacement Cost

You will note that Figure 33.3 does not include replacement costs. If I hire replacements who are as capable as my regular employees, there would be no foregone profit and overhead expenses but instead a replacement cost item equivalent to the salary of regular employees, assuming no recruitment costs. Why is this so? It's because the replacements would simply be taking over functions or responsibilities that would otherwise have been idle. The cost analysis would then be presented as shown in Figure 33.4.

We could have the same cost set-up as that shown in Figure 33.1 with a situation in which the replacements do not work as efficiently as the regular employees. In this case, one may have to estimate, as a cost item, the reduction in profit. As the inefficiency of replacements vibrates down the end of the production line, other employees will suffer some degree of inefficiency in performing their own tasks. Hence, one should also estimate, as another cost item, how much less efficiently the overheads are going to be utilized.

To illustrate what the cost analysis might look like, let us assume that the replacements are half as efficient as the regular employees.

TR = total return
TC = total cost
VC = variable cost per unit output
FC = fixed cost per unit output
TVC = total variable cost
TFC = total fixed cost

Q = quantity produced
P = price per unit of output
$\$$ = profit per unit of output
TQ = total quantity produced
$T\$$ = total profit

A business venture is profitable if

$$TR > TC \tag{1}$$

Since: $TR = TQ \times P$
$TC = TVC + TFC$
$P = VC + FC = \$$

we can express equation 1 as

$$[TQ + P] > [TVC + TFC]$$

or alternatively written as:

$$
\begin{array}{cc}
Q_1\,(VC_1 + FC_1 + \$_1) & VC_1 + FC_1 \\
+ & + \\
Q_2\,(VC_2 + FC_2 + \$_2) & VC_2 + FC_2 \\
+ \qquad\qquad > & + \\
\cdot\ \cdot\ \cdot & \cdot\ \cdot\ \cdot \\
+ & + \\
Q_n\,(VC_n + FC_n + \$_n) & VC_n + FC_n
\end{array}
$$

or:

$$\sum_{t=1}^{n} VC + \sum_{t=1}^{n} FC + \sum_{t=1}^{n} \$ \; > \; \sum_{t=1}^{n} VC + \sum_{t=1}^{n} FC \tag{2}$$

Equation 2 can be rearranged as:

$$\sum_{t=1}^{n} VC + \sum_{t=1}^{n} FC + \sum_{t=1}^{n} \$ \quad - \quad \sum_{t=1}^{n} VC + \sum_{t=1}^{n} FC \quad = \sum_{t=1}^{n} \$$$

$$TR - TC = T\$$$
$$TR = TC + T\$ \tag{3}$$

Hence, we see that total return is the mirror image of total costs plus profit. Rewriting equation 3, we have:

$$TR = TVC + TFC + T\$ \tag{4}$$

Since no production has been made during training, no variable costs are incurred but simply fixed (overhead) costs and foregone profit.

Hence, $$TR = TFC + T\$ \tag{5}$$

These are represented in Table 1 as the two figures: (1) Overhead for TFC
(2) Profit for $T\$$

Figure 33.2

Cost items	Salary Factor	Student A	Student B	Student C
Salary per week		200	300	400
Benefits	0.33	66	99	132
Overhead	1.59	300	450	600
Lost Profit*		40	59	79
Tuition		500	500	500
Administration	0.33	66	99	132
Travel		Nil	Nil	Nil
Total		1,172	1,507	1,843

*If company books are not readily available, one may assume a rate of return that is high enough to maintain the allocation of resources to where they are currently employed. In this example, I assumed 7% (it could be higher with your company), of the sum of salaries, benefits and overheads. [*For a production line person, this figure could be drastically higher, for example 200 to 300% of salaries, benefits, and overhead. For a staff person, it may be zero; the 7% figure is used as an average for the overall organization.*]

Figure 33.3. Cost for a one-week training course with no replacement.

Cost items	Salary Factor	Student A	Student B	Student C
Salary per week		200	300	400
Benefits	0.33*	66	99	132
Replacement	1.00	200	300	400
Tuition		500	500	500
Administration	0.33	66	99	132
Travel		Nil	Nil	Nil
Total		1,032	1,298	1,564

*It could be that the salary factor is 0.66 if the replacement is provided benefits as well as the person who is away on training.

Figure 33.4. Cost for a one-week training with equally efficient replacements

This means that I will pay the replacements half the regular salary, lose half the regular profit, and utilize half the capacity of overheads. The salary factor for replacements and overheads will then be 0.50 and 0.75 respectively. Figure 33.5 shows an analysis of the training cost.

Summary

What I have shown are cost analyses of training under three situations. Our computation of total costs of training, as we have seen, depends upon the identification and valuation of relevant cost items. Obviously, the least cost is entailed if equally efficient replacements can be sought, but this may not be possible, especially in as short a period as one week, unless the company has a pool reserve of qualified workers. However, there are possible avenues to ease the seemingly high cost of training. Take a look at those possibilities and take advantage of them.

Cost items	Salary Factor	Student A	Student B	Student C
Salary per week		200	300	400
Benefits	0.33	66	99	132
Replacement	0.50	100	150	200
Lost Profit		20	30	40
Overhead	0.75	150	225	300
Tuition		500	500	500
Administration	0.33	66	99	132
Travel		Nil	Nil	Nil
Total		1,102	1,403	1,704

Figure 33.5. Cost for a one-week training course with replacement half as efficient as the regular person

Part

Sample
Lesson Designs

34

How to Begin

Introductions are inevitable before a course can start. Just as inevitably, they are a source of problems.

There appear to be innumerable ways of carrying them out: each person introduces himself, paired people introduce each other, or the class can be split into groups that introduce themselves. All to no avail. The introductions are still dull. And, probably worse, they fail to communicate anything to anyone. Students don't hear each other—or, if they do hear each other, they fail to remember.

If the course leader introduces himself and provides details on course mechanics, the students also fail to hear or remember his comments. If you doubt this, think of the number of times students have asked you in the middle of a course about details you have already given them in the introduction. Frustrating, it is.

We have found a simple solution to the problem. Don't have the students introduce themselves to each other. Don't introduce yourself and don't provide any details on the course mechanics. That makes it sound like you shouldn't do anything, but that's not quite the intent. What you do is take the emphasis off the usual approach where the course leader is the center or focus in the introductions. Put the onus squarely on the students.

A method for doing this is outlined here. It has been tried by a number of different instructors in a wide variety of courses and has worked successfully every time. In each case, the instructor didn't have the students introduce themselves or each other, didn't introduce himself or the course.

Instead, the instructor put a visual on the overhead projector displaying the information shown in Figure 34.1. The instructor stressed that the students should feel free to ask any questions. The class was told to break into small groups of four, five, or six and take five minutes to decide what they wanted to ask.

FORM GROUPS
Decide what questions you want to ask me about:

A. my background
   my experience
   my present activities, etc.

B. the course—its hours
              —its content
              —its format
              —etc.

Please feel free to ask any question you feel is important to you.

Figure 34.1

If the class is composed of students who don't know each other, the first thing that occurs is mutual introduction within the group. One might also add that these mutual introductions are extremely short, crisp, and to the point. Usually they amount to just a name exchange. Why there is only a name exchange is hard to tell. They probably feel that the sharing of any more information is futile; they don't need it and would probably forget it anyway. The significance of this brevity really strikes home when one compares it to the usual long introductions. We are forced to consider whether the students need to know anything about each other and whether or not they remember any of it.

A good technique to help the students and yourself is to get the students to put on their name tags any pertinent information you or they may want. For an example, see Figure 34.2.

When you announced the group activity you gave them five minutes in which to form their questions. Don't cut their discussion off at five minutes unless they have stopped talking. Wait for a decrease in the level of talking; it usually takes ten minutes. Then start your take-up, the sharing and processing of the group's work.

How you do the take-up will set the tone of your whole course. If you want your students to be explorative, creative, and expansive in their approach to the course, then provide them the freedom to be this way in the take-up. If you want them to be ordered, neat, and precise, then structure your take-up that way. The structured type of processing we leave to each instructor to design in his own way from the information provided in the explorative take-up.

Figure 34.2

Explorative Take-up

Ask "Group One to give one question; any question is OK." Asking the class in this way is significant from three standpoints:

1. No Group One has been designated as yet, nor should one be indicated in your statement. Let the class decide; the group that catches on will *grab* the initiative and become Group One.

2. You have asked for one question, not all their questions. You don't want to have one group monopolizing the take-up. You limit each group to one question per turn. This limitation increases the listening. Obviously, the group that asked the question has a stake in the answer, and the other groups have a stake in checking out what is said so that they don't duplicate a question that has already been answered.

3. "Any one question is OK" tells Group One that you don't necessarily want its first or even best question. You are trying to say that any question is satisfactory as far as you are concerned.

Having received your question from Group One, answer it truthfully, whether you like the question or not. Some questions will be unexpected. They will involve thoughts and ideas you hadn't considered. Admit this to the students and try and answer the question to the best of your ability.

Continue going from group to group in order. Go around about once or twice. Then, to stimulate more participation, call on the next group to ask the next question. If it isn't ready quickly, go on to the next. If that group isn't ready either, don't wait—go on to the next. Often these rapid-fire questions will get you back quickly to the original copy. This trick gets the students to think of other questions they want to ask. In other words it increases their explorative nature.

Somewhere in your take-up, the group approach to asking questions will disintegrate. Someone may ask two questions at once that you'll have to answer together because they are logically connected.

Another way the sequence can be broken occurs when Group Four asks a question that leads you to answer in such a way that Group Three feels it has the next logical question. Forget your rule of sequence; answer its question.

You may also see someone who hasn't spoken yet in the introduction. If he has a question to ask, let him speak out of turn. Don't miss this opportunity to bring a new person into the discussion.

Using the suggestions that have been outlined, the order and formality of the introductions should rapidly start to break down. The atmosphere should become informal enough to allow the students to relax and become themselves.

Achieving this relaxation is vital. If it doesn't occur, you will learn very little about your students. If the formality does break down, you will learn a great deal that will help you in the lessons to follow.

For example, you will learn who are the talkative students and who are the silent ones. You will learn who is afraid of what. You will learn who was forced to come, who's seriously trying to learn and who's there just to have fun. Nobody is going to stand up and say these things, but they will be communicated indirectly.

For example, one student might ask, "Are we going to deal with laser communications in this course?" How he asks the question can tell you such things as: he already knows that subject; or, he has taken it before but doesn't understand it; or, he doesn't think he could ever learn it. It might also tell you that he wants to learn about laser communications.

What the student means by his question can be explored by the instructor (if he feels it is appropriate) asking, "Why did you ask that?" This question, if asked at the appropriate point, always triggers an explanation. You can also ask the rest of the class if there is interest in learning more about that area.

The answers to these questions can set the stage for other parts of your course. You will already have had an expressed interest in the parts to come and you can relate back to this interest at the appropriate time.

Exploring the Instructor's Background

Although the visual (Figure 34.1) that started the group activity highlights three areas, (1) the course content, (2) the instructor's background, and (3) any question they feel is important, an interesting phenomenon usually occurs. The students tend to ignore the instructor's background. If they do ask about your background through a broad, all-encompassing question, keep the answer short, simple, and to the point. One minute is the most it should take. Then you should add that if they want more detail, they should ask another question.

Because of the low emphasis on the instructor, the students place a high emphasis on the course and its content. This emphasis gives the instructor a perfect chance to avoid a lecture on the course's purpose, objective, and major areas of study.

Student questions about the course allow a meaningful dialogue and interchange on the course's purpose, objective, and content *as they see them*. The key to focusing on the students' viewpoint is to use their questions as an opportunity to ask for their feelings and thoughts on the point at hand. Often this exploration will lead the instructor right into the course itself.

As a final note, allow yourself between three quarters of an hour and one hour for this activity. Once you have tried it, you are likely to want to use it on all future courses.

35

A Quiz to Improve Self-Awareness

Are you ready for a bit of fun? This column is devoted to provoking your thoughts about the type of management you practice from day to day. The late Douglas McGregor had some definite and controversial ideas on this subject. To find out where he would place *you*, go through Figures 35.1 and 35.2. How close did your estimate come to your actual score?

For each question, check the choice that most accurately describes **your** activities. Be sure to make one choice for each question.

	USUALLY	OFTEN	SOMETIMES	SELDOM
1. I supervise my subordinates closely in order to get better work from them.	☐	☐	☐	☐
2. I provide my subordinates with my goals and objectives and sell them on the merit of my plans.	☐	☐	☐	☐
3. I set up controls to assure that my subordinates are getting the job done.	☐	☐	☐	☐
4. I believe that since I carry the responsibility, my subordinates **must** accept my decisions.	☐	☐	☐	☐
5. I make sure that my subordinates' major workload is planned for them.	☐	☐	☐	☐
6. I check with my subordinates daily to see if they need any help.	☐	☐	☐	☐

Figure 35.1. Management behavior

Marit Stengels was co-author of this column.

Figure 35.1. (Continued) USUALLY OFTEN SOMETIMES SELDOM

7. I step in as soon as reports indicate that the job is slipping. ☐ ☐ ☐ ☐

8. I have frequent meetings to keep in touch with what is going on. ☐ ☐ ☐ ☐

9. I back up spontaneous but unauthorized decisions made by my employees. ☐ ☐ ☐ ☐

10. I push my people to meet schedules if necessary. ☐ ☐ ☐ ☐

(For more realistic results, do **not** score this questionnaire until you have completed Figure 35.2.)

Read the definitions of X and Y shown below and then try to estimate on the scale where your attitudes lie.

THEORY X

- The average human being has an inherent dislike of work and will avoid it if he can.
- Because of this human characteristic of dislike of work, most people must be coerced, controlled, directed, threatened with punishment to get them to put forth adequate effort toward the achievement of organizational goals.
- The average human being prefers to be directed, wishes to avoid responsibility, has relatively little ambition and wants security above all.

THEORY Y

- The expenditure of physical and mental effort in work is as natural as play or rest.
- External control and the threat of punishment are not the only means of bringing about effort toward organizational goals. Man will exercise self-direction and self-control in the service of objectives to which he is committed.
- Commitment to objectives is a function of the rewards associated with their achievement.
- The capacity to exercise a high degree of imagination, ingenuity and creativity in the solution of organizational problems is widely, not narrowly distributed in the population.
- Under the conditions of modern industrial life, the intellectual potentialities of the average human being are only partially utilized.

On the scale below, indicate where, in terms of McGregor's Theory X and Theory Y, you would classify your own basic attitudes toward your subordinates.

−20	0	+20
THEORY X	neutral	THEORY Y

Using the table in Figure 35.3, score the questionnaire you completed in Figure 35.1. When you are finished, be sure to compare your attitude estimate with your actual score.

Figure 35.2. Attitudes toward Theory X and Theory Y

(Descriptions of Theory X and Theory Y from Douglas McGregor, *The Human Side of Enterprise*, Copyright 1960, McGraw-Hill, pp. 33-34 and 47-48. Used with permission of McGraw-Hill Book Company.)

How to Score Your Questionnaire

Score all questions except number nine as follows:

> −2 for **usually** (that you checked)
> −1 for **often**
>   1 for **sometimes**
>   2 for **seldom**

Reverse the process for question number nine. Score 2 for **usually**, 1 for **often**, −1 for **sometimes** and −2 for **seldom**.

Total your score.

Figure 35.3. Scoring table for management behavior

RATING ATTITUDE VERSUS BEHAVIOR

If your estimate was considerably more Y-oriented than your score, you're in good company! The estimate represents your attitude, while your questionnaire score is a rating of your behavior. This quiz has been used in a number of supervisory training sessions. One of the results usually has been that the more management training a person has had, the more Y-oriented his attitude appears. The clincher comes when his behavior rating is considerably lower (nearer to Theory X) on the scale and he sees an apparent difference between his attitude and his behavior.

As a device for measuring attitudes and behavior, this quiz, at best, can only indicate general patterns. Nor is it intended to make specific measurements. Its real purpose is to trigger *self-awareness* and to illustrate the *difference between attitude and behavior*. And it does this successfully and meaningfully.

The quiz can be used with great effect in almost any management or supervisory training seminar. It acts as a take-off point for discussion and thought about leadership styles.

Did *you* do the quiz in Figures 35.1 and 35.2 when you started reading this column? If you did, chances are that you probably became quite involved with it. It is this same high degree of involvement that has made this presentation so successful in the courses where it has been used. The participants complete their *own* questionnaires, discuss *their* ideas and walk away with a greater self-awareness because they were allowed to retain and reshape their ideas in their own way. They were, after all, analyzing *themselves*.

Using the X/Y Theory Presentation

Using the X/Y Theory presentation in a seminar is a simple procedure. In sessions where it has been used, the portion that appears in Figure

35.1 is handed out and completed first. Then the second part (as it appears in Figure 35.2) is handed out and completed.

At no time should the instructor indicate a preference for either Theory X or Theory Y. He merely guides the discussion so that participants can form their own opinions.

Despite this fact, most people conclude that *they* should be Y-oriented. This comes to light very clearly on the attitude diagram in Figure 35.2, where people rate themselves as being high on the Y-factor.

Neither Theory is Right or Wrong

The fact is that neither theory is right or wrong, especially once you apply it to a particular situation. For example, a radically Y-oriented (in behavior and attitude) manager could not operate efficiently in a company that is run on extremely X-oriented principles. If general company policy is based on Theory X, then the Y-oriented groups within the company will be forced to act in varied X/Y combinations.

All other things being equal, the amount of Y-behavior retained by these groups will correspond with the amount of autonomy they have from the rest of the company. The more X-factors in a company that Y-oriented groups are forced to cope with, the more frustrated and less efficient they'll become.

Unfortunately, this may lead an X-oriented company to view their behavior as proof that the Y Theory doesn't work. And they are right. In their company, it *can't work*. The reverse of this is also true. An extremely X-oriented individual would be inefficient working where top management is Y-oriented.

In a seminar, the instructor lets his group arrive at its own version of these conclusions. Then he shows a film *Styles of Leadership* (Roundtable Films), which is presented in a unique way. (This film and its presentation is discussed in detail in the column, "How to Make Effective Use of Films.")

There is one final step that can be added to this process. It is illustrated in Figure 35.4. Our results show that most groups tend to choose superiors whose attitudes would closely coincide with their own.

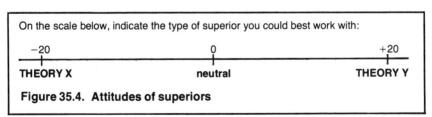

On the scale below, indicate the type of superior you could best work with:

−20	0	+20
THEORY X	neutral	THEORY Y

Figure 35.4. Attitudes of superiors

Success with the Presentation

Our criterion for success with this presentation is the already-mentioned degree of self-awareness. This isn't exactly the type of thing you can measure after the close of a session. Yet, if you listen to the session and to what the participants are saying, you can become jubilantly aware that they are starting to look at themselves critically. That's success!

No attempt has been made here to cover the X/Y Theory in depth. If you are interested in further reading, Douglas McGregor's book, *The Human Side of Enterprise* (McGraw-Hill, 1960) is an excellent place to start.

If you completed the questionnaire, we would like to hear your results, both from the behavior questionnaire and the attitude diagram. Your response can be jotted on a postcard and sent to Patrick Suessmuth anonymously, if you wish.

36

A Behavior-Modification Activity

Training has been defined as changing behavior. Most of us know that changing behavior is hard to do. The simulation activities presented in this article, although oriented to supervisory safety training, are also suitable for use in the modification of workers' behaviors. For example, consider the following training situation:

A large warehousing facility has been plaqued with a high frequency of back injuries. The training officer is called in and the workers are trained to lift the merchandise properly. The result of the training is nothing—there is no decrease in the number of back injuries.

The warehouse manager and the trainer discuss the problem and decide that a follow-up session is needed to supplement the first effort because the language problems and other related training difficulties probably reduced the effectiveness of the original session. The second refresher session is conducted and again, there is no reduction in the number of back injuries.

The decision at this point is to try another session, but, fortunately, the district supervisor forces the warehouse manager and trainer to find out if the men can lift things properly. A survey shows that all the men know how to lift things correctly, but they have not been doing it. Why?

On investigation, it is discovered that under normal working conditions no one reacts to picking-up behavior—either proper or improper. Only the safety officer really cares. The supervisors are brought together and are trained to reinforce, reward, or praise workers for lifting things properly. The result of this program is that the long awaited drop in back injuries is finally achieved.

Reinforcing techniques work on manufacturing lines too, for example:

The practice in one plant is for quality control to send a red slip up the production line detailing quality defects. A dramatic effect occurs when quality control changes to only informing the line when quality passes standard. To do this, a green slip is sent up the line when quality meets standard. *Result*: no change in quality. The reject rate remains the same, although no feedback on poor quality is being provided. *Benefit*: a 16 percent increase in total production for the unit being tested. *Conclusion*: the negative quality control of the red slip was depressing production; it was having little or no effect on quality, although most people felt that it was essential.

The training of supervisors and managers to use reinforcing techniques is only now beginning. The following simulation activity fits into this area.

MATCH ACTIVITIES

Objectives

1. To increase the supervisor's understanding of the effect of reward systems in motivating people to work in a safe manner.
2. To increase the supervisor's understanding of his responsibility for designing new and improved safety practices, when current practices impede his unit's productivity.

Time Required

At least two hours.

Group Size

Approximately twelve members.

Materials

1. Six books of matches with striking surface on the front, i.e., the same side as the flap or cover that protects the matches.
2. A copy of Observers' Instructions for each participant.
3. A copy of Reinforcement Applied to Motivation for each participant.
4. Modified book of matches.

Learning Activities

1. Start by securing agreement that not only must employees be trained in how to work safely, they must also be motivated to work in a safe manner. Explain that the group activitiy will provide a deeper look into the concept of motivation.

2. Ask for three volunteers to help you by role playing as workers in a little activity. Have these people sit at a table in the front of the room. Brief them on what their job will be, using the Briefing Details for Workers shown in Figure 36.1.

3. Hand out the Observers' Instructions (Figure 36.3) to the remainder of the participants.

4. Have the three volunteer "workers" do their work. Tally the results. Congratulate the winner.

5. Ask the three "workers" to repeat the activity, but with one change, which is explained in the Briefing Details for Workers, shown in Figure 36.2. Have the "workers" do Match Activity 2. Tally the results. Congratulate the winner and have the "workers" return to their regular seats.

6. Have the observers report on differences they noted between Match Activity 1 and Match Activity 2. (The prediction is that established procedures, such as not closing the cover all the way, will be violated in the first activity and followed rigidly in the second activity.)

7. Ask the participants for their ideas on the reasons for these differences. Continue probing until you get the following key points on the chalkboard:
   a. In the first activity, the "workers" were rewarded for quantity of production only.
   b. In the second activity, the "workers" were rewarded for production, but only if they followed procedures exactly. In fact, they were "punished" if they deviated from prescribed procedures.

8. Point out that rewards and punishment have a lot to do with the way people work. Develop the concepts of positive and negative reinforcement, using Reinforcement Applied to Motivation (see Figure 36.4) as a guide, but putting it in your own words. Tie these concepts into what happened.

9. Ask the group for examples from their own job experience that relate to these concepts. Allow time for discussion.

10. Compare the productivity of the "workers" during Match Activity 1 with their productivity during Match Activity 2. (Productivity was probably less during Match Activity 2.)

11. Pose the questions: "Do these differences in productivity create a dilemma for the supervisor who wants to enforce safe practices on the job? If so, what is the best solution?"

12. Allow for free discussion of the questions in the previous item (11) but be certain that the following point is developed: When safety procedures are seen as an impediment to production, it is the responsibility of the supervisor to create ways of modifying the practice or changing the system (in conjunction with the safety engineer, if necessary) so that productivity can be increased without compromising safety. Under no condition can the supervisor disregard safety as a means of promoting productivity.

13. Call attention to the reason for insisting on a closed matchbook cover: to prevent the whole book from flaming when a match book is struck, although this practice is a productivity impediment.

14. Show the modified matchbook as an example of how the safety aspects can be retained while the impediment to productivity is removed. (Construct the modified matchbook by using Figure 36.5 as a guide.)

15. Summarize by securing agreement that what people are rewarded for strongly influences what they will be motivated to do. Ask each participant to review his operations and come up with at least one concrete example of how the reward system could be modified (even slightly) to improve safety.

BRIEFING DETAILS FOR WORKERS

Your job here today will be to:
1. Pick up the book of matches and open the cover;
2. Tear *one match* from the booklet;
3. Close the cover by returning it to its original position;
4. Strike the match;
5. Blow out the match;
6. Lay the match on the table to form a row;
7. Repeat steps 1 through 6.

The activity will last for 1½ minutes. Work as fast as you can. You will get one point for each burnt match placed in a row during the allotted time period. The winner will be the person with the most points.

Figure 36.1. Match Activity 1

BRIEFING DETAILS FOR WORKERS

The instructions are the same as those for Activity 1, except that this time each worker will *lose one point* for each time he doesn't *close the matchbook cover completely*.

Figure 36.2. Match Activity 2

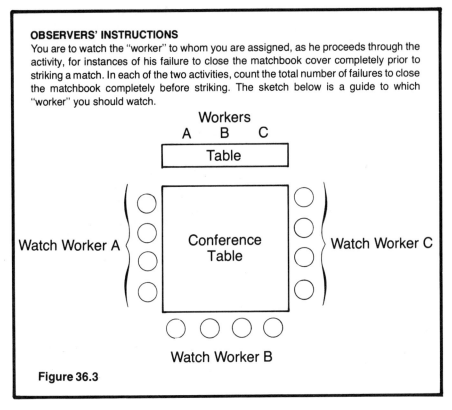

OBSERVERS' INSTRUCTIONS
You are to watch the "worker" to whom you are assigned, as he proceeds through the activity, for instances of his failure to close the matchbook cover completely prior to striking a match. In each of the two activities, count the total number of failures to close the matchbook completely before striking. The sketch below is a guide to which "worker" you should watch.

Figure 36.3

Evaluation

Each participant should develop at least one modification in his reward system based on the concepts discussed.

You may want to change this activity and the handouts to use positive reinforcement techniques instead of negative techniques. To do this requires that the lesson be modified as follows:

- Complete learning activities 1 through 4 as previously outlined.

- Change learning activity 5 in the following manner:

Brief the observers, out of earshot of the workers, that this time they are to gather around the workers they are to observe and verbally give a point each time the task is done correctly. They can reward the workers in any way they want to, when it is justified. Also, stress that the observers cannot tell the workers why they scored the points except by saying that the observers followed the instructions correctly. Be sure someone keeps track of the total points scored. Finally, when all is ready, ask the workers to repeat the activity.

- Learning activities 6 through 15 should be modified as you feel it is necessary. You should realize that, initially, production will drop more in this second activity and pick up significantly by the end.

Reinforcement Applied to Motivation

Reinforcement can easily be understood if we think for a moment about the way children behave toward parents and vice versa. When a small child says, "Da-da," for the first time, the father usually picks the child up and fondles it lovingly. Since the child likes this expression of love, it will tend to repeat the word "Da-da," so that it can get more love from the father. In this example, the expression of love by the father, in response to the word "Da-da" by the child, increased the likelihood of the child repeating the word "Da-da." Anything that *increases* the likelihood of a person repeating some behavior he has already exhibited *reinforces* that behavior, or more specifically, *positively reinforces* it.

Let's look at another example. When a small child creeps toward the top of a steep staircase and appears to be in danger of falling down, the father will usually move the child away. If the child repeats the behavior, the father may spank the child. Since a child usually doesn't like to be spanked, it probably will stop creeping toward the top of the staircase, particularly when it can associate the spanking with the creeping. Anything that *decreases* the likelihood of a person repeating some behavior is said to *negatively reinforce* that behavior.

These concepts apply to adults as well as children. Adults who receive compliments, bonuses, or awards for a job well done are more likely to do a good job in the future. Thus compliments and awards are reinforcers of good work. Since most people like to receive compliments and awards, they will usually try to do whatever is necessary to get them. In this sense, we can say that *prospect* of compliments, bonuses, or awards *motivates* people to do good work.

Conversely, most people like to avoid reprimands or punishment. A worker who drops an expensive part, and thereby ruins it, is usually reprimanded. The reprimand decreases the likelihood of the behavior being repeated. It is a *negative reinforcer*. The prospect of avoiding a reprimand *motivates* the worker to exercise care.

Now let's examine these concepts in terms of how they can affect safety in the job situation. Certainly a worker will wish to avoid injury to himself. Therefore, we might assume that he would be motivated to work safely. This is not necessarily true for the following reasons. Most workers who are injured on the job have not experienced that injury for that reason before. The concept of negative reinforcement doesn't apply since a negative reinforcer tends to decrease the likelihood of behavior being *repeated*. However, the negative reinforcement necessary to motivate people to work safely can be provided by the supervisor punishing or reprimanding actions by the worker that are likely to result in injury. The alert supervisor can provide the conditions under which the worker will be motivated to avoid reprimand. The supervisor who pays only lip service to safety will not provide these conditions and, in effect, contributes to unsafe operations and injury.

The supervisor who rewards *faster* work and greater production effectively provides conditions that will tend to motivate people to produce a large quantity of work quickly. If the supervisor leaves the impression that safety can be overlooked to get these rewards, the workers will do exactly that.

The supervisor who vacillates back and forth with his reward system—rewarding high production during one period of time and safe practices during some other period—will effectively confuse the worker to the point where the worker won't be motivated strongly to follow either course of action.

Thus, the effective supervisor must reward *both* safe practices and high production in tandem. He must never create the impression that either takes precedence over the other if he wants his workers to be motivated to work safely while producing satisfactory quantity.

Figure 36.4 .

Modifications

Do Match Activity 1 (MA 1) as it is. Then do Match Activity 2 (MA 2), but change it to allow the group verbally to positively reward correct behavior by worker A, to negatively reward worker B, and to say nothing to worker C.

Do MA 1 as it is, then do MA 2, but allow the group verbally to correct behavior. Finally, repeat the original MA 2, which allows a comparison of productions in activity 1 and activity 3 when learning is complete.

There is an infinite number of other variations possible with this exercise; hopefully the above will start you off.

Credit for this simulation goes to Richard J. Stox, Manager Training and Education, International Telephone and Telegraph Corporation, New York.

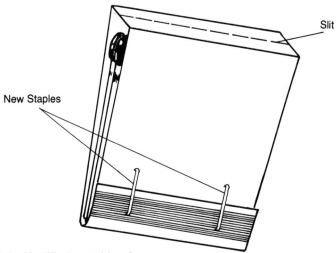

Figure 36.5. Modified matchbook

37

Your Own Communication Game

Training done in the "art of communicating" can provide some real enjoyment along with its practical benefits. The communication simulation featured here is no exception. It is almost totally spontaneous in its application.

You start out with a problem: *communication through several levels*. This subject may be explored in a number of ways. One of the most popular approaches is through an old parlor game in which each person receives and passes on a message. This message is passed in turn until the last person receives it and repeats what he heard to the group. Inevitably, the message is distorted completely by the time it reaches the last person. This makes it easy to make the point that verbal communication through several levels is unreliable. And, from here, you can move into the Communication Game.

The Purpose of the Communication Game

The Communication Game is designed to teach trainees that written communication is not infallible either. It illustrates vividly the barriers that exist in any organization when communication through a number of levels is necessary.

In addition, the game teaches corrective measures by showing how to find the barriers that exist and the specific actions that may be taken to correct these barriers, such as the following:

• Written communication must be complemented by face-to-face communication, if it is to be successful. Letters and memos should be followed up personally to ensure that the recipient interpreted the message correctly.

Marit Stengels was co-author of this column.

- Whenever possible, by-pass intermediate levels to be sure the proper level gets the message as it originated. A simple way to by-pass channels is to send carbons to intermediate levels simultaneously as you send the original message to the person who should get it.

- Write clearer and more carefully-worded letters. It is suggested that the Communication Game be preceded by lessons on letter and memo writing.

The Communication Game[1]

While Figure 37.1 to 37.5 are meant primarily to show you how the game can be built, you may also find these sketches helpful in understanding how it works.

The objective is to teach the trainees that written communication is not infallible. The game consists of written messages that are passed through six levels.

Figure 37.5 shows six four-inch squares that are each cut into three pieces. These pieces are distributed among the players so that no one player has three pieces that will fit together to form a square. The players' task is to exchange pieces back and forth until they have the matching ones to make a square.

The rules of the game make this activity meaningful:

1. Only the leader of the group is told what the task is. The explanation given to him is along these lines: "You're the leader of your team.

---

[1]A reader of this article, E. O. Malott, Jr., Vice President for Research & Development, American Management Association, pointed out the history of this activity to me. He wrote, "that it fails to give credit to Alex Bavelas as the originator of the techniques described." He went on to say, "I would cite for you the description appearing on pages 493-506 in the book, *Group Dynamics*, by Dorwin Cartwright and Alvin Zander, published by Row Peterson & Co. in 1953. In turn, that chapter cites the material as having been originally presented in the *Journal of the Acoustical Society of America*, 1950, No. 22, pages 725-730. Also, it was presented in a chapter of the same title in *The Policy Sciences*, David Lerner and Harold D. Lasswell (Editors), Stanford University Press, 1951. In addition, you will find a related description of the first experiment in Chapter 14 of *Managerial Psychology* by Harold J. Leavitt, published by the University of Chicago Press, 1958 (reissued in a Phoenix paperback edition, 1962)." [See also Bavelas, The five squares problem: An instructional aid in group cooperation. *Studies in Personnel Psychology*, 1973, 5, 29-38. An adapted version appears in J. W. Pfeiffer & J. E. Jones (Eds.), A *Handbook of Structured Experiences for Human Relations Training* (Volume I, Rev.). La Jolla, Calif.: University Associates, 1974.—EDITOR]

Your task is to get each person in your group to exchange pieces of the square until he gets a four-inch square. These exchanges must be arranged through written communication. Only you know what the task is and it is your job to communicate this by written message to the team members."

2. There is an absolute rule of no talking while the game is in progress; this includes the leader. All communications are to be written. This rule must be emphasized and enforced if the game is to be successful.

3. Each player must at all times have two, three, or four pieces in front of him. This is to prevent one player from collecting all the pieces. The onus is on the leader to see that players do not abuse this rule.

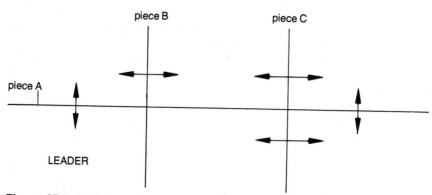

Figure 37.1. Top view of simulation. Arrows show direction of mail flow through five letter slots.

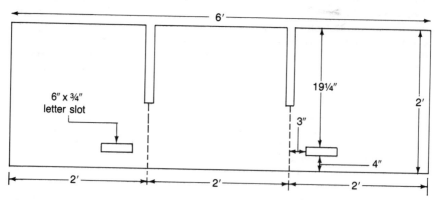

Figure 37.2. Piece A

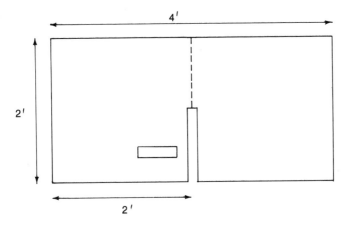

Figure 37.3. Piece B

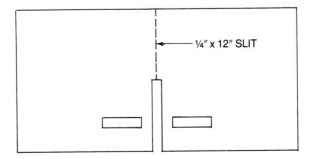

¼" x 12" SLIT

Figure 37.4. Piece C

What You Can Expect

In giving your instructions, you can expect to have some communications problems. The leader will seem to have absorbed your instructions. Experience has shown that he probably hasn't. The best way to overcome this is to get the man to repeat the instructions back to you and to get him to ask you questions.

A second problem will occur during the activity. You'll find that the rule stating each player must have two, three, or four pieces in front of him is being violated in some way. No matter how you stress this, the dynamics of the game will cause this rule to be forgotten.

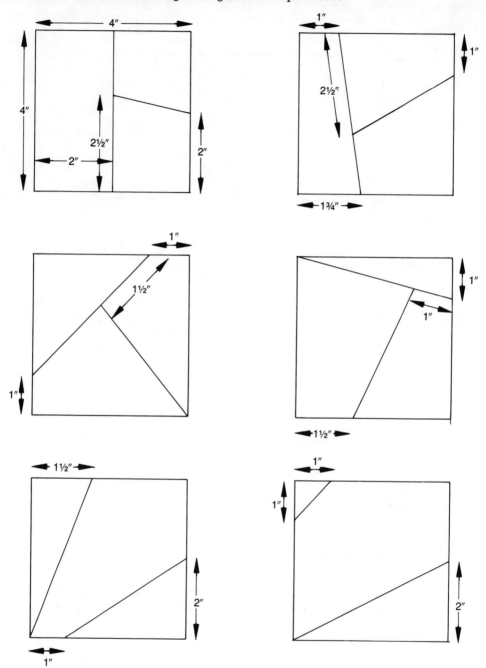

Figure 37.5. Measurements for making the six four-inch squares of three pieces each

The solution is to stress the rule when giving your instructions to the leader but don't worry about it being violated once the game is in operation. The breaking of this rule will not likely affect the overall learning the students are experiencing. This communication loss can make for interesting discussion in the session following the game.

You'll notice that at the beginning of the game, the leader is placed in a unique position with only one letter slot, not two as in most of the work stations. This is done to create a further barrier to communication and also to simulate the type of situation that exists in organizations: the boss communicates down to the levels below him. Upwards, communication for the leader is to the instructor.

The various letter slots create an interesting situation. If you check back in the instructions to the leader, you'll find that he is told that communication is through written messages only. Neither he nor the other members of the group are told how to send messages on to other people but in practice, they all tend to assume that the notes *must* go through the letter slot.

This point can be brought up in the summary when the group members can be asked why they didn't pass notes around or over the top of partitions dividing each member of the group from the others, especially in cases where there was no slot for passing a note.

Two other things may be done with this activity. A new, naïve person can be inserted into the work station receiving information from the leader, while the game is already in progress. This simulates, to some extent, the situation where a new employee fills a vacancy that has occurred because of a resignation or a retirement. The other possibility is to set up the game so that there are two leaders in the same group. The learning implications in this situation are obvious.

Group Size

If the class consists of more than twelve people, it is advisable to have more than one group game layout. It has been found that one unit should exist for each eight to ten people. The extra people can serve as observers and are allowed to move from group to group in the room so that they can compare different groups' levels of achievement in the oral reports given after the game.

Building the Game

To build the game, all you need for the main framework (as outlined in Figures 37.1 to 37.4) is a supply of large sheets of cardboard which can be obtained at most stores. A furniture store is the best source if you want a ready and free supply of sheets of cardboard.

To build the pieces for the four-inch squares, any stiff cardboard is suitable, provided that it is the same on both sides. Painted wood or plastic pieces also work.

Pads for writing letters or memos are also needed. These can be color coded or size coded so that the source of a memo can be traced in the discussion period.

Credit for this idea goes to Frank Laverty, Chairman of Administrative Studies, School of Business, Algonquin College.

38

Variations on the Communications Game

A communications game was described in the previous article. Briefly, the game involved six people separated from each other by cardboard walls. Their task was to build six four-inch squares, one in front of each person, with the aid of written communications only, (see the article for a detailed account of how the game works).

We wrote this game with the idea that the possibilities in using it were infinite. And they are. Doug Oxby, Training Officer, Ontario Department of Health, sent the following variation on how to use the game's concepts:

OXBY'S VARIATION

Figure 38.1 presents the Players' Instructions and Figure 38.2 provides the Instructions for Observers. In reading these figures, note that this use of the game is designed to stress planning and work performance rather than communications.

You will notice that this use of the game prevents players from handling the pieces during the planning period and that it does not tell them the number of pieces in each square.

Oxby suggests that, prior to plunging into the use of this exercise, we carefully plan what we are going to do. The reason for this, he states, is that the concept can very easily become a meaningless task unless carefully planned in advance.

Marit Stengels was co-author of this column.

PLAYERS' INSTRUCTIONS

1. The Task

• The objective is to produce a number of squares, with sides 4" long. The precise number of squares to be made will depend on the number of members in the group.

2. The Parameters

• No trading during the planning period.
• No trials during the planning period.
• At the conclusion of the game, no pieces will be left over.
• No extraneous instruments are to be used in the game, such as rulers, pencils, paper, etc.

3. The Rules

• Groups are allowed up to one hour of planning time, under the direction of an appointed or elected leader, who acts as chairman.
• A group must signify to the umpire when it is ready to begin the task performance part of the game, and in any event, must begin this part when one hour's planning time has elapsed.
• Task performance time (when pieces can be traded and exchanged freely) will be measured competitively.

Figure 38.1

INSTRUCTIONS FOR OBSERVERS

The following items are furnished as a guide for observing what the leader does and how the group behaves.

1. How did the leader present the problem?

• In presenting the problem, did the leader have the attitude of asking for help?
• Did the leader present all the facts?
• Was the leader's presentation of the problem brief and to the point?
• Did the leader scrupulously avoid suggesting a solution?

2. What things occurred during the discussion?

• Did all group members participate?
• Was there free exchange of feelings between group members?
• Did the group use social pressure to influence any of its members?
• On which members of the group was social pressure used?
• Did the leader avoid taking sides or favoring any person?
• Was the leader permissive?
• What were the points of disagreement in the group?

3. What did the leader do to help problem solving?

• Did the leader ask questions to help the group explore ideas?
• Were all ideas accepted equally by the leader?
• Who supplies the final solution?
• What did the leader do, if anything, to get unanimous agreement on the final solution?

Figure 38.2

Frank Laverty, Chairman of Management Studies, School of Business, Algonquin College, has also submitted a modified version of the Communications Game. We quote from a letter he sent us:

"I have added a few refinements to my use of the game. I use it a second time with the same group but use a second puzzle made from wallpaper."

LAVERTY'S VARIATION

Materials

1. The Communications Game (see the previous article).

2. Six cards, about five to six inches in size, are cut in different shapes. Each card is pasted with a mosaic of pieces of different wallpapers. All the pieces are cut from wallpapers resembling wood grains. There should be several wallpaper designs on each card, as shown in Figure 38.3. Wallpapers with wood-grain patterns can be found at wallpaper stores. Old sample books will often do the trick. Cards should be large enough so that they can't be passed through the letter slots. Careful consideration should be given to your choice of wallpaper; it should provide the student with some chance of succeeding with the activity.

3. *Only one wood-grain pattern is repeated (is the same) on all six cards.*

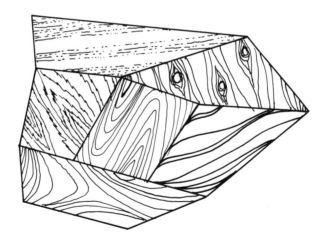

Figure 38.3. Pieces of wood-grain-patterned wallpaper arranged on card.

Method

1. The leader is briefed that the task is to identify which wood grain is the same (is repeated) on each card. The cards must remain in their cubicles.

2. Written communications are used at first (later participants are allowed to talk through the cubicle openings).

3. Because it has not been mentioned that the participants are not restricted in any other way, it is surprising that they do not hold their cards up to the hole for visual identification purposes. They seem tied to communications as written or spoken, and they forget visual communciations.

4. During the game, the last man in the chain is treated as an isolate. The participants on each side of him are advised that they may not communicate to him or answer his communications. In fact, it is a five-level game with a sixth person isolated.

It is interesting to observe the actions of the isolate, who does not know the task. After the isolate has displayed anxiety, anger, and frustration (usually about thirty minutes), the trainer floods him with notes (previously prepared) that criticize his participation. Even though he is being criticized unjustly, he is relieved because he feels he is part of the game. When the talking period is allowed and he is isolated again, he becomes more frustrated.

One thing noted is that after the game (even when he has been advised of the test), the isolate usually sits apart from the group because it takes time to get over his inner reactions. In fact, he continues the isolation pattern that has been imposed on him.

[We have not run this game, but if you do, you must know your isolate extremely well. Well enough, in fact, to be able to predict how he will react under the conditions set up in this activity. If you don't feel you can do this effectively, then the isolation procedure should be avoided. On the basis of the trainer being able both to predict the isolate's behavior and to feel competent to manage the situation, the technique has merit.]

5. The action can be recorded on video tape. The summary includes statements by the isolate, participants, observers, and a review of the video action. This game builds on the first use of the model with the squares so that the group can consider communications, organization, planning, human behavior under stress, isolate symptoms, etc.

Laverty writes, "We have found it to be a very useful technique. The video does not bother the participants because they are so involved in the game."

ANOTHER APPLICATION

There is still another use of the communications game; this time involving the same basic materials originally described.

The major change is in the size and shape of the pieces, and the way the squares are divided into pieces. In this case, the pieces can be fitted together to form either a six-inch square or a triangle measuring 8½ x 8½ x 12 inches. Figure 38.5 illustrates how to cut the six-inch squares in such a way that a triangle can also be made with the three pieces from each square.

In this activity, there are two leaders, one with the instructions to make the six-inch squares and the other with instructions to make the 8½ x 8½ x 12 inch triangles. Figure 38.4 shows how to position the leaders.

In taking up (processing) this activity, you can discuss any number of management functions, as well as communications and unity of command.

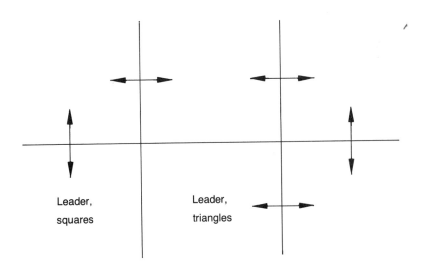

Leader, squares

Leader, triangles

Figure 38.4. Top view of the game, showing position for seating two leaders

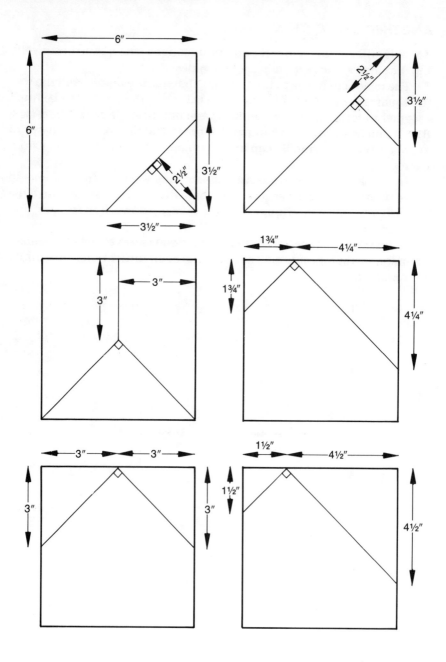

Figure 38.5. Measurements for making the six six-inch combined squares and rectangles

39

Ring-Toss and Goal Setting

We continue the theme that learning should be enjoyable. To this end, the ring-toss activity can be used to determine some of the variables that go into setting goals and objectives.

When you are starting this activity with a class, do not tell the students its purpose. Research shows that students' behavior will be affected by knowledge of the objective. In this case, you want their natural behavior, the behavior they have been exhibiting on the job. Simply tell them that this activity will give them some insight into themselves and their behavior, both on and off the job.

(However, as a variation, you can tell the students the purpose of the activity and exploit the effect this knowledge has on their accomplishing the objective.)

Ring-Toss Equipment

Either buy a ring-toss game or make your own. You simply need two short sticks or pegs, each fastened to bases so that they'll stand upright as targets, and a set of at least six rings, which can be made from heavy rope and tape. You also need masking tape and a tape measure or ruler.

Part 1

Procedure

1. Set up the two stick targets outside the classroom about fifteen to twenty feet apart.

Marit Stengels was co-author of this column.

2. Place masking tape on the floor between the sticks. Mark off one-foot intervals on the masking tape.

3. Send out two people at a time to make three throws each. When they come back in, have them post their names, the distance (or distances) from which they threw, and whether or not their throw was successful (placed the ring on the peg). Figure 39.1 shows a typical data sheet. Ask the students to circle those distances that represent successful throws.

4. Continue to send people out to play the game until each person has been out three times.

		Part 1			Part 2		
1	N	8	7	(4)	5	(5)	5
2	*	20	20	20	5	(5)	20
3	*	20	20	20	(5)	(5)	20
4	*	14	14	12	5	5	5
5	*	10	10	8	5	(5)	6
6	*	4	5	6	(5)	5	5
7	*	10	12	12	(3)	(4)	5
8	X	(1)	(1)	(1)	(3)	(4)	5
9	*	20	20	20	6	6	6
10	*	15	15	15	5	4	(3)
11	*	14	13	9	(9)	9	8
12	N	10	5	(1)	(6)	7	(7)
13	N	10	5	(2)	5	(5)	(5)
14	N	10	8	3	(3)	4	(3)
15	N	7	5	5	(3)	4	(4)
16	*	7	7	7	(3)	(4)	(4)
17	X	(4)	(4)	(4)	(6)	(6)	6
18	X	(1)	(1)	(1)	(2)	(3)	5
19	X	(3)	(3)	(3)	(3)	(4)	5
20	N	(6)	12	9	(10)	11	(11)
21	*	8	8	6	3	(3)	(4)
22	X	(2)	(2)	2	(2)	(3)	(4)
23	*	14	12	10	(5)	(6)	6
24	N	(1)	2	(3)	(6)	(7)	8

Sum of the distance of successful throws
Part 1: 41 feet   Part 2: 188 feet

Figure 39.1. Typical data sheet from the game, except that here the students got only three throws in Part 1 as opposed to the nine that were planned

5. Divide the number of successful throws made from a particular distance by the total number of throws attempted from that distance. Develop a probability graph out of these figures similar to the example shown in Figure 39.2.

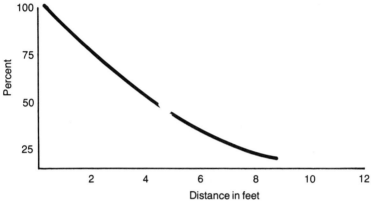

Figure 39.2. Probability curve

Discussion

1. Discuss the low-, medium-, and high-risk points on the curve.

2. Discuss the process of setting a realistic goal: estimate, perform, analyze and measure, make improvements, and make a new estimate. If anyone changed this distance during the activity, you might ask him why.

3. Discuss the resources that were used to help the student in setting his objective, for example:

   a. He may have leaned over—keeping his feet on the line. Thus, he has used his physical resources such as a long arm.

   b. He may have practiced—using the resource of time.

   c. He may have used the posted scores of the people who left the room before him to estimate his own chances of success from a certain distance.

4. Discuss the risks taken on the job: by the different students, entrepreneurs, accountants, doctors, etc.

Part 2

The second part of the activity is more complex because it involves both personal and group goal setting and is a closer approximation of the on-the-job situation.

Procedure

1. Divide the class into groups of five or six.

2. Explain that after a waiting period of ten minutes, each person in each group will have three throws and then each group's score will be totaled. Watch carefully what they do in this ten-minute period (don't tell them what to do). Some may practice, others may just sit there and talk. Be sure to question them about this behavior later during the discussion.

3. Have everyone throw and then total each group's score.

Discussion

1. What extra resources were used in this part of the activity?
   Available were the probability curve, each person's previous scores, and group opinion.

2. How was this second game different from the first?
   The players had more resources and they were subjected to group pressures. As a result, there was probably some conflict between personal and group objectives.

3. Which game was more realistic?
   This discussion should lead to a consideration of the pressures on a supervisor when he sets goals. There will be pressure from his immediate supervisor, his subordinates, his own sense of pride, his awareness of previous standards, and his estimation of the cost of failure.

4. As a summary, discuss the factors that affect the setting of realistic objectives, using the following guidelines:

   Estimate. Pressures (internal and external), knowledge of resources (people, feedback, time), cost of failure.

   Perform. Skill (technical, interpersonal).

   Analyze and Measure. By how much did I fail? Why did I fail? Here is a chance for you to use the people resources at your disposal.

   Improve. This step again asks you to go back to all your resources. The success of this step depends on how well you analyze your performance.

   New Estimate. Its accuracy and realism depends on how well you carried out your analysis and improvements.

Analysis and Improvements

Participants in the ring-toss game fall into three groups that have been identified in the first column in Figure 39.1.

1. Those who consistently aim high and miss (marked with an *);
2. Those who consistently aim low and get the ring on the peg (marked with an X); and
3. Those who calculate (marked with an N), i.e., those who use feedback to modify the distance from which they throw to increase the probability of success.

Goal-Setting Process

Let us look at the goal-setting process for each of these groups.

1. The people who are marked with an asterisk (*): aim higher and miss.

   Estimate. Their estimate was quite high. The cost of failing to put the ring on the peg was considered low.

   Perform. They missed the peg 100 percent of the time. The average distance from the peg was 9.9 ft.

   Analyze and Measure. Since they did not revise their distances in any major fashion, we must conclude that for them the major criterion consisted of how far away they stood and/or how *close* they got to the peg.

   Improve and New Estimate. For some of them, improvement probably meant getting the ring closer to the peg. These people either did not change the distance they stood from the peg (players 2, 3,9,10,16); lowered the distance only slightly (4,5,21); or increased their distance despite the fact that they did not get the ring over the peg (6). Notice that I am careful not to say "succeed" because these people succeeded to some extent by their own criteria—obviously getting the ring over the peg was not one of their main criteria for success.

2. The people who are marked X: consistently aim low and get the ring on the peg.

   Estimate. Their estimate was quite low. They must have considered the cost of failing to put the ring over the peg as being quite high.

   Perform. They were 87 percent successful in getting the ring over the peg. The average distance from the peg was 2.2 ft.

   Analyze and Measure. It must be concluded that their only criterion for success was getting the ring over the peg. Generally they stood quite close and did not increase their distance after a successful throw.

   Improve and New Estimate. They did not attempt to improve but stuck to their original estimate.

3. The people who are marked N: use feedback and calculate.

Estimate. Their estimates varied from 1 to 10 ft.

Perform. They were moderately successful (28 percent) in getting the ring on the peg. The average distance from the peg was 10 ft.

Analyze and Measure. They had two criteria for success: (1) getting the ring over the peg, and (2) the distance they stood from the peg. Most of them started quite far from the peg.

Improve and New Estimate. They all looked for improvement. Those who started too far away decreased their distance until they made a successful throw. Those who started close increased their distance (players 20 and 24) after they made a successful throw.

Results

In the second part of the activity, most people behaved like those of group 3 (marked N). Their estimates varied from 2 to 9 ft. They were moderately successful: 57 percent from an average distance of 5 ft. Their criteria for success were two-fold: the distance from peg and getting the ring over the peg; and they revised their estimates upward or downward based on positive or negative feedback. In Part 1, the sum of the distances of successful tosses was 41 ft.; in Part 2, it was 188 ft.

The data are certainly suggestive. They can be used to show how group pressures alter behavior, how to go about setting realistic goals, what factors go into goal setting; or the data can be construed as favoring groupthink or worker participation in goal setting. In short, the activity has enough flexibility to allow you to lead the discussion into several different areas—the ones most relevant to your training goals.

Interaction Dynamics Activity

Simulation activities are usually fun for the students and easy to administer for the instructor. This is true for the interaction dynamics simulation outlined here. I call it interaction dynamics because that title allows me flexibility in choosing the use I make of this simulation. I have taught (a) decision making, (b) group-interaction characteristics, (c) problem solving, (d) management styles, and even (e) how to manage—all based on similar procedures for the activity but with totally different processing of the data generated.

Before proceeding, please read the handout, Interaction Dynamics, shown in Figure 40.1, which describes the purpose, procedure, and rules of the activity. This outline is handed out before the activity is started. The entire activity, including processing, may require from two to three hours of time.

Classroom Set-up

Divide your class into at least three teams. I use the word *teams* rather than *groups* because it has more of a note of competition than does groups, and competition is a key part of the activity. The reason for having at least three teams is to allow each team to have more than one competitor. It also allows the timing of the activity to be such that there is always continuous activity in the classroom.

The ideal number of teams is four, although as many as six teams can be formed. Each team should have from three to six members, and at least one student observer should be appointed. This provides a range in class size of ten to forty students.

The classroom should have the team tables or work areas separated from each other. This is to reduce the possibility of one team overhearing the plans of another team. In other words, the tables are separated to

INTERACTION DYNAMICS

Introduction

1. This session is designed to dynamically develop the basic attitudes and approaches of each group member in order to facilitate the understanding of these attitudes and approaches on the job.

2. The following is a problem-solving approach that participants may find useful:
   A. Pinpoint the problem;
   B. Consider all the factors relevant to the problem;
   C. Form conclusions from these factors and set a suitable objective;
   D. Decide on a plan to meet this objective;
   E. Use this plan;
   F. Consider the feedback from its use and make necessary changes;
   G. Ensure that the plan meets the objective.

Structure

3. The class will be divided into at least three teams. Each team will be watched by an observer.

4. Each team will be given a set of chips (small round disks used in games of chance) and will be identified by the color of its chips.

5. Sets of problem worksheets are attached.

6. The problem grid (hidden from the teams) consists of three layers of clear plastic, each of which is divided into squares.

7. Points will be scored whenever a team succeeds in placing three chips on the grid in a straight line in any spatial direction.

Rules

8. The following should be read very carefully; no other information will be given:
   A. Each team will be allowed fifteen minutes to read and understand these instructions and to make preparations;
   B. Each team will have thirty seconds in which its representative may deliver instructions to the umpire and observe the grid;
   C. Only one chip may occupy a square at any given moment;
   D. Each team selects a square on which it wishes its chip to be placed and three alternate squares;
   E. On the Instuction Sheet, list only the four choices that the team has chosen;
   F. When the team is called by the umpire, its representative will take a completed Instruction Sheet and a chip to the umpire, who will place the team's chip in position on the grid in accordance with the instructions;
   G. The members of each team will take turns as representatives. Once the sequence of representatives has been set, it must not be changed;
   H. The representative may inspect the board and report what he sees to his team, as long as he does not go overtime;
   J. A scoreboard showing the teams' points will be maintained;
   K. The umpire will clear the problem grid of chips from time to time without interruption and without telling the teams;
   L. The decisions of the umpire are final; no reason will be given for any refusal to follow the instructions passed to him by a representative; the team involved must discover the reason(s) on its own.

Figure 40.1. This student handout sheet gives all the information needed to play the interaction dynamics simulation game

reduce spying, although spying is allowed. In fact, anything is allowed as long as the rules are not violated (see Figure 40.1).

A separate table should be near a flipchart or chalkboard, but isolated from the students. On this isolated table set up the tiered three-level-playing surfaces shown in Figure 40.2. Place the extra chips and instruction sheets behind the play area. Cover the whole playing area and extra materials with a cardboard box. This should effectively hide the playing surfaces from the class as they enter the room and also during the fifteen-minute preparation period (see Rule A in Figure 40.1, which is handed out to all teams before the start of the activity).

Once play starts, the carton *is not* removed. The carton is opened along one of its side seams and adjusted so that only the instructor can see the playing surfaces. What the class sees from the team areas is the carton. In other words, when the instructor stands behind the table he can see the playing areas as he looks out at the class.

You will remember that the extra chips and instruction sheets were placed at the back of the play area. What this means, now that we have the carton opened, is that to get at these extra materials, you or the students have to reach between the playing surfaces to get more materials. This is done to make it difficult for the students to get more materials once they run out. Using this arrangement, it takes quite a while for the students to spot these extra materials, which of course adds to their problems in this activity.

Role of the Umpire

The umpire is you, the instructor. You break the class up into teams and appoint the observers. You introduce the activity but you don't explain anything about the simulation itself—just the purpose of the lesson.

Give one set of the student handout materials (Figures 40.1, 40.2, and 40.3) to each student. Give each team three chips (these could be colored poker chips) and three instruction sheets. After doing this, you can tell the teams they have fifteen minutes to prepare for the activity, or you can keep quiet. By saying nothing, you provide the groups with the further problem of what they are now supposed to be doing. In using either approach, be sure to note the time so that you will know when to call up the first team representative.

While the teams are preparing, brief the observers, giving them their instruction sheets (Figures 40.5 and 40.6) and clues about what you want them to look for. I have included two different sets of observer instructions.

I designed Instructions for Observers: 1 for the times when I use the activity to develop general management skills or problem-solving

A1	A2	A3
A4	A5	A6
A7	A8	A9

On a single level, points may be scored either diagonally or straight across or up and down

Points may also be scored vertically or diagonally through the three levels (A1-B1-C1 or A3-B5-C7)

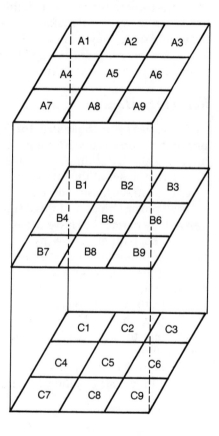

Figure 40.2.

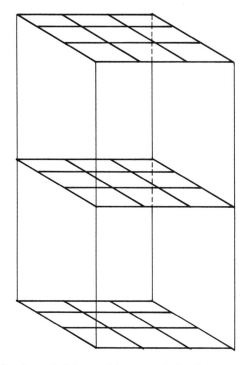

Figure 40.3. Copies of this problem worksheet come with the handout materials

INSTRUCTION SHEET

ALTERNATE PLAYS

1. _____

2. _____

3. _____

4. _____

Figure 40.4. Form used by participants to indicate first choice of play and three alternatives

INSTRUCTIONS FOR OBSERVERS: 1

1. Do not at any time during the course of the game participate in the processes of the team you are observing. You are not to converse with the team on any matter, even if you observe a flagrant breach of the rules.

2. Watch the way your team behaves as it seeks to meet the various problems that arise, with particular regard to the following points:

    A. Did any one person take the lead, or was leadership exerted by more than one person?
    B. Did the team identify the problems inherent to the activity before play actually began? Did it subsequently identify further problems as they arose?
    C. Did the team members establish a cause for each problem?
    D. Did they consider all the facts?
    E. Did they form conclusions from the facts?
    F. Did they select an objective?
    G. Did they examine possible ways of achieving the objective?
    H. Did they consider the advantages and disadvantages of each possible solution?
    I. Did they select the best solution in the light of these advantages and disadvantages?
    J. Did they prepare an appropriate plan?
    K. Did this plan provide objectives for each player and for the team as a whole?
    L. Were objectives changed to meet changing problems?
    M. Was there effective communication?
    N. Were all the available resources fully used?
    O. Did all team members make a full contribution?
    P. What were the effects of success or failure on the morale of individuals and on the team as a whole?
    Q. Did the team attempt to break or circumvent the rules? Did it succeed?
    R. Did the leadership change at any time (e.g., when morale was at its highest or lowest)?

3. Prepare a brief report of your observations in narrative form for verbal presentation to all participants at the end of the session. This report should highlight any significant departure from the problem-solving principles taught in the course.

4. Throughout the activity you are free to move around, to consult with other observers and to look at the problem board.

Figure 40.5

INSTRUCTIONS FOR OBSERVERS: 2

In the group, analyze what goes on in terms of:

1. How did interpersonal relationships promote or delay problem solving?
2. How did other groups affect your group?
3. How did you resolve problems as they occurred?
4. How did your group use the resources available to it?
5. When an obstacle occurred how did you tackle it and solve it?
6. Watch and be sensitive to what goes on in your group and others.

Figure 40.6

skills. The sheet, Instructions for Observers: 2, is used in courses when I want the class to study the characteristics of decision making or group interaction.

During this preparation period, student questions may be answered if the answers don't tell the students what they are to do or how the game is played. Questions that you don't feel should be answered can be handled with a forlorn look, a shrug of the shoulders, and a verbal "I'm sorry!" If you're really feeling devilish you then can smile. This smile will negate the previous three behaviors and often sets the group to discussing you rather than the task.

The Play

Once the fifteen-minute preparation time is over, don't announce that the time is up, just call out "Red." Red is one of the team colors and you are telling the red team that it has the first chance to put a chip on the playing surfaces. When you say "Red," you are expecting the red team to send up its first representative *who will hand you, the umpire, a red chip and its filled-out instruction sheet*. Note, I said *will hand you*. This doesn't mean that the team representative puts the chip on the playing surface. Rule F is the key here; it says both chip and instruction sheet are handed to you, the umpire.

Now a standard rule for the umpire is: don't help anyone except your observers. When the team representative comes up, stand aside so he can get at the playing area. Don't offer to take the chip and instruction sheet from the representative. The best procedure is to keep your hands in your pockets and lean lackadaisically against the wall. What usually happens is that the representative puts the chip on the playing surface and leaves. As he leaves, walk over to the playing surface, remove the chip and give it back to the team representative with an apologetic "I'm sorry!" Whatever you do, don't offer an explanation.

Now back to when you call "Red." Often nothing happens other than everyone wonders what it means. Wait thirty seconds and call "White," then thirty seconds later, call "Blue," and so on, round and round the teams. (Rule B covers this behavior.)

Once the representatives are coming up, remember that they have only thirty seconds from the time you called the team color to complete their play. This means you must police the representative who has only thirty seconds in total. Now watch it; Rule B says the representative only has thirty seconds. That doesn't exclude other team members from coming up at any point in time to watch or see what is happening. Nor does Rule B restrict how long other team members can stay in the playing area and watch. Whatever you do, don't volunteer this information until you take-up (process) the activity.

Watch that Rule G isn't violated. Sometimes teams tend to use the same person as the representative. This naturally means that, as the umpire, you will say nothing to the team concerning why, although it hands the chip and instruction sheet to you, you continually reject their moves. At the start of the game, I relax this rule slightly until the team successfully manages to get a chip on the playing surface. Once the team gets its first chip on, then I apply Rule G. Then, if the same person comes up twice in a row and hands me the materials, I just hand them back and say "I'm sorry!"

Instruction Sheets

The students, in their efforts to get a chip on the playing surface, usually rewrite and cross out their playing alternatives on the instruction sheet often to the point where it is next to impossible to read the sheets. If this happens, hand the sheet back with the usual, "I'm sorry!"

Other things that are totally unacceptable are instruction sheets that have been torn in half and substitute instruction sheets. Substitute sheets usually appear once the team has run out of the original ones. Only the printed sheets are permissible.

No Materials

You will remember that each team received three chips and three instruction sheets. These are quickly used up, once a team starts getting chips on the playing surface. I suggest, that every time you, as the umpire, place a chip on the playing surface, you destroy the accompanying instruction sheet. This will prevent reusage of these sheets and also will result in their being used up.

Once a team has used up its materials, it will try all kinds of things. You will find its representatives coming up and removing one of its chips from the playing surface and handing this to you. The teams will make paper chips. They will give you written instructions to move one of their already played discs. Naturally you reject all these, making sure their chips remain where they were originally placed.

Sometimes the groups say things such as "We've run out of chips" or "We don't have any instruction sheets left." Neither of these statements request more materials, so you say "I'm sorry!" What you want is a specific request for more materials such as, "Can we have more chips?" This, of course, means you respond by reaching through the playing surfaces and giving the team some more chips. This may seem a bit petty but remember this activity is meant to create problems to test the teams' abilities to overcome them.

Frustration Stoppages

You can expect teams that have been unsuccessful in trying to get more materials to get frustrated. If the frustration level gets too high it is advisable to stop the game. You can do this at any time. The rules do not say how long the activity will last. Besides, you are the umpire and Rule L says all your decisions are final.

When you stop the game, you can proceed with an open discussion of why the groups are all tied up or whatever the situation calls for. You also can just let the team members use the stoppage to consider what they are doing and how they are working together as a team. Instructions for Observers: 2 can serve as an excellent format for team discussion of how it has done. Sometimes the stoppage may only be to help one team that is so frustrated or hung-up that you feel help is essential.

To start the game again just call out the next team's color and proceed. The total length of the actual playing time, excluding any stoppages, usually will be about forty-five minutes. With stoppages, introduction, and processing the activity requires from two to three hours, so plan your lesson accordingly.

It may be advisable to stop the game if all or most of the teams are failing to get chips on the playing surface. Discuss the problem and restart the game. If only one team is failing to place chips, you can help them with a clue, such as; "Read the rules carefully." In case they didn't hear you, you can check with the next representative sent up by the team to discover whether or not they got the message. Even telling a team to read the rules carefully may not correct the problem. They still may fail to place chips on the playing surface. At this point, I usually get specific and say, "Read rule F."

Umpire Rulings

Rule L says the umpire's decisions are final. The rule even states that you don't have to explain any of your behavior. This certainly resembles a situation in which what the boss says is final and cannot be questioned by any subordinate.

A further ramification, which is vital to the operation of the activity, develops from Rule L. That is, *the umpire can make his own rules to suit the circumstances*. This should help you as a beginning umpire. Don't hesitate to use it when unusual and unexpected things happen, such as the following situation.

The red team is way ahead on points and is really doing well. Its representative takes all the remaining chips of the other teams to stop them from scoring any points. As the umpire, what do you do? I would stop them and say, "Sorry," taking back the materials.

Now, let's reverse that situation. The red team is totally at sea and is going nowhere. Its representative takes all the remaining chips of the other teams. As the umpire, I would do nothing. In fact, I might support them and even go so far as to tell the other teams that they will have to deal with the red team to solve this problem.

As the umpire, you can adjust the rules to suit the situation. I have even gone so far as to set up the activity as outlined here and then, without telling the students, I used a completely different set of rules than they have been given.

Miscellaneous

The most powerful spot in the exercise is B5. It is central and lines of three can be built in more directions from there than anywhere else on the playing surfaces.

Two or three points can be scored at one time by just adding one chip to the playing surfaces, e.g., Blue has chips on B7, C7, A4, A1, A5 and A3 and adds its chip on A7. The result is three points for Blue.

It is permissible for the umpire to remove all chips at any time from the playing surface, (see Rule K). Therefore, when all playing spots have a chip on them, you can clear the chips from the playing surfaces, or you could remove them at the start just after all teams have figured out how to get the chips on the playing surface.

41

A Pawn-Checker-Chess Simulation

We have probably all heard that "learning should be fun." It isn't always, but we trainers are to blame for that. The trainer *is* responsible for making the learning experience fun, and simulation activities such as the one described here can do the trick.

Goals

Used in management development, the main goal of this activity is to make students realize how ineffectively they use the resources they have available to them in any work situation.

Process

The instructor should be at least vaguely familiar with how pawns move in the game of chess. Even that is not essential; the instructor does not have to know the rules. Knowing the rules and how to do the activity is the problem of each team.

At the outset, *don't* tell the students that the purpose of the activity is to explore the resources available to the work group. Tell them that this is a management development activity relating directly to the work situation. You can challenge them to try to reason out the purpose as they go along, but don't expect them to spend their time doing so. They will become so wrapped up in the activity that they will forget about trying to figure out what it is all about.

Ask for a show of hands of those who can play chess. Be sure that they hold up their hands long enough for you to remember who can play. Then divide the room into teams of five or six people and *be sure to wind up with an even number of teams*. Each team should have, *must* have, a chess player on it. The teams are then paired off.

Marit Stengels was co-author of this column.

251

Materials Utilized

1. A chess set, table, and an appropriate number of chairs for each pair of teams.
2. Pads of paper and pencils for each team.

Rules

1. The pawns move as pawns are moved in chess.

2. Each team must move within one hour of the previous move or within one hour of when you say "Start the activity." (The hour may seem long but they rarely, if ever, use the full time. It serves as a period in which proper planning can be done. You may get some negative feedback about the hour of planning time but don't let it bother you. Students will see the reason for it at the end of the activity, if the discussion goes right.)

3. The team with black chess pieces has the first move.

4. The goal of the game is to move any pawn from one team's back-row starting position (the bottom row on each side of the checker board) to the back row of the opposing team. The first team to do this wins.

5. The activity can extend over more than one training session. It is better if the students play for two hours and then break and come back a week later or the next day. Doing this gives the students a chance to bring in an expert, if they think of it, or to study some chess books, or to bring in a chess set and board from home. In other words, the break allows the students to develop and utilize outside resources.

Time Required

A. To complete the activity, the teams usually need a total of some four hours.

B. If the groups finish at different times, the first groups through can take an extended coffee break; *or* play a second and third game, using a five-minute time limit between moves; *or* they can leave, if it is close to the end of the class time, and you can have the remaining groups complete the activity before they leave.

What to Watch for

A. The impatience of the people who must wait to make their next move while the opposing team is in a prolonged planning session.

B. Players who opt out or leave their teams.

C. People who consider the whole thing silly and hence affect their team's efforts.

D. If a player quits a team and starts to leave the class, catch him and talk to him. He has done you a favor because something obviously is wrong on his team. Tell him it is a team fault and you are glad he left his team; it is something you had hoped would happen. Explore this opt-out situation in the discussion that follows the activity. Give the person who was opting out a chance to express his feelings. Check with his team to see if the other members experienced the problem. Ask how they solved it. Go back to the problem team. Ask what the feeling is now and how this problem should have been handled.

E. The ingenuity or creative ideas that are being applied by the players.

F. The use of secrecy.

G. How the teams use their resources. (See the resources list that follows.)

H. Because the one-hour time allowance leads to comments and friction within the teams, people may feel the time between moves should be five minutes.

I. How do the chess players train the non-players? Do they train them?

J. Are the rules of chess totally explored? Usually they aren't. Examples of things overlooked include: (1) the possibility of a draw or tie game; (2) when a player moves his pawn and removes his hand, the move is final and can't be changed; (3) when a player moves his pawn and does not remove his hand, the move can be taken back but that pawn and no other has to be moved on the move to be played; (4) two spaces may be moved on the first move of any pawn, not just as an option in the first move of the game for each team.

K. The style of play used by each team. Is the team offensive-minded or defensive-minded? Does it have a "come-to-us" or an "attack-them" approach? Or does the team take a "lets-get-it-over" approach? Or does it play a conservative game? In other words, what is each team's operational philosophy?

L. What leadership pattern emerges in each team? Authoritarian? Democratic? Is each move decided by a different man as predetermined by a batting order similar to that used in a baseball game's line-up? Does the total team provide the leadership by getting agreement from all members before making a move? Is there no leadership either by an individual or by the team itself?

M. How does the team solve internal problems?

N. How does the team solve problems in playing the game?

O. How does the team arrange the team's seating and the position of the master game board on which both teams make their moves?

P. Do the teams foresee problems?

Q. How do they plan and organize themselves?

R. Are the teams planning six or seven moves ahead?

S. Does one team try to maneuver the other team through stalling tactics, by changing its pattern of attack, or by changing its planning workplace in such a way that it disturbs the other team?

T. Do the teams consider other alternatives to the ones they are presently using?

U. Does any team ever stop playing in order to consider how it as a team should be managing the activity? Do the teams review their ways of attacking it?

V. Watch for the pitfalls of boredom, smugness, feeling secure, poor use of time, a defeatist attitude, complacency after a move, team dissension.

W. Does any team shatter, i.e., not work on the activity as a team but revert to individualism?

X. Does the whole team know the rules or not? What is the effect on the team when some people don't really know the rules?

Y. How do teams attack the problem?

Z. Does any team consider the resources available to it?

Discussion

Have an *open discussion* following completion of the game. This is vital. The students will have lots of pent-up feelings. An open discussion means that you do not direct them in any way. It means you keep out of the discussion except to: (a) police a situation where two or three people are all saying the same thing and don't realize it; (b) help a silent person break into the conversation (all that is needed is for you to use the person's name, indicating you want him to have his say; the rest will shut-up and listen to him); (c) clarify a point that is important, but the person trying to express it has failed to communicate it to the class; (d) focus attention on a point that has been expressed but overlooked by the class in its enthusiastic discussion. Preferably, you should not make the point. Have the person who expressed the idea re-explain it to the class. If you do it, discussion will focus on you and hence it becomes closed rather than open.

The open discussion should last for at least one and a half hours.

If the class gets off on a meaningless/irrelevant tangent, *do not* attempt to bring it back on course. The class will do this eventually, although it may take it fifteen minutes to get there. Remember, you are trying to get the students, not yourself, to use their resources. If you bring them back on track, then they don't really have the opportunity to develop *their* resources. This self-directing experience, and the development of a correcting mechanism, are a vital part of the learning experience. Note the self-correcting element because it may prove useful to you to discuss it in the summary of the open discussion.

To Trigger Discussion

All you have to do in order to evoke discussion is ask, "Who is confused about the purpose of the activity?" Most students will readily admit to being confused. Then ask, "Who *thinks* he has an idea what the activity was about?" The wording of this last question is critical. Don't ask, "Who knows?" Under these circumstances, nobody would admit that he knows. But some may *think* they know, and this question will trigger them to speak. Asking, "Who has an idea what the activity is about?" will also work, for the same reason. Ask the students who think they know the purpose of the activity *to explain it to the others, not to you*.

That should trigger your discussion.

Likely Topics to be Discussed

- The role of the manager.
- Who should lead.
- Should the person who is knowledgeable about chess carry the rest of the team? Should the non-experts depend on the expert and not learn how to play chess?
- How well should the non-experts learn how to play chess?
- Who should make decisions?
- The one-hour time period.
- The man who quit the team (if one did).
- Can a group solve all its problems?
- Did the teams use all the resources and skills they had?
- Should there be 100 percent agreement; i.e., should all team members be in agreement on each and every decision?

Facilitating Discussion

The students will wonder during their discussion if they should be talking as much as they are while *you*, the instructor, are saying so little. This requires you to praise or reinforce the discussion at the times when it is really on the track. Nodding the head, smiling, murmuring approval, and saying, "Yea," are all strong enough reinforcement to keep the discussion going; and at the same time they don't disrupt the ongoing conversation.

Students want and need this type of feedback because they worry that they are not on the right track or they are not correct.

Let them know they are on the track when the occasions arise. Use pauses in the conversation, glances in your direction, and questions directed to you as opportunities to offer reinforcement to the students. They want and need to hear it.

Omit the reinforcement, especially in the early stages of the discussion, and you are likely to have no discussion at all.

If, during the discussion, the fact that a man quit a team has not been explored, bring it up and have it discussed as outlined in point D under What to Watch For.

Summarize the discussion and comment on the highlights and significant points in the open discussion. The students expect this kind of wrap-up by the teacher and they need it; it serves to reinforce remembering the significant points in the discussion. This is the time for you, the trainer, to discuss with the class the points you feel are important.

Listing Available Resources

Following the summary of the discussion, divide the class back into the teams used in the pawn-checker-chess game. By means of an overlay on the overhead projector, or by using the blackboard, have each team decide what resources were available to each team.

At about the half-hour to three-quarter-hour mark you should find that each group will have just about played out the possibilities it can think of. Wait for this point before telling the students that there are at least twenty-five resources that they should come up with. Saying so at this point will start them working again. Initially they probably listed only about half of the twenty-five or so resources available to them. Most groups will then re-attack the problem and come up with about twenty.

An interesting factor to note at this point is that the losing teams will probably come up with fewer resources than the winning teams. This might be worth discussing *after* the resources have been listed. So might the fact that the groups tended to quit after they had done almost half of the task.

Resource List Procedure

Ask each team in turn for one resource and post it if the other teams have it. If the other teams do not have it, stimulate a discussion until agreement on the wording, meaning, and implication of the resource has been reached. (See the article, "How to Make Case Studies Come Alive" for more about this technique.) Once you have agreement, post the resource on the list that you are building. (This posting rewards the class for its efforts and leads to more and better consideration of other resources to be posted.)

If the other teams don't have a point that is suggested by one team, then this point must be discussed and the class must agree on whether or not it should be on the list. Ask the class as a whole, "Is that a resource?", or "Shall I post it?", or simply, "Why is that a resource?."

No matter what happens, allow or stimulate some discussion on each resource.

Resources Available

1. Group planning, using teamwork.
2. The individuals themselves.
3. Knowledgeable people, i.e., those who can play chess.
4. Brainpower: learning ability.
5. A teaching resource.
6. Time.
7. Group objectivity or the group's ability to keep itself on the track toward reaching the objective.
8. Outside information, such as libraries, consultants, and reference material.
9. Communicating: the ability to express ideas to others and gain their understanding.
10. Choice of a method of leadership.
11. Rules of the activity: its regulations and policies.
12. Freedom of movement.
13. Spying, counter intelligence, and espionage, or, more simply, observing the other teams.
14. Secrecy in planning moves.
15. The condition of the room or the room's layout.
16. Simulations: setting up other chess boards on sheets of paper.
17. Analyzing and evaluating the other group's style, as opposed to spying.
18. Psychologically maneuvering the other group (see point S in What to Watch For).
19. Cheating or trying to break the rules.
20. Group-developed compatibility.
21. Curiosity, inquisitiveness, and a desire to learn.
22. Re-evaluating the process of how the team is working on the problem (see point U in What to Watch For).
23. Flexibility.
24. Preconceived ideas, or lack of any.
25. Having a questioning approach.
26. An attitude of thinking positively.
27. The motivation of group members.
28. Room facilities such as pads, tables, boards, etc.

42

Valuable Source of Activities Uncovered

Good usable activities, whether they are cases, role-plays, or simulations, are often hard to come by. In fact, most of us collect them so that we will have them should the training need arise. Well, I've found a tremendous collection of structured experiences and training instruments developed by users for users: The Pfeiffer-Jones Series in Human Relations Training. The credit goes to John Kenny, Training Officer with the Ontario Ministry of Education, who first drew my attention to these valuable sources.

To give you an idea of what these training tools are like, we have reprinted, with permission, three of them. If you study these three samples, you will see that you can easily figure out how to plan and administer the activity from the information given.

Pfeiffer and Jones permit you to freely reproduce and adapt the materials for educational and training purposes. The actual wording of this right to reproduce includes the following:

> Our reproduction policy gives users the freedom to duplicate (and adapt) . . . materials *for educational and training purposes.* We ask only that such materials be identified with the credit statement given on the copyright page. (Some materials . . . are copyrighted by others; in that case, permission to reproduce the materials for any purpose must be obtained from the copyright holder, unless otherwise indicated.) *If University Associates materials are to be reproduced in publications for sale or are intended for large-scale distribution, prior written permission of the editors is required.*

From this you can see that here is a source of useful training ideas that can be used without further costs.

CONTENT

The Pfeiffer-Jones series includes the six volumes of *A Handbook of Structured Experiences for Human Relations Training* and yearly volumes of *The Annual Handbook for Group Facilitators*, published since 1972. There is also the *Reference Guide* to *Handbooks* and *Annuals*, which classifies the contents of the series.

The content of the books ranges through such topics as leadership, problem solving, decision making, nonverbal communications, group dynamics, process observation, stress, listening, organizational simulations, and many, many more. Now, naturally, with such a large collection of activities, not all are necessarily going to interest every reader. In my case, I feel that about half of the activities are helpful in my training work. The other half, while not presently applicable, may be of use in the future.

Change to Fit

Another point that I find useful is that these simulations are easily changed to fit the training need you may have. For example, my title for the activity, "Residence Halls," is "Developing Group Commitment." This material would have to be changed for most industrial courses. You can easily adjust the ranking sheet shown so that it deals with a particular topic in which you have an interest. I have used it to deal with motivation and am presently considering adapting it to deal with decision making and problem solving.

RESIDENCE HALLS:
A CONSENSUS-SEEKING TASK

Goals

    I. To study the degree to which members of a group agree on certain values.

    II. To assess the decision-making norms of the group.

    III. To identify the "natural leadership" functioning in the group.

Reprinted from J. William Pfeiffer and John E. Jones (Eds.), *A Handbook of Structured Experiences for Human Relations Training* (Vol. I, Rev.), La Jolla, CA: University Associates, 1974, 72-74. Used with permission.

Group Size

Between five and twelve participants. Several groups may be directed simultaneously in the same room. (Synergistic outcomes are more likely to be achieved by smaller groups, *i.e.*, five to seven participants.)

Time Required

Approximately one hour.

Materials

    I. Copies of the Residence Halls Ranking Sheet for all participants.

    II. Pencils for all participants.

Physical Setting

It is desirable to have small groups seated around tables and to have the groups far enough apart so as not to disturb each other. Lapboards or desk chairs may be utilized instead of tables.

Process

    I. The facilitator forms groups and announces that they will engage in an activity to accomplish the goals spelled out above.

    II. He distributes copies of the Residence Halls Ranking Sheet. The facilitator functions as a timekeeper according to the schedule on the sheet. One or more members may function as process observers. (See "Process Observation," *Vol I*: Structured Experience 10.)

    III. After the allotted time, the group discusses the process in terms of stated goals.

Variations

    I. The ranking sheet can be easily revised to fit situations other than residence halls. The content may be the goals of the organization or group, characteristics of an ideal leader, desirable characteristics of teachers (principals, ministers, counselors, supervisors, employers, etc.), or any other relevant list. One suggestion might be to conduct a problem census of the organization or group and to use that list as the items to be rank-ordered.

II. When several groups in the same organization (class, institution, etc.) engage in this experience simultaneously, it is sometimes helpful to summarize the rank orders for the several groups and to have a discussion of the agreements and disagreements among the groups.

Similar Structured Experiences: *Vol I:* Structured Experience **11;** *Vol II:* **30;** *Vol. III:* **64, 69;** *'72 Annual:* **77;** *Vol. IV:* **115.**
Lecturette Sources: *'73 Annual:* "Synergy and Consensus-Seeking," "Value Clarification."

RESIDENCE HALLS RANKING SHEET

Rank the following functions of the residence-hall system according to the importance *you* attach to them. Write the number 1 in front of the most important, the number 2 before the second most important, etc. You have ten minutes for this task.

After members of your group have finished working individually, arrive at a rank ordering *as a group*. The group has thirty minutes for the task. Do *not* choose a formal leader.

Individual Rank	Group Rank	
_____	_____	Residence halls exist to help college students develop social maturity.
_____	_____	Residence-hall organizations should militate for improving the quality of student life.
_____	_____	The residence hall is where students develop business and social contacts that will be helpful after graduation.
_____	_____	Residence halls provide a "home away from home" where the resident is accepted and wanted.
		The residence-hall system encourages worthwhile fellowship.
_____	_____	The residence hall is an experiment in living, through which the student comes to know his prejudices and tries to overcome them.
_____	_____	Participation in residence-hall activities is training for leadership in adult life.
_____	_____	Residence halls support and enhance the classroom learning experience of students.
_____	_____	In the residence-hall system, students are treated as adults, not as adolescents who need to be controlled.
_____	_____	Residence halls function as laboratories for democratic action.

LUTTS AND MIPPS:
GROUP PROBLEM-SOLVING

Goals

    I. To study the sharing of information in a task-oriented group.

    II. To focus on cooperation in group problem-solving.

    III. To observe the emergence of leadership behavior in group problem-solving.

Group Size

From six to twelve participants. Several groups may be directed simultaneously in the same room.

Time Required

Approximately forty-five mintues.

Materials

    I. Copies of the Lutts and Mipps Instructions Form for all participants.

    II. A set of Lutts and Mipps Information Cards for each group (26 cards in a set).

    III. Copies of the Lutts and Mipps Reactions Form for all participants.

    IV. Paper and pencil for each participant.

Physical Setting

Members of each group are seated in a circle.

Reprinted from J. William Pfeiffer and John E. Jones (Eds.), *A Handbook of Structured Experiences for Human Relations Training* (Vol. II, Rev.), La Jolla, CA: University Associates, 1974, 24-28. Used with permission.

Based on a problem by Rimoldi, *Training in Problem-Solving*, Publication No. 21, Loyola University Psychometrics Laboratory.

Process

I. Lutts and Mipps Instructions Forms are distributed.

II. After participants have had time to read the instruction sheet, the facilitator distributes a set of Lutts and Mipps Information Cards randomly among the members of each group. Participants begin their task.

III. After about twenty minutes, the facilitator interrupts and distributes the Reactions Forms, which are to be completed *individually*.

IV. The facilitator leads a discussion of the problem-solving activity, focusing on information-processing and the sharing of leadership in task situations. Group members are encouraged to share data from their reaction forms.

SOLUTION: 23/39 wors

Variations

I. The problem can be simplified by handing out data sheets that include both answers and questions.

II. The problem can be made more difficult by adding redundant or unnecessary information.

III. The same structure can be used with a different problem more relevant to the group.

IV. A competition among the groups can be set up: The winner will be the group that achieves the correct solution in the least amount of time.

Similar Structured Experiences: *Vol II*: Structured Experience 29; *'72 Annual*: **80**, *Vol IV*: **102, 103, 117**.

LUTTS AND MIPPS INSTRUCTIONS FORM

Pretend that lutts and mipps represent a new way of measuring distance and that dars, wors, and mirs represent a new way of measuring time. A man drives from Town A, through Town B and Town C, to Town D.

The task of your group is to determine how many wors the entire trip took. You have twenty minutes for this task. Do *not* choose a formal leader.

You will be given cards containing information related to the task. You may share this information orally, but you must keep your cards in your hands throughout the task.

Lutts and Mipps Information Cards

To make a set of cards, type each of the following sentences on a 3″ x 5″ index card (a total of 26). A set should be distributed randomly among members of each group. Each group must have all twenty-six cards.

1. How far is it from A to B?
2. It is 4 lutts from A to B.
3. How far is it from B to C?
4. It is 8 lutts from B to C.
5. How far is it from C to D?
6. It is 10 lutts from C to D.
7. What is a lutt?
8. A lutt is 10 mipps.
9. What is a mipp?
10. A mipp is a way of measuring distance.
11. How many mipps are there in a mile?
12. There are 2 mipps in a mile.
13. What is a dar?
14. A dar is 10 wors.
15. What is a wor?
16. A wor is 5 mirs.
17. What is a mir?
18. A mir is way of measuring time.
19. How many mirs are there in an hour?
20. There are two mirs in an hour.
21. How fast does the man drive from A to B?
22. The man drives from A to B at the rate of 24 lutts per wor.
23. How fast does the man drive from B to C?
24. The man drives from B to C at the rate of 30 lutts per wor.
25. How fast does the man drive from C to D?
26. The man drives from C to D at the rate of 30 lutts per wor.

Lutts and Mipps Reactions Form

1. Whose participation was most helpful in the accomplishment of the task?
2. What behavior was helpful?
3. Whose participation seemed to hinder the accomplishment of the task?
4. What behavior seemed to be a hindrance?
5. What feeling reactions did you experience during the problem-solving exercise?
6. What role(s) did you play in the group?

PRISONERS' DILEMMA:
AN INTERGROUP COMPETITION

Goals

I. To explore trust between group members and effects of betrayal of trust.

II. To demonstrate effects of interpersonal competition.

III. To dramatize the merit of a collaborative posture in intragroup and intergroup relations.

Group Size

Two teams of no more than eight members each.

Time Required

Approximately one hour. (Smaller teams take less time.)

Materials

I. Copies of the Prisoners' Dilemma Tally Sheet for all participants.

II. Pencils.

Physical Setting

Enough space for the two teams to meet separately without overhearing or disrupting each other. For step VII, two chairs for team representatives should be placed facing each other in the center of the room.

Process

I. The facilitator explains that the group is going to experience a "risk-taking" situation similar to that experienced by guilty prisoners being interrogated by the police. Before interrogating prisoners suspected of working together, the questioner separates them and tells each one that the other has confessed and that, if they both confess, they will get off easier. The prisoners' dilemma or risk is that they may confess when they should not or they may

Reprinted from J. William Pfeiffer and John E. Jones (Eds.), *A Handbook of Structured Experiences for Human Relations Training* (Vol. III, Rev.), La Jolla, CA: University Associates, 1974, 52-56. Used with permission.

fail to confess when they really should. (The facilitator carefully avoids discussing goals.)

II. Two teams are formed and named Red and Blue. The teams are seated apart from each other. They are instructed not to communicate with the other team in any way, verbally or nonverbally, except when told to do so by the facilitator.

III. Prisoners' Dilemma Tally Sheets are distributed to all participants. They are given time to study the directions. The facilitator then asks if there are any questions concerning the scoring.

IV. Round I is begun. The facilitator tells the teams that they will have three minutes to make a team decision. He instructs them not to write their decisions until he signals them that time is up, so that they will not make hasty decisions.

V. The choices of the two teams are announced for Round 1. The scoring for that round is agreed upon and is entered on the scorecards.

VI. Rounds 2 and 3 are conducted in the same way as Round 1.

VII. Round 4 is announced as a special round, for which the payoff points are doubled. Each team is instructed to send one representative to the chairs in the center of the room. After representatives have conferred for three minutes, they return to their teams. Teams then have three minutes, as before, in which to make their decisions. When recording their scores, they should be reminded that points indicated by the payoff schedule are doubled for this round only.

VIII. Rounds 5 through 8 are conducted in the same manner as the first three rounds.

IX. Round 9 is announced as a special round, in which the payoff points are "squared" (multiplied by themselves: *e.g.*, a score of 4 would be $4^2 = 16$). A minus sign should be retained: *e.g.*, $(-3)^2 = -9$. Team representatives meet for three minutes; then the teams meet for *five* minutes. At the facilitator's signal, the teams write their choices; then the two choices are announced.

X. Round 10 is handled exactly as Round 9 was. Payoff points are squared.

XI. The entire group meets to process the experience. The point total for each team is announced, and the sum of the two team totals is calculated and compared to the maximum positive or negative outcomes ($+126$ or -126 points). The facilitator may wish to lead a discussion about win-lose situations, zero-sum games, the relative merits of collaboration and competition, and the effects of high and low trust on interpersonal relations.

Variations

I. The competition can be carried out using money instead of points.

II. Process observers can be assigned to each team.

III. Teams can be placed in separate rooms, to minimize rule-breaking.

IV. The number of persons in each team can be varied.

V. In Round 10, each team can be directed to predict the choice of the other. These predictions can be posted before announcing the actual choices, as in the following diagram. (Actual choices are recorded in the circles after the predictions are announced.)

Predicting Team	Predicted Choice	
	Red Team	Blue Team
Red	◯	
Blue		◯

Similar Structured Experiences: *Vol. II:* Structured Experience **35, 36;** *'72 Annual:* **83.**
Lecturette Sources: *'72 Annual:* "Risk-Taking and Error Protection Styles"; *'73 Annual:* "Win-Lose Situations."

PRISONERS' DILEMMA TALLY SHEET

Instructions: For ten successive rounds, the Red team will choose either an A or a B and the Blue Team will choose either an X or a Y. The score each team receives in a round is determined by the pattern made by the choices of both teams, according to the schedule below.

PAYOFF SCHEDULE

AX—Both teams win 3 points.
AY—Red Team loses 6 points; Blue Team wins 6 points.
BX—Red Team wins 6 points; Blue Team loses 6 points.
BY—Both teams lose 3 points.

SCORECARD

Round	Minutes	Choice		Cumulative Points	
		Red Team	Blue Team	Red Team	Blue Team
1	3				
2	3				
3	3				
4*	3 (reps.) 3 (teams)				
5	3				
6	3				
7	3				
8	3				
9**	3 (reps.) 5 (teams)				
10**	3 (reps.) 5 (teams)				

*Payoff points are doubled for this round.
**Payoff points are squared for this round. (Retain the minus sign.)

The LEGO® Man

LEGO Man is without doubt in a class of activities that will help determine the future of training. This exercise consists of a planning part, an assembly part, and finally a feedback part on the results of the earlier efforts. I realize that LEGO bricks aren't part of every trainer's kit, but maybe you can borrow from your children's stockpile or seek help from your neighbors' kids. Of course, you could always buy them.

Figure 43.1 presents some of the results I've had with this structured experience. I've found it useful after the activity to point out some of the following:

A. The group didn't really read the instruction sheet carefully and this made the task even harder.

B. Planning can be done serially in two ways: one thing after the other, or parallel, with two or three things being done at the same time.

C. The lack of any attempt by the group to plan the planning effort. I usually indicate, as a rule of thumb, that 20 percent of the planning time should be spent on planning the planning.

D. This ties in with C. The activity encourages and demonstrates vividly the effects of increased planning time (see Figure 43.1), which shows that more time spent in planning results in less time spent on assembly. Good use of this planning time is also worth considering. In other words, effective use of planning time is also essential but is not measured in this activity.

Class Number	Group Number	Planning Time	Assembly Time
Class No. 1	1	97 minutes	7¼ minutes
	2	68 minutes	15 minutes
Class No. 2	1	95 minutes	13 minutes
	2	46 minutes	20 minutes
Class No. 3	1	31 minutes	6½ minutes
	2	28 minutes	19 minutes
Class No. 4	1	54 minutes	3 minutes
	2	48 minutes	6 minutes

Figure 43.1. LEGO Man data from four classes of two groups each. Note how the planning and assembly times are inverted; the longer the planning time, the shorter the assembly time in each class

INTERGROUP MODEL-BUILDING: THE LEGO® MAN

Goals

 I. To extract the learnings from a competitive teamwork experience, in terms of leadership style, developing alternatives, dominance and submission within teams, and distribution of work and resources.

 II. To diagnose the dynamics of an intact group in terms of role-taking.

Group Size

Teams of 8 to 15 participants each.

Time Required

Approximately two hours.

Materials Utilized

 I. Sets of special plastic interlocking building blocks of red and white, in the shape of squares, rectangles, and pegs. (LEGO by

From W. Brendan Reddy and Otto Kroeger, "Inter-group Model-Building: The LEGO® Man." In J. W. Pfeiffer and J. E. Jones (Eds.), *The 1972 Annual Handbook for Group Facilitators*, pp. 36-42. Copyright 1971 by W. Brendan Reddy and Otto Kroeger. Used by permission of the authors.

Interlego AG. See note below on obtaining sets specially assembled for this structured experience.) Each set of building blocks contains exactly 48 pieces, including 11 red 8's, 12 white 8's, 3 red 6's, 2 white 6's, 6 red 4's, 6 white 4's, 3 red 2's, 3 white 2's, 1 red peg, and 1 white peg. Each team will have one set, and one set will be used by the facilitator to construct the model before the experience begins.

  II. LEGO Man Instructions Sheet for each team.

 III. Model Construction Diagram for the facilitator.

 IV. Chalkboard or newsprint sheets and felt-tip marker.

  V. Scratch paper and pencils if teams wish to use them.

 VI. LEGO Man Planning and Assembly Table. (Optional.)

VII. LEGO Man Planning and Assembly Time Graph. (Optional.)

Physical Setting

  I. Large room with a work table for each team placed approximately fifteen feet apart.

 II. Table, which displays the model, near the center of the room, also approximately fifteen feet from any team's table.

Process

   I. The facilitator assembles the model LEGO Man in advance of the experience and places it on the table in the center of the room.

  II. If the teams are not intact groups, the facilitator forms teams in any appropriate way. He asks each team to choose an observer. (The facilitator may serve as observer if he desires to and if the number of teams makes this feasible, or he may employ staff observers.)

 III. The facilitator asks observers to distribute a set of building blocks among the team members at each table, alloting each member approximately the same number of blocks. He also asks them to give a copy of the LEGO Man Instructions Sheet to their teams and to ask team members to wait for further instructions before handling the materials.

 IV. The facilitator explains to the observers that they are to monitor team member behavior during the process of planning and assembly of the model. He also explains the task of timing the planning and assembly periods for their individual groups. Both phases will be timed, although the teams will be aware of only the assembly-time factor.

V. The facilitator tells the teams that they will be competing with each other in assembling an exact replica of the model LEGO Man on the center table. He explains that they are free to structure their time and resources in any way they find useful. He then reads the LEGO Man Instructions Sheet aloud.

VI. When all teams have completed their models, the facilitator announces the winner. He then discusses the times of the individual teams in both the planning phase and assembly phase and reviews representative times of other groups for the teams to use in seeing how they "fit in" with other group norms. The facilitator may put the LEGO Man Planning and Assembly Table on a chalkboard or newsprint or distribute copies of the table to the teams.

VII. The facilitator may also wish to incorporate the LEGO Man Planning Production Time Graph into the discussion by reproducing the graph as a poster or by distributing copies to the teams. He discusses outcomes of various types of groups, focusing on characteristics of fragmented, smooth, and conflicted groups.

VIII. He then gives a lecturette on the dynamics of problem-solving in terms of interpersonal functioning.

IX. The observers are asked to give their individual teams feedback on how members used resources, how they worked together on an interpersonal basis, what kind of leadership behavior was observed, and what roles were played in an intact group, if applicable. The teams continue to discuss the facilitator's input and the observer's feedback in terms of how they saw their team functioning.

X. The teams are then asked to share their learnings with the group as a whole. (The facilitator may structure the times alloted for IX and X in a way that seems appropriate to the particular group.)

The facilitator may wish to introduce the variable of "outside consultants" by allowing members of the team which have completed assembly of the LEGO Man first to offer their services to teams who have not yet completed the task. Observers should be alerted to the possibility of new behaviors when the "outside consultant" is introduced into the on-going efforts of the team.

To obtain special sets of LEGO blocks for assembly of the LEGO Man write to the following address:

> Dr. W. Brendan Reddy
> Community Psychology Institute
> 109 West Corry Street
> Cincinnati, Ohio 45219

LEGO MAN INSTRUCTIONS SHEET

Each team has a set of 48 Lego Blocks (11 red 8's, 12 white 8's, 3 red 6's, 2 white 6's, 6 red 4's, 6 white 4's, 3 red 2's, 3 white 2's, 1 red peg, 1 white peg).

You are to assemble these pieces *exactly* like the model, which is in the center of the room.

You are to spend whatever time you wish preparing to assemble your pieces. You can work together as a group in any way which you think will be most helpful in preparing to assemble and in assembling the pieces.

There are some ground rules, however:

1. Only one person may leave the table at a time to look at the model. The model may not be handled in any way. The pieces on your model cannot be taken from the table you are working on.

2. Until you are ready to start the assembly, you may not exchange the pieces or put any two pieces together. The pieces must stay in front of each person. They can be handled by that one person, but not fitted together nor lined up in any orderly arrangement.

3. When you are ready to start assembling, you should advise your observer so that he can clock the time.

4. When you are finished assembling, your observer will note the time. He will not tell you the time until all team times are in. You are to bring the assembled man to the center table, where the facilitator will determine whether the assembly has been completed properly.

5. If the facilitator finds an error when the assembly is completed, he will advise the team that the model is not correct, but he will not tell what the error is. The observer will start timing again, adding to the original time.

6. Remember, you can have all the time you want to prepare as a group for the assembly, but let your observer know when you are ready to start assembling.

Lego Man Planning and Assembly Table
In Minutes

Group	Activity	Mean	Standard Deviation
Total (N = 110 groups)	Planning	53.46	28.62
	Assembly	11.04	9.48
Managers (N = 14 groups)	Planning	63.28	4.43
	Assembly	6.41	3.59
Teachers (N = 11 groups)	Planning	35.06	25.12
	Assembly	17.53	13.01
Administrators (N = 11 groups)	Planning	24.72	20.20
	Assembly	27.98	18.01

Record Time: Planning, 93 minutes; Assembly, 38 seconds.

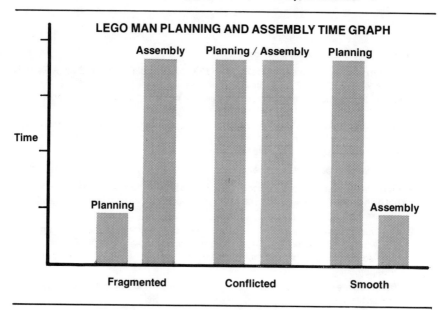

LEGO MAN PLANNING AND ASSEMBLY TIME GRAPH

GROUP TYPE

Fragmented groups. Autocratic leadership, subgroupings, and minority pressure forces these groups into making rather quick decisions without considering quality alternatives. Openness is not a norm. They exhibit minimal effort and minimal gain.

Conflicted groups. They are cautious, suspicious, and while they consider many alternate plans, they are not able to move toward consensus. They tend to use majority vote, usually as a desperate move; however, there is little commitment to the plan or outcome. They exhibit maximal effort and minimal gain.

Smoothly functioning groups. They tend to be trusting, cohesive, and exhibit high interaction and sharing. They test for consensus without threatening members and seem committed to the plan and outcome. They are characterized by minimal effort and maximal gain.

Model Construction Diagram

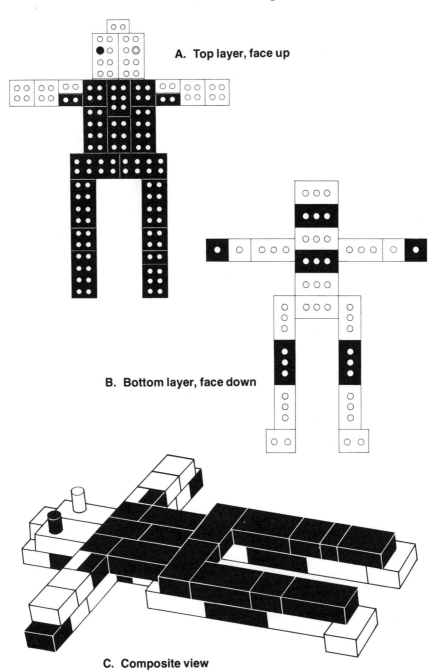

A. Top layer, face up

B. Bottom layer, face down

C. Composite view

Bridge Building:
An Intergroup Competition

This column provides a further use for the LEGO® bricks you used in
"The LEGO Man." This activity also involves both planning and as-
sembling. In this case, the students have to plan and build a bridge.
Before proceeding, please read the following:

- Figure 44.1, the bridge contract;
- Figure 44.2, letter from the Upper and Lower Hoe Council;
- Figure 44.3, contract terms;
- Figure 44.4, cost factors.

THE BRIDGE CONTRACT

You are the project team employed by Bridge Builders Ltd.

You have been asked to advise the Company whether or not it should accept a contract
in the terms set out.

You have to evaluate the possibilities and advise your General Manager (Teacher) on:

a. a feasible design

b. the potential profit to the company if it takes the contract.

Stage 1

You have 40 minutes in which to conduct your evaluation of the situation.

You may use the materials to test your theory but may not prefabricate to assist Stage 2.

Stage 2

After the planning stage you will have the time you nominate in your plan to carry out the
activity.

Figure 44.1

LETTER FROM THE UPPER AND LOWER HOE COUNCIL

Bridge Over the River Wadden

You are invited to apply for the contract to build a bridge over the River Wadden between Upper and Lower Hoe. The requirement for a bridge has been occasioned by the collapse of the previous bridge. The Court of Inquiry into the collapse reported as follows and all contractors must accept this finding:

"The River Wadden is a raging torrent, 850 mm. wide at the point where the collapse occurred. Our soundings indicate the major cause of failure was the total unsuitability of the river bed for any sort of supporting pier for a bridge. All future bridges must therefore be single-span structures."

Contract price $3,000,000 plus additions indicated in attached terms.

Yours etc.

Figure 44.2

CONTRACT TERMS

(i) A fixed price of $3,000,000 will be paid for the following additions:

Span 850 mm.	No supplement
Span 860 mm.	$100,000 addition paid
Span 870 mm.	$250,000 addition paid
Span 880 mm.	$500,000 addition paid
Span 890 mm.	$800,000 addition paid
Span 900 mm.	$1,100,000 addition paid

(ii) The center point of the bridge must be 100 mm. above a line drawn between the two bases (Diagram A).

(iii) There must be some means of access by nonmechanical means from ground level to the main span of the bridge, i.e., there must be a ramp.

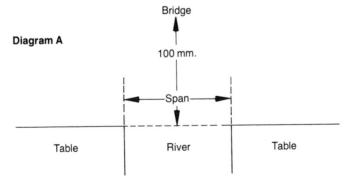

Diagram A

Figure 44.3

COST FACTORS

Cost factors are as follows:

Land:	Donated by Council
Bricks:	$500,000 per 50 irrespective of size
Labour and Administration:	$200,000 per construction minute

Figure 44.4

In studying these figures, you should readily see that the council has set the price it will pay, i.e., $3,000,000 for the basic 850 millimeter bridge. It has also indicated it will pay more for use of longer spans. The reason for the council's willingness to pay extra for longer spans is based on the fact that the students have been asked to plan the bridge and predict their profit. We did not ask the groups to submit a tender to build the bridge; we asked them to predict profit. By having a range of prices from the council, the student teams can vary designs and yet choose a bridge length that will allow them a profit.

Materials Required

1. Adequate LEGO bricks: at least two hundred per group or bridge to be built.

2. Spans: one complete set of spans for each group. Spans can be made from a board 4″ to 6″ wide and ½″ to ¾″ thick. The length of the spans doesn't necessarily have to be exactly as indicated in Figure 44.3, but if they aren't, be sure the river is exactly the same width as your shortest span.

3. A copy of all four figures (44.1-44.4) to give to each group.

4. Two tables or student desks per group so that you can separate them to form the river.

Process

It is suggested that "The LEGO Man" activity (previous column) be done in one of the sessions preceding this one. It will help the group plan more effectively when tackling this activity. My procedure would be as follows:

1. Introduce the activity by referring back to the group's experience with "The LEGO Man." I'd check what was learned and how the members would plan it if they had to do the activity again.

2. Introduce the bridge activity by passing out Figures 44.1 through 44.4. You can have the figures preassembled to speed up their distribution.

3. Set up the tables or desks for each group so that they are separated by a distance exactly equal to the shortest span member each group could use.

4. Pass out clusters of about two hundred LEGO bricks per team.

5. Announce that the forty-minute design and profit-prediction time has started. Be sure to note the time; it can be embarrassing later if you don't know when the planning period began.

6. At the forty-minute point, ask each team for its design and the profit figure. You will probably have to push here to get these two pieces of information. What you can do is to have some of the teams separate all the LEGO pieces and place them into piles of fifty for costing purposes, while other members draw out the design and write out their estimated profit. (At the thirty-five-minute mark, you may want to call out "Five minutes left." Teams often lose track of time.)

7. When all teams have handed in the design and profit estimates, give each team the span length it wants. You may have to check that the tables are still the right distance apart. They are often moved during the planning stage. When all is ready, start the assembly time.

8. Give each team its total for assembly time; accurate to the second because each second is worth \$33,333.

9. When all the teams have completed the assignment, have each team assess how it has done and prepare a report to present to the class on how it would proceed if it had to do the task again. Allow about fifteen to twenty minutes for this.

10. Have reports presented and close off the activity.

This activity was sent to me, with kind permission to have it reprinted, by Peter Mumford, Head, Staff Development and Training Unit, Department of Brighton Polytechnic, Brighton, England. Peter indicated in his letter to me that he "usually uses the bridge activity as the sixth or seventh stage in a program. This allows the group to have worked together for some time. It lends itself to some unusual solutions . . . the observer is asked specifically to watch for ways in which the group encourages (or discourages) ideas as well as the development of discipline in the group so that ideas are captured and built upon instead of being lost in a mass of verbiage."

45

A Training Session on Discipline

Objectives

1. To develop understanding of the true meaning of discipline.
2. To develop understanding of the value of a positive approach to discipline.
3. To develop understanding of effective ways of creating and maintaining a well-disciplined unit.

Materials

Figure 45.1: Definition of a well-disciplined unit.
Figure 45.2: Steps to Positive Discipline.
Figure 45.3: Steps in Negative Discipline.
Figure 45.4: Discipline questionnaire.
Figure 45.5: Effective Discipline.

Learning Activities

1. Begin by saying that most people would agree that each supervisor is responsible for establishing and maintaining discipline among the employees he supervises.
2. Say that we would like to discuss effective discipline techniques, and would like to begin by asking each participant to complete a short questionnaire. Pass out the questionnaire (Figure 45.4).

This outline of a training session on discipline was given to me by Dick Stox, Manager, Training and Education, International Telephone & Telegraph, New York. Full credit for it goes to Dick Stox, who developed it and field tested it numerous times prior to allowing me to use it.

Discipline

Place a check mark next to the statements that portray effective discipline techniques.

1. My people know that if I say nothing, everything must be all right.
2. If I find somebody doing something wrong, I let him know right then and there.
3. You have to use judgment in discipline. For example, I wouldn't land as hard on a good worker for breaking a rule, as I would on a poor worker.
4. I have a good relationship with the union steward. If one of my people needs a little discipline, I get the steward to take care of it.
5. If the productivity of one of my people drops off, I call him in right away and let him know what the score is—that I'll only tolerate 100 percent effort.
6. I review the work rules periodically with my people, explain carefully why they are necessary, and then enforce them.
7. As soon as Personnel tells me that absenteeism in my unit is getting out of hand, I crack down immediately.
8. If the scrap rate of one of my workers rises above acceptable standards, I tell him about it right away and give a timetable for improvement.
9. If I hear about an employee violating a work rule, I call him in right away for a reprimand.
10. I ease off on discipline when morale is low.

Figure 45.4

---

3. Tabulate the results. (To protect anonymity, arrange to have no one report his own results.)

4. Announce the correct answers. Only question 6 outlines effective discipline techniques. Be prepared for some disagreement. Say that they will have a chance to discuss each item in detail later in the session. Suggest that, first, it will be helpful to discuss the subject of discipline generally.

5. Display Figure 45.1. Secure agreement that there are two aspects to a well-disciplined unit:

- High productivity.
- Adherence to rules.

6. Draw attention to examples of well-disciplined units outside the industrial situation, such as football teams and marching bands, to reinforce the key points made in the previous learning activity.

Definition

A well-disciplined unit is one that is operating at high productivity, while adhering to all necessary rules and regulations.

Figure 45.1

---

7. Ask, "What does the word *discipline* itself mean?" Mention that it comes from the same root as the word *disciple* and means *to teach so as to mold*.

8. Secure agreement that most disciplinary action in industry has gone far afield from the idea of *teaching* and *molding*—that many people think of discipline merely as punishment.

9. Make the point that all of us will want to achieve discipline and improve productivity by *positive* means and every effort should be expended in this direction.

10. Develop the key point that if discipline is *teaching* and *molding*, then *training* and *motivating* must be important aspects of achieving discipline.

11. Display Figure 45.2, Steps to Positive Discipline. Discuss each point.

STEPS TO POSITIVE DISCIPLINE

1. Ensure that workers know the standards of performance desired;
2. Teach them how to attain these standards;
3. Encourage them as they make progress;
4. Compliment them when they perform at standard;
5. If they slip from standard, determine the reasons why and take appropriate action (e.g., retraining);
6. Repeat steps 3 and 4.

Figure 45.2

---

12. Describe how each step on Figure 45.2 applies to the achievement of key unit standards, such as:

- Productivity
- Attendance
- Tardiness
- etc.

13. Point out that even the best supervisor who has been following the positive discipline approach will, on occasion, have an employee who continues not to perform up to standard, or continues not to follow the rules.

14. Suggest that just as a football coach may have to "bench" a player, so must a supervisor occasionally reprimand, warn, or even suspend a worker. Indicate that these things are called *negative discipline*.

15. Ask, "If we can assume that a worker who has been positively disciplined will be happy, then what is our assumption about how a worker who has been negatively disciplined will feel?" Secure agreement that he probably will be unhappy or even angry.

16. Indicate that people who are angry frequently look for ways to lash out in some destructive way against those who made them angry. Secure agreement that the supervisor who finds it necessary to discipline negatively must try to act in a way designed to reduce anger to a minimum. Suggest that he do this by following thirteen key steps. Display Figure 45.3 and discuss.

17. Return the questionnaires completed earlier. Discuss each item in light of the key points made in the session. Develop complete understanding of the "discipline traps" inherent in the questionnaire items.

18. Summarize the session by saying that the effective supervisor employs positive discipline techniques *constantly*, and uses negative discipline only when other techniques have failed—that he relies on the high morale generated by his overall positive approach, coupled with his careful handling of negative discipline situations, to minimize employee anger over being "punished."

19. Conclude by handing out Figure 45.5, Effective Discipline.

STEPS IN NEGATIVE DISCIPLINE

1. Get all the facts and only the facts—pay no attention to hearsay and rumor;
2. Determine that negative disciplinary action has been taken consistently against other employees who have committed similar infractions;
3. Ensure that the employee knew it was an infraction;
4. Talk to the worker in private;
5. Confine the discussion to the facts of the infraction only, keeping personalities out of it, and not implying that the worker is a "bad" person;
6. Keep calm;
7. Give the worker a chance to express his views and feelings;
8. Get the worker to agree to the facts;
9. Fit the punishment (reprimand, suspension, etc.) to the facts in a consistent manner;
10. Don't harbor a grudge—consider the incident closed once the appropriate punishment has been given;
11. Don't forget to positively discipline, when appropriate, any present or future actions of this worker;
12. Be as friendly as possible;
13. Document the action taken.

Figure 45.3

Figure 45.5. Effective discipline

It is a fundamental concept in industry that the supervisor is responsible for maintaining discipline among the employees he supervises. Since there is often a lack of agreement among supervisors about just what the words "maintaining discipline" mean, it might be worthwhile spending a few moments discussing the subject.

Actually a well-disciplined unit is one that is operating at high productivity, while adhering to all necessary rules and regulations. Therefore, if a supervisor wishes to have a well-disciplined unit, he must see to it that all his workers are properly trained, and then motivate them to attain the standards of performance desired.

Incidentally, the word discipline comes from the same root as the word *disciple* and *means to teach so as to mold*. Unfortunately, many people have forgotten the teaching and molding aspects of discipline, the positive aspects, and tend to think of discipline as punishment or reprimand, which are negative aspects. Probably all will agree that it's healthier in the long run to accentuate the positive, rather than the negative. The question is, how do we do this effectively?

We can accentuate the positive by doing essentially the same things that all good athletic coaches do—make sure our "players" know what standards of performance are desired, teach them what to do to attain these standards, and compliment them when they perform as they should or encourage them as they show progress toward reaching the standards set.

Now for some examples. Let's assume a supervisor has a worker who hasn't had a product defect in a week (or a month, etc.). He should compliment this worker to let him know that his efforts are appreciated, and to encourage him to perform similarly in the future. On the other hand, if the supervisor has a worker who has had ten defects in a week, he should conduct any retraining necessary to assure the worker knows how to do the job correctly, and then compliment him and encourage him as his defect rate begins to drop. If a worker has a perfect attendance record, the supervisor should compliment him. If he has a poor attendance record, the supervisor should try to determine the reasons why, do what he can to help the worker to overcome his problem, and then encourage him as his record *begins* to improve—not wait until it's perfect.

Obviously, there are many more examples that could be given, but you can see the pattern emerging. Positive, effective discipline begins with teaching, and is *attained* and *sustained* through the motivating forces of encouragement and compliments.

Unfortunately, even the best supervisor, who has been following the positive discipline approach, will on occasion have an employee who continues not to perform up to standard, or continues not to follow the rules. Just as an athletic coach occasionally has to "bench" a player, so must a supervisor occasionally reprimand, warn, or even suspend a worker. We can call these things *negative* discipline.

While one can assume that a worker who has been positively disciplined will be "happy," we can equally assume that a worker who is negatively disciplined (or punished) will be "unhappy" or even angry, and we know that angry people frequently look for ways to lash out in some destructive way against those who have made them angry. Therefore, the effective supervisor, who finds it necessary to punish, must try to act in a way designed to reduce anger to an absolute minimum. He does this by:

• Getting all the facts and only the facts—paying no attention to hearsay and rumor;

• Determining that negative disciplinary action has been taken consistently against other employees who have committed similar infractions;

- Assuring himself that the employee knew it was an infraction;
- Talking to the worker in private;
- Confining the discussion to the facts of the infraction only, keeping personalities out of it, and not implying that the worker is a "bad" person;
- Keeping calm;
- Giving the worker a chance to express his views and feelings;
- Getting the worker to agree to the facts;
- Fitting the punishment (reprimand, suspension, etc.) to the facts in a consistent manner;
- Not harboring a grudge—considering the incident closed once the appropriate punishment has been given;
- Not forgetting to positively discipline when appropriate, any present or future actions of this worker;
- Being as friendly as possible;
- Documenting the action taken.

In summary, the effective supervisor employs positive discipline techniques constantly, and uses negative discipline only when other techniques have failed. He relies on the high morale generated by his overall positive approach, coupled with his careful handling of negative discipline situations, to minimize employee anger over being "punished."

Also, remember, every supervisor always has someone ready to help him to discipline effectively, and that person is the Industrial Relations Manager. Call on him for guidance.

46

Determining a Problem's Importance

Don't read this article. It can't be important to you, since you don't even know what it's about.

Still reading? That must mean that determining importance *is* important to you. I wonder how you determined that this article was important enough for you to take the time to read it.

Let me test you as I test all people who present problems or training requests to me. This test is very direct and simple. If I were meeting you face to face, I would be less blunt in administering the test, but alas, when learning to write I never thought it was important for me to learn to be subtle.

So here goes:

Test 1

Ask yourself, "Is determining a problem's importance important to me?" or "Is reading this article important to me?" If your reaction to those questions is "That's a somewhat naïve question to ask," I agree. The answer obviously is yes, or you wouldn't be reading this. Whenever someone asks me for help with a problem, I always ask if the problem is important and I invariably get "Yes!" In fact, I have had people communicate to me nonverbally, "Of course it is. Why do you think I called you in the first place?"

On analysis, this last nonverbal statement leads to this conclusion: if your telephone rings and you are called into a meeting with someone, obviously the problem is important in the other person's eyes. How important? You don't know. You do know it is as important as the value of your combined time during the meeting. In most cases that turns out not to be very valuable. Let me show you why with Test 2.

Test 2

Again, let's apply Test 2 to your continued reading of this article. Remember, this is an attempt to find out how important something is to someone. Or, if you prefer, we could say this sets up a *standard* by which anyone can *measure* the intensity, depth, or criticalness of the vague, undefined word "important." Let's find out *how* important.

Step 1. Picture your organization's worst employee. If that employee isn't too bad, mentally conjure up a situation involving a fictitious, incompetent employee who should have been fired long ago.

Step 2. Let the person chosen have at least four or more continuous years of service in your organization. (Ignore the important problem of badly managed organization here.)

Step 3. Let us also accept the fact that firing people with four or more years' service in your organization requires a lot of diligent effort, but can be done when it has to be done.

Step 4. Answer this: Would reading this article rank as high in importance as the firing of that incompetent person? I expect most people answered, "No, reading this article is less important." If you answered, "Yes," keep reading—you have a real need for importance determination. If you didn't answer, don't read on. Go and do something important.

Other Important Determiners

To those of you who are still with me, here are some other ways I eliminate problems from the importance area:

- The person with the problem isn't willing to commit any or enough resources to eliminate the problem. If a problem is important, then the money, people, time, resources, or whatever usually become available to work on the problem.

- The problem may be voiced as important, but the voicing may be from the wrong person. If, for example, a department manager feels his department is understaffed but top management says "not so" and refuses extra budget to correct the problem, then the problem is not important to the people who can solve it. Therefore, it does not fit into the "important problem" category.

- In situations involving people who aren't performing up to established standards, a simple test of importance is to ask, "After doing everything possible to correct the situation, would you be willing to fire this person?" The answer to this question will give you a fix on the relative importance of the problem: "Yes" means it's definitely important; "We would transfer the employee" indicates moderate importance; and "No" suggests an unimportant problem.

- Another check of importance is to ask "What is the worst that will happen to your organization if you do nothing about this situation?" Answers can range from "Nothing" to "Bankruptcy." Listening carefully should enlighten you concerning how much effort should be spent on this particular problem.
- If, having got this far, you still have a problem, it's time to do a cost/benefit analysis. This is done in three stages:

Stage one. Ask, "What is the problem costing you now?" Don't be surprised if they can't tell you. Press for an answer in dollars and cents. Press gently, but be aware that if no answer is forthcoming, the problem probably isn't important.

Stage two. Sit down with the person and work out what it is going to cost to correct the problem. Some, but not necessarily all of the costs you should include in this are: the salaries of people involved in correcting the situation, benefits for these people, new or changed facilities, overhead, maintenance costs, start-up costs, educational/training costs, research costs, etc. You may add on other costs because they vary drastically depending on the situation.

Stage one costs should be a minimum dollars-and-cents figure.

Stage two costs should be a maximum dollars-and-cents figure.

Stage three. Here we combine the two cost figures; the formula for this combination is shown in Figure 46.1.

Problem Costs versus Correction Costs are weighted in this fashion because it is virtually impossible to get firm figures—and the range may be such that the answer may be affected, for instance:

It has been estimated that problem X costs between $5,000 and $10,000 and the correcting cost will be between $8,000 and $12,000. This could be stated:

Problem Cost (Max.)	$10,000.00
Correction Cost (Min.)	8,000.00

or

Problem Cost (Min.)	$ 5,000.00
Correction Cost (Max.)	12,000.00

Given the first statement, one might be very willing to implement a solution to this problem, but given the second, one would probably look again.

Let's consider a few more examples as set out in Figure 46.2. Check the box you would consider most appropriate for each example.

There are, of course, no firm answers to these examples, but most people would choose to reconsider the correction in cases 1, 2, and 3 and to proceed with the correction in cases 4 and 5.

It is important to note here that these costs may be one time costs or may be ongoing costs. If the problem costs $5,000 per year and will take $12,000 to correct forever, the equation is obviously different than if the problem costs $5,000 per year and takes $12,000 per year to correct.

Stage one	or	Problem cost	(the minimum figure)
Stage two		Correction cost	(the maximum figure)

Figure 46.1

Example	1	2	3	4	5
Est. Problem Cost (Min.)	$ 5,000	$ 7,000	$ 1,000	$ 6,000	$20,000
Est. Correction Cost (Max.)	12,000	8,000	1,000	4,000	1,000
Proceed with correction					
Reconsider correction					

Figure 46.2

47

An Involvement Inventory

Here is another instrumented questionnaire from the Pfeiffer-Jones Series in Human Relations Training (see the previous column, "A Valuable Source of Activities Uncovered").

If you wish, why not try the inventory on yourself? Then you can compare your results with those of twenty small group facilitators and ten managers (see Figure 47.1).

THE INVOLVEMENT INVENTORY[1]

Development. The Involvement Inventory is the outgrowth of the first author's [Richard Heslin] curiosity about some differences between himself, his wife and his friends. The differences at first appeared to involve whether people approached life in an active or passive way. However, the differences became more complex when we looked carefully at the people and their orientations. Plato's three-fold view of people seemed to be relevant to the active-passive orientations. He described three kinds of men: philosophers, warriors, and the rest of us. His philosophers were concerned with intellect, his warriors with courage and will, and the rest with self-gratification. In current terminology these emphases are roughly analogous to cognition (ideas), motivation (getting things done), and emotions (feelings).

In order to measure these orientations, statements were written to indicate an active orientation regarding feelings and interpersonal involvement, *i.e.*, an open, expressive, extroverted manner. Statements were also written to measure an active orientation toward objects and

---

[1]From Richard Heslin and Brian Blake, "The Involvement Inventory." In J. E. Jones and J. W. Pfeiffer (Eds.), *The 1973 Annual Handbook for Group Facilitators*, pp. 87-94. Used with permission.

the material world, *i.e.*, a task-accomplishing, project-completing set. Finally, statements were written that described a person who was very active in his approach to ideas and the pronouncements he hears from people, *i.e.*, statements indicating an analytic, questioning, examining set.

Thus the Involvement Inventory is based on a philosophy that there are three important phenomena in life with which a person must interact: (1) people, (2) objects, and (3) ideas. The person's comfort and ability to cope with the experiences he has with these phenomena affect whether he is able to reach out to them, grasp them and use them, or is tentative in his approach to them, or even avoids encountering them. These may be thought of as phenomenological arenas in which he may expend whatever amount of energy he chooses in meeting the challenges which present themselves within the arenas.

In summary, the Involvement Inventory measures three characteristics of people:

A. *Affective*, or feeling, involvement with people,

B. *Behaviorial* involvement in accomplishing tasks, and

C. *Cognitive* involvement with analyzing pronouncements encountered.

The ABC scales taken together represent a generally active involvement in and orientation toward life. A low scorer on the A scale tends to be affectively passive, emotionally controlled, and interpersonally cautious. A low scorer on the B scale tends to be a follower, finds it difficult to plan ahead, and finds doing projects distasteful. A person who scores low on the C scale tends to be accepting of information he receives, uninterested or unwilling to challenge information that comes to him, and willing to believe pronouncements of others.

The Involvement Inventory has been subjected to extensive testing and refinement. The present version of the instrument has been found to be reliable (A = .76, B = .78, C = .76, total = .78) and valid (*e.g.*, compared to low scorers, high A scale scorers prefer spending spare time with friends, high B scale scorers are involved in far more activities, and high C scale scorers are more likely to reject parental religious and political views). The correlation among the scales is A-B .37, A-C .18, B-C .49, or an average of .34. These correlations indicate moderate overlap in content.

Scoring

The response categories are weighted as follows: Disagree = 1; Unsure, probably disagree = 2; Unsure, probably agree = 3; and Agree = 4. For statements that are reversed items, agreement indicates low involvement; the weighting is: Disagree = 4; Unsure, probably disagree = 3; Unsure, probably agree = 2; and Agree = 1. Statements that are reverse weighted appear in the latter portion of each scale. (A scale = statements 1-39, B scale = statements 40-74, C scale = 75-102.) The totals of the three scales can be added together for the overall involvement score.

Uses of the Instrument. The Involvement Inventory can be used to explore issues of life style. A person can get some insight into (1) how much energy he is expending beyond meeting the maintenance needs of his life and job, (2) whether that energy is focused in one of the three phenomenological arenas of life and (3) which one or two arenas are the focus of his energy and involvement.

The Involvement Inventory can be used to help a person generate a personal agenda for a workshop if he concludes that he is distributing his time and energy in a way that is not fruitful or if he feels that the way he copes with the three arenas is getting in his way at work or home. Participants in a workshop can be given this inventory on the first day. Scoring of their responses can be done by them or by clerical assistants. It is important that the participants get their scores relatively early so that they can use the information in the workshop. The facilitator may have the participants post their scores on the A, B, and C scales and on the total instrument using newsprint and felt-tipped markers. Make a group frequency distribution for each of the 4 scores using a chalkboard or newsprint. Have the members form into small groups (2-6 people) to interpret each other's score patterns and check out how the respondent sees his own scores. The instrument is also a useful device to teach the concepts of high and low involvement in each of the three arenas and in combinations of the three.

If the facilitator wishes to compare his group's scores with those of another group, the following norms are included as an example. The group illustrated was composed of 20 individuals functioning on some level as small group facilitators who were involved in a workshop in Montreal. Their backgrounds were fairly diverse and included industrial management, education, the clergy, and clinical psychology. Ages ranged from 25 to 55 years. The medians for this group were: A scale = 116, B scale = 100, and C scale = 86. The median for the total equalled 300. For purposes of identifying significantly high or low scores, the middle fifty per cent ranged from 107 to 122 for the A scale, 88 to 109 for the B scale, and 78 to 92 for the C scale. The total ranged between 289 and 320.

INVOLVEMENT INVENTORY

Directions: Indicate your level of agreement with each statement by placing a check in the appropriate space on the answer sheet. Do not spend a lot of time on any one item. Respond with your initial reaction.

1. I like to get close to people.
2. I find it easy to express affection.
3. When I become angry, people know it.
4. When I am happy, I like to shout and whoop it up.
5. I am the kind of person who would shout a friend's name across a crowded room if I saw him come in the door.
6. I know I would stand up in a group and call a liar a liar.
7. I enjoy the shoulder to shoulder contact with other people in a crowded elevator.
8. The wise thing for a person to do is argue his case with a policeman who has pulled him over for speeding.
9. I like to flirt with someone I find attractive even if I'm not serious.
10. I prefer dogs to cats.
12. I have struck up a conversation with another person while waiting for an elevator.
13. The thought of participating in one of these "sensitivity training" groups where people tell each other exactly how they feel really appeals to me.
14. If someone is driving down the street and sees a friend walking in the opposite direction, he should honk his horn and wave to him.
15. It is a thrill to walk into a party alone with a large group already there.
16. I like to dance the latest dances at a party.
17. If I am required to have continual close contact with someone who has irritating habits, I would bring them to his attention.
18. After I have been reading for some time, I have to spend some time talking with someone, otherwise I feel lonely.
19. If I were emotionally attached to someone, I could sing a song or say a poem to him (her).
20. I get nervous when people get personal with me.
21. I am able to hide my feelings when I feel sad or angry.
22. People consider me a serious person.
23. When I am angry, I become quiet.
24. I never am wholly relaxed with other people.
25. I wish I were more relaxed and free-wheeling in my dealing with my friends.
26. I have never spoken harshly to anyone.
27. If a friend of mine was concerned about something that he was embarrassed to speak about, I would probably let him work it out himself.
28. I become embarrassed when the topic of conversation touches on something the other person wants to avoid.
29. If someone challenged something I said in a decidedly hostile manner, I would probably break off the conversation at the first convenient opportunity.
30. It is best to forget an unpleasant person.
31. I get as much kick out of watching an exciting game of football or basketball as I do playing a game.
32. Even though I may want to, I feel nervous about putting my arm around the shoulder of a friend.
33. There are many times when I have held back from saying what I knew I should say because I didn't want to hurt someone's feelings.

INVOLVEMENT INVENTORY (CONTINUED)

34. If a person does something to hurt a friend, he should do something to make it up to him rather than mentioning or apologizing for the hurt.
35. If I were riding on a train and the car I was in had only one of a pair seats empty, I would go on to another car looking for a double seat that was empty so that I wouldn't have to sit with someone.
36. I am never quite sure how to handle it when someone flirts with me.
37. If a good looking married man puts his arm around a woman in a friendly manner while talking to her, she should disengage herself at the first appropriate chance.
38. When people tease me in a group, I often do not know what to say in response.
39. I prefer watching television to sitting around and talking.
40. I always have at least four projects going at once.
41. I am the one who gets others going and in action.
42. I tend to take charge in my groups and direct the others.
43. I like to take risks.
44. I would rather build something than read a novel.
45. I have a very strong need to run things and organize things, even though doing so cuts into time I might devote to other activities.
46. I love to repair things.
47. I love to work with my hands building things.
48. I have strong "arts and crafts" interests.
49. I do good work with my hands.
50. Nothing is quite so enjoyable as winning in competition.
51. I enjoy persuading people.
52. I enjoy playing competitive athletics.
53. It would be fun to try to make a radio (or woman's suit) using only a very basic blueprint (or pattern).
54. As an accomplishment, I get a bigger kick out of the Panama Canal than out of the Theory of Evolution.
55. Even though I may delegate tasks to people who are helping me, it makes me nervous to do so because I know if I want it done right, I should do it myself.
56. I find that I work faster than most people I know.
57. I have always enjoyed constructing model airplanes, ships, cars, and things like that.
58. I prefer to follow and let someone else take the lead.
59. I like to keep my risk low.
60. I prefer to be involved in an activity that another person rather than myself has organized.
61. I doubt that I could produce and market a product successfully.
62. I would rather read a play than make something.
63. I wouldn't know where to begin if I had to build something like a fireplace.
64. I avoid taking chances.
65. I would rather play solitaire than build a birdhouse.
66. I prefer to join a group that is already well established, rather than join a new one.
67. For me the greatest joy is in finding out about things rather than in doing things.
68. Life is so short that we should spend more time enjoying it and less time rushing around doing various projects.
69. I average more than seven hours of sleep a night.
70. I prefer to stick with one task until it is done before taking on another task.
71. I find it more gratifying to work out a successful compromise with the opposition, than to compete with and defeat them.

72. When I am bored, I like to take a nap.
73. True contentment lies in coming to a harmonious adjustment with life rather than continually trying to "improve" it.
74. I envy the people in some religious orders who have time for peaceful contemplation and well-organized daily routine.
75. I love to try to spot the logical flaw in TV commercials.
76. You take a big chance if you don't listen to more than one version about something.
77. I would not hesitate to write to any source or official to get the information I need on some problem.
78. I try to read two or three versions of a problem I am trying to understand.
79. I enjoy debating issues.
80. I enjoy analyzing two opposing views to find where they differ and where they agree.
81. When someone tells me something that does not sound quite right, I often check his source.
82. My acquaintances turn to me for new slants on the issues of the day.
83. I have more information about what is going on than my associates.
84. It is almost always worth the effort to dig out the facts yourself by reading a number of viewpoints on an issue.
85. I don't believe that any religion is the one true religion.
86. I don't believe in life after death.
87. It is a good idea to read one or two foreign newspapers as a check on our Associated Press and United Press International dominated newspapers.
88. Government response to such things as air pollution, water pollution, pesticide poisoning, and population explosion leads one to believe that it does not have the public welfare as its main interest.
89. It is fun to search far and wide to gather in all of the appropriate information about a topic to be evaluated.
90. I like a friendly argument about some issue of the day.
91. If people were forced to describe me as either short-tempered or overcritical they would probably say that I am overcritical.
92. I have trouble finding things to criticize in something I read.
93. Most of what I read seems reasonable to me.
94. I wish someone would put out a book of *known facts* so that people would know what is right these days.
95. I don't like to argue ideas.
96. You should take the expert's word on things unless you know for sure that they are wrong.
97. I would rather read a summary of the facts in an area than try to wade through the details myself.
98. I get almost all of my news information from television.
99. As with most people, 95 percent of my opinions come from personal acquaintances.
100. Once I have made up my mind on an issue, I stick to it.
101. If people were forced to describe me as either selfish or narrow minded, they would probably say that I am narrow minded.
102. Most of my acquaintances would describe me as productive rather than as individualistic.

INVOLVEMENT INVENTORY
Answer Sheet

Column headers (repeated for each group): Disagree | Unsure, Probably Disagree | Unsure, Probably Agree | Agree

Disagree	Unsure, Probably Disagree	Unsure, Probably Agree	Agree		Disagree	Unsure, Probably Disagree	Unsure, Probably Agree	Agree		Disagree	Unsure, Probably Disagree	Unsure, Probably Agree	Agree
1. ___	___	___	___	35. ___	___	___	___	69. ___	___	___	___
2. ___	___	___	___	36. ___	___	___	___	70. ___	___	___	___
3. ___	___	___	___	37. ___	___	___	___	71. ___	___	___	___
4. ___	___	___	___	38. ___	___	___	___	72. ___	___	___	___
5. ___	___	___	___	39. ___	___	___	___	73. ___	___	___	___
6. ___	___	___	___	40. ___	___	___	___	74. ___	___	___	___
7. ___	___	___	___	41. ___	___	___	___	75. ___	___	___	___
8. ___	___	___	___	42. ___	___	___	___	76. ___	___	___	___
9. ___	___	___	___	43. ___	___	___	___	77. ___	___	___	___
10. ___	___	___	___	44. ___	___	___	___	78. ___	___	___	___
11. ___	___	___	___	45. ___	___	___	___	79. ___	___	___	___
12. ___	___	___	___	46. ___	___	___	___	80. ___	___	___	___
13. ___	___	___	___	47. ___	___	___	___	81. ___	___	___	___
14. ___	___	___	___	48. ___	___	___	___	82. ___	___	___	___
15. ___	___	___	___	49. ___	___	___	___	83. ___	___	___	___
16. ___	___	___	___	50. ___	___	___	___	84. ___	___	___	___
17. ___	___	___	___	51. ___	___	___	___	85. ___	___	___	___
18. ___	___	___	___	52. ___	___	___	___	86. ___	___	___	___
19. ___	___	___	___	53. ___	___	___	___	87. ___	___	___	___
20. ___	___	___	___	54. ___	___	___	___	88. ___	___	___	___
21. ___	___	___	___	55. ___	___	___	___	89. ___	___	___	___
22. ___	___	___	___	56. ___	___	___	___	90. ___	___	___	___
23. ___	___	___	___	57. ___	___	___	___	91. ___	___	___	___
24. ___	___	___	___	58. ___	___	___	___	92. ___	___	___	___
25. ___	___	___	___	59. ___	___	___	___	93. ___	___	___	___
26. ___	___	___	___	60. ___	___	___	___	94. ___	___	___	___
27. ___	___	___	___	61. ___	___	___	___	95. ___	___	___	___
28. ___	___	___	___	62. ___	___	___	___	96. ___	___	___	___
29. ___	___	___	___	63. ___	___	___	___	97. ___	___	___	___
30. ___	___	___	___	64. ___	___	___	___	98. ___	___	___	___
31. ___	___	___	___	65. ___	___	___	___	99. ___	___	___	___
32. ___	___	___	___	66. ___	___	___	___	100. ___	___	___	___
33. ___	___	___	___	67. ___	___	___	___	101. ___	___	___	___
34. ___	___	___	___	68. ___	___	___	___	102. ___	___	___	___

THE INVOLVEMENT INVENTORY
Scoring

1. The A scale (affective or feeling involvement with people) includes items 1 through 39. Items 1 through 19 are weighed differently than items 20 through 39. Draw a line under item 19 on the scoring sheet. Add the checks in each column for items 1 through 19 and place the sum in the spaces below. Multiply each column total by the multiplier beneath it. Add the four products across and put the total in the blank designated (A).

x1	x2	x3	x4

_____+_____+_____+_____=_____ (A)

Draw a line under item 39. Add the checks in each column for items 20 through 39 and proceed as you did with items 1 through 19 (notice that the multipliers are reversed from those for items 1 through 19).

x4	x3	x2	x1

_____+_____+_____+_____=_____ (a)

2. The B scale (Behavioral involvement in accomplishing tasks) includes items 40 through 74. Draw a line under item 57. Proceed with the scoring as above.

x1	x2	x3	x4

_____+_____+_____+_____=_____ (B)

Draw a line under item 74 and proceed as above.

x4	x3	x2	x1

_____+_____+_____+_____=_____ (b)

3. The C scale (Cognitive involvement with analyzing pronouncements encountered) includes items 75 through 102. Draw a line under item 91 and proceed with the scoring as above.

x1	x2	x3	x4

_____+_____+_____+_____=_____ (C)

Total the remaining columns and proceed as above.

x4	x3	x2	x1

_____+_____+_____+_____=_____ (c)

4. Obtain scale scores by adding the totals for each two-part scale. Then, obtain the total involvement score by adding the three scale scores.

$A + a =$ _____

$B + b =$ _____

$C + c =$ _____

Total involvement score = _____

Student	A scale	B scale	C scale	Total
1	74	88	81	243
2	81	60	74	215
3	107	116	92	315
4	96	72	101	269
5	94	77	78	249
6	88	103	94	285
7	94	77	78	249
8	75	82	69	226
9	103	122	82	307
10	87	98	97	282

Middle 40 percent range: 88 to 94 for the A scale
77 to 98 for the B scale
78 to 92 for the C scale

Figure 47.1. Individual results for a group of ten managers

48

Holding a Meeting with No One There — Delphi Style

If you've been trying to teach participative management, but haven't been able to use the concept yourself because of the cost involved in talking to other managers in your organization, the Delphi technique *may* well be the answer to your problem.

The Delphi technique is a method of solving problems, reaching decisions, and achieving group consensus via the mails. It consists of a number of stages:

1. An open-ended questionnaire is developed on an issue that concerns a group;

2. The questionnaire is mailed to the group concerned;

3. The group concerned answers and returns the questionnaire;

4. The group's answers are summarized by the coordinator;

5. A new questionnaire is built on summarized answers;

6. This questionnaire is mailed to the same group again;

7. Stages 4, 5, and 6 are repeated (as many as four times), eventually leading to an outcome on the issue that is acceptable to the group.

Using this technique, you can have input on training programs as they are being developed. After you have proved its worth, you might wish to teach it to others in your organization for their own use. The technique is simple and we'll do a run-through on a training survey so that you can see how it works. Here's the situation:

Your management has asked you (the training officer) to submit a list of the courses, with reasons and justification, that you are going to offer next year at the organization's Central Training School. (Your organization has offices and plants scattered all across the country.)

You have considered doing an organization-wide needs analysis to determine your training requirements, but you have rejected it because of the travel costs involved, the lack of time to do the analysis properly, etc. A general meeting of all the local training representatives was considered but discarded because bringing everyone together proved to be impossible.

The dilemma here is that you know if you talk to a number of people, each will have ideas and no agreement will result. You also know that if you decide what courses to give, you'll be guessing and won't have agreement across the country.

The reasons and justification for the courses you plan to offer can be provided by the Delphi technique and here is how it will do it.

STEP ONE

Design a questionnaire to send to the group. Care must be taken here. You must have a clear, easily understandable questionnaire. In fact, you should never send this questionnaire out to your organization without testing it first on a few typical respondents. Before trying to construct the questionnaire, you should consider:

1. Should you go back to top management and ask for clarification of what is wanted from you? In this case, for example, is management questioning the past effectiveness of the Central Training School's offerings, or is it simply concerned with what future offerings should be made?

2. What do you want to find out after you have determined the reason for the survey, via an exploration of the issue with management?

3. Later in the Delphi process, you'll want to consider to whom this questionnaire should be sent and how you will publicize the results of the process. Both of these answers will affect your initial work in developing the questionnaire.

In this case, the question has three parts, assuming management is simply concerned with finding out what future courses should be offered. Your question and the form it takes are shown in Figure 48.1.

STEP TWO

Who should get this questionnaire? Central and regional management? Local training representatives? Local managers and supervisors? The work force itself? To decide this, let's develop criteria and use them to determine who will receive the questionnaire.

Criterion 1. People who will be affected by the decision reached.

Criterion 2. People who would have information related to the questions asked.

Course Survey—First Questionnaire for Central Training School 19___

In the spaces below: 1. List the course titles you feel the central training school should offer.
2. List, in point form, one or two reasons you feel the course should be offered.
3. List in point form, why Central Training School should offer this course over local training facilities.

COURSE TITLE   **REASONS**   **WHY CENTRAL**

Figure 48.1

Criterion 3. People who (we hope) will take the time to answer the questions.

Criterion 4. People who would consider the outcome of the exercise worthwhile to their needs and interests.

Criterion 5. People whose answers will be seen as representative of the group affected by the decision. (This criterion is used if the sample population determined by the first four criteria is too large.)

Apply the criteria to the people to whom you want to send the questionnaire. Remember that each person must fit all of the first four criteria. If the list gets too long, you apply Criterion 5. Research has shown that as the numbers increase above twenty-five to thirty people, the amount of new and significant information added is minimal for the work involved in summarizing the answers submitted. However, it may be desirable to include more than that to enable all those concerned to have a say in the decision.

Suppose, in this situation, we decide to send the questionnaire to the local training representative as one group, and to all local managers and supervisors as a second group.

STEP THREE

The Delphi technique requires that one never sends out a questionnaire without first having someone talk to each recipient. This should ensure that

- they will send it back;
- they know its purpose;
- they know the time required to complete it;
- each person knows there will be at least one follow-up questionnaire;

- they will get a copy of the final report; and
- each person knows that the result will affect his world. Finally,
- the most important part—thank each person solidly; and
- express your interest in seeing and including his answers in the survey.

Because of the numbers and distribution of local managers and supervisors in our training survey, telephoning each person would be difficult so we delegate. Delegate by calling each local training representative, and treat him as previously outlined. When you have his agreement, ask him if he'd be willing to contact all his local managers and supervisors personally and get them to do the questionnaire too. Indicate that you'll do all the data summarizing and all the work following his initial contact by telephone and his relaying of the initial letter, which you'll provide.

Finally, tell him you will be developing two reports out of this, one on the courses recommended by training representatives and the other on the courses recommended by the local managers and supervisors. If asked to do one just for a local area, indicate that you feel that will create too much extra work, but that you will keep his request in mind *if* local discrepancies tend to show up.

STEP FOUR

A covering letter goes with each questionnaire. This letter *must* be sent out the same day that the person agrees to take part in this decision-making process. A sample of a suitable letter is presented in Figure 48.2. The key features in the letter are:

- The opening thanks for help;
- An explanation of why his ideas are needed;
- An explanation of how the results will be used;
- The next to last paragraph tells the person what to do and gives him a due date;
- The last paragraph simply restates thanks to the person for offering help.

Other points about the letter and questionnaire are:

1. Field test both locally in your office before sending them out. They must be right. They must be clear enough to ensure that you will get the type of response you want.

```
Dear _____:

Thanks for agreeing to help the Central Training School decide on the courses it should
offer next year. Your answers to the attached questionnaire are needed to help us keep
our programs relevant to the needs of the total organization.

Here's how your answers will be used. We will pool all answers received and develop a
subsequent questionnaire to establish the actual courses the school will offer. You will
have ample opportunity throughout to comment and critique ideas and suggestions
made.

Attached is the first questionnaire; please complete it and return it in the enclosed
envelope. We need your answers by _____, in order to include them in the
development of the second questionnaire, which will be distributed on _____.

Again, thank you for offering to help.
```

Figure 48.2. The letter

2. Have each letter typed. Don't send copies. An original letter gives a personal touch to the process, suggesting that you feel the person receiving it is important.

3. Send the letter out on the same day the person consents to take part. The people volunteering should get the questionnaire while their thoughts are still fresh, not after they have forgotten about offering to help.

4. Keep the letter short—no longer than one page. Remember, the responders are busy people and long letters take time to read.

5. Enclose a return envelope to simplify the returning of the questionnaire.

STEP FIVE

When preparing to analyze the questionnaire, plan your response processing early. Don't wait for the questionnaires to be returned before figuring out how to compile the data. Even if the survey only involves ten people, preplanning is necessary to cope with the multiple answers.

The best procedure for coping with the data, without a computer, is to transfer each item to a 3″ x 5″ card. Each card in our example would contain three pieces of information: course title, reasons it is being offered, and why the course should be held at the Central Training School rather than locally.

A separate card for each course title on every questionnaire must be made.

After the cards are made, sort them by course title into piles—a separate pile for each course. Then make a short list of reasons why each course should be offered at the training center. Once this short summary has been written, you are ready to construct Questionnaire 2.

Questionnaire 2

Figure 48.3 is an example of how the second questionnaire would look. A covering letter similiar to the first one should be sent with the second questionnaire. Some features of the second questionnaire are:

- It summarizes all responses to the first questionnaire;
- It has a stepped set of clear, simple instructions;
- It is short, and should take less than thirty minutes to complete;
- Its items are not numbered; using the alphabet to label the items eliminates the confusion in tabulating the results that can result from two numbering systems operating at the same time;
- It allows comments, concerns, and clarification, etc. to be expressed about items or priority value to be set;
- Allowing additional items to be added is optional. If you plan to send a third questionnaire, the additional items area is critical, and so is the comment area.

Analyzing Questionnaire 2

Again—preplan. Prepare a tabulation sheet (see Figure 48.4) and log all the second questionnaire's data as they are received. Design a Priority-Value Report Sheet (see Figure 48.5). Write a letter to use when sending the final report of the survey.

In this case, you should send the coming year's calendar of courses, which is based on the Priority-Value Report Sheet. This should go out immediately after completion of the survey to show the respondents that your section is action-oriented. Of course, this means that while the second questionnaire is being done, course outlines, instructors, room schedules, etc., should be tentatively plotted in anticipation of final survey results.

Sometimes, the data with the comments and additional items may make the issuance of further questionnaires necessary. I leave you to design further loops on this.

Before you start using the Delphi approach, be prepared to follow-up on those few people who do not respond quickly to your questionnaire. Write or telephone to remind laggards that the information is important.

Course Survey—Second Questionnaire for Central Training School 19___

INSTRUCTIONS:

Step 1: Review the following summarized list of responses from the first questionnaire. Make any comments about the items listed you feel are needed. Keeping comments brief and clear will be helpful to our analysis of this questionnaire.

Step 2: Select the 10 items you feel are the most important. Set priorities by assigning the most important course a 10, the next most important a 9, etc., down to and including a value of 1.

Step 3: Use the enclosed envelope to send us your response by _____.

PRIORITY VALUE	COURSE TITLE, REASON AND WHY HELD AT CENTER	COMMENTS, CONCERNS, CLARIFICATIONS, ETC.
_____	a. **Assessment Interviewing** Increased staff recruiting in the next year, throughout the organization	
_____	b. **Support Staff Development** No programs local or central for support staff development	
_____	c.	
	d.	
	e.	
	etc.	

ADDITIONAL PROGRAMS:

_____

_____

_____

Figure 48.3

ITEM LETTER	EACH INDIVIDUAL PRIORITY VALUE, SEPARATED BY COMMA	COMMENTS, CONCERNS, CLARIFICATION, ETC.
a	4,7,9,3,6,7,7,4,5,......	An assessment center might be better
b	10,9,10,8,9,10,9,9,9,......	Lower staff members are really demanding this
c	.,.,.,.,.,.,.....	....

Figure 48.4. Second questionnaire tabulation sheet

PRIORITY-VALUE REPORT SHEET

ITEM	No. SURVEYED PLACING VALUE ON ITEM	INDIVIDUAL VALUES	TOTAL VALUE	PRIORITY RANK
a—Assessment Interviewing				
b—etc.				
c—etc.				

Figure 48.5. When all data is in and tabulated, this report sheet is completed and sent with related support documentation to each person who participated in the survey.

REFERENCES AND READINGS

Dalkey, N. G. (Ed.), *Studies in the Quality of Life: Delphi & Decision-Making.* New York: Lexington, 1972.

Delbecq, A. L., Van de Ven, A. H., & Gustafson, D. H. *Group Techniques for Program Planning: A Guide to Nominal Group & Delphi Processes.* Glenview, IL: Scott Foresman, 1975.

49

Reactions to Group Situations: Part 1

There has been a lot of interesting research on behavior of people in learning groups and groups in general. We all are part of any number of groups. Groups are the essence of our life style today. For this reason, a study of how people react in groups is vital for trainers from two points of view:

1. So that trainers will know and understand how they personally react in groups, since whenever they instruct they are in a learning group;

2. So that they can recognize student reactions in their classrooms and hence adjust better to their students' individual needs.

This article and the next one develop both of these concepts. They also provide you with a questionnaire and a lesson plan on how to use it, so that your students can gain greater insight into their own reactions in groups.

First Stage

To gain an understanding of how you react in groups you should complete the questionnaire, You in Groups, presented in Figure 49.1. To do it, simply follow the instructions at the top of the questionnaire. Many of you may decide not to work on the questionnaire at this time. That's OK, as long as you realize that by reading on and not doing it now, you will not be able to do it later and get a valid assessment because the other material that follows in this article will influence your answers fairly significantly.

Figure 49.1. YOU IN GROUPS QUESTIONNAIRE[1]

Instructions: In each situation below, read the opening incomplete statement and rank the choices from 5, for your most likely reaction to the opening statement, to 1 for your least likely reaction.

Work quickly. There are no "right" or "wrong" reactions. Rank as your first reaction dictates. Don't worry about reasons for your 5,4,3,2,1 rankings. Your first impressions are best to help you explore how you react in groups. **Please write five answers for each statement.**

1. When Vic made a proposal, I . . .
   _____ (a) started talking with my neighbors.
   _____ (b) didn't know what to do.
   _____ (c) helped Vic analyze the proposal.
   _____ (d) said, "That would be wasting our time."
   _____ (e) was bored.

2. When the leader lost interest, I . . .
   _____ (a) tried to get the group to support Willie who was deeply involved.
   _____ (b) told her to stand on her own feet.
   _____ (c) said, "Let's see how we might solve the problem."
   _____ (d) became thirsty and asked if anyone else wanted a drink.
   _____ (e) waited, because I didn't think the group was close to an answer.

3. When Tom thought he needed a lot of help, I . . .
   _____ (a) told a joke.
   _____ (b) wouldn't help.
   _____ (c) asked others to help him later.
   _____ (d) kept on working.
   _____ (e) tried to get him involved again.

4. When Bernie agreed with Robin, I . . .
   _____ (a) accomplished a lot more.
   _____ (b) was glad.
   _____ (c) asked the leader if their agreement was acceptable.
   _____ (d) lost interest in what we were supposed to be doing.
   _____ (e) was suspicious.

5. When I realized a few people were taking digs at each other, I . . .
   _____ (a) looked out the window.
   _____ (b) said, "It will help if all of you would share some responsibility for this."
   _____ (c) asked those involved if they didn't have something else to do.
   _____ (d) disliked Bobbie's idea of how to solve the situation.
   _____ (e) hoped they wouldn't say something they later regretted.

----

[1]My development of this questionnaire was influenced by reading, first, H. A. Thelen's "Reactions to Group Situations Test" (in J. W. Pfeiffer and J. E. Jones (Eds.), *The 1974 Annual Handbook for Group Facilitators*. La Jolla, CA: University Associates, 1974, 91-96) and, second, A. A. Zoll's *Explorations in Managing* (Reading, MA: Addison-Wesley, 1974).

6. When Val said we could be finished in another hour, I . . .
_____ (a) resented Val's comment.
_____ (b) thought we ought to proceed onward.
_____ (c) winked at Dale.
_____ (d) looked to the leader for guidance.
_____ (e) wanted to leave.

7. When several members dropped out of the discussion, I . . .
_____ (a) also wanted to.
_____ (b) changed the subject to a lighter topic.
_____ (c) suggested a new approach to the situation.
_____ (d) asked them what they thought they were doing.
_____ (e) said, "Come back into the discussion, we need your ideas."

8. When Carol liked my ideas, I . . .
_____ (a) asked for Carol's help.
_____ (b) was glad the session was almost over.
_____ (c) defended it from being changed by others.
_____ (d) gladly backed Carol up.
_____ (e) thought we would now be able to work.

9. When everyone felt angry, I . . .
_____ (a) was pleased some were defending my point.
_____ (b) suggested we take a break and cool off.
_____ (c) agreed with Bob and Janice.
_____ (d) asked if they saw any solution.
_____ (e) suggested we cut the argument short and work on the issue.

10. When Sam asked the leader what her ideas were, I . . .
_____ (a) got sore at Sam for not being self-reliant.
_____ (b) felt free to doodle.
_____ (c) wanted help too.
_____ (d) went right on working.
_____ (e) winked at Frankie.

11. When no one was sticking to the topic, I . . .
_____ (a) changed the subject.
_____ (b) pushed the original topic.
_____ (c) wished the leader would bring us back to the point.
_____ (d) told everyone to act like adults and stick to the point.
_____ (e) asked Pat what point we were on.

12. When the group made little of my idea, I . . .
_____ (a) asked the leader to expain my idea.
_____ (b) was pleased when Mel explained my idea.
_____ (c) wished the meeting would end.
_____ (d) said they didn't want any ideas.
_____ (e) realized they needed my ideas.

13. Together, Chris and I . . .
_____ (a) thought this might move us toward our goal.
_____ (b) asked the others for their ideas.
_____ (c) abandoned the discussion because it was useless.
_____ (d) turned to Lee, who we thought felt the same way.
_____ (e) resisted what the others suggested.

Figure 49.1. You in groups questionnaire (continued)

14. When Leslie said, "I don't see that we are getting anywhere in this meeting, I . . .
_____ (a) felt we could do well together.
_____ (b) wondered what to do next.
_____ (c) wondered why Leslie wasn't considering my views.
_____ (d) thought of a way to explain where the meeting was going.
_____ (e) thought this meeting was like all the others.

15. When the group remained silent waiting for the leader to speak, I . . .
_____ (a) started to describe a personal experience to those near me.
_____ (b) encouraged Alfie to make his comment.
_____ (c) thought the leader should break in.
_____ (d) summarized what we were accomplishing.
_____ (e) told the leader to do something.

16. When Jean began a side conversation with Jackie, I . . .
_____ (a) became annoyed with them.
_____ (b) suggested that they stick with the original topic.
_____ (c) thought that I'd like to leave the room.
_____ (d) felt much more warmly toward them.
_____ (e) wanted to ask their advice.

17. When I felt angry enough to boil, I . . .
_____ (a) became silent.
_____ (b) expressed my anger.
_____ (c) turned to Lyn to share my anger.
_____ (d) asked if anyone had a suggestion to help.
_____ (e) tried to get on with the topic.

18. When Gerry reported the results to date, I . . .
_____ (a) just didn't feel like working.
_____ (b) thought we would probably begin to make progress now.
_____ (c) felt grateful to Gerry for really expressing what we both felt.
_____ (d) questioned the report.
_____ (e) did not know what to do.

19. When Peg got the leader to do the assignment she was in charge of, I . . .
_____ (a) tried to get on with the task.
_____ (b) told the rest of the group what happened to me in coming to the meeting.
_____ (c) agreed to help also.
_____ (d) said, "In this case, surely the least Peg could do was help herself."
_____ (e) asked the leader if Peg could use my help too.

20. When no one was sticking to the point, I . . .
_____ (a) wanted someone to ask what the point was.
_____ (b) discussed what I thought the point was with Wally.
_____ (c) realized the group needed me to clarify what the point was.
_____ (d) asked them what they thought the point was.
_____ (e) realized the group was never going to get back on topic.

21. When the group wanted my views about the task, I . . .
_____ (a) thought of what I might tell them.
_____ (b) agreed that my views might be helpful.
_____ (c) asked the leader, "How do you want my views expressed?"
_____ (d) wondered why they wanted my views.
_____ (e) got up and left.

22. When Barby turned toward me, I . . .
_____ (a) shrank from her.
_____ (b) wished she would help me.
_____ (c) found a friend.
_____ (d) told her to leave me alone.
_____ (e) thought of what I might tell her.

23. When Bev said, "The leader should keep us on the right track," I . . .
_____ (a) turned to see what the leader's reaction was.
_____ (b) asked Bev what the right track was.
_____ (c) was enjoying what we were doing.
_____ (d) felt like staying on the track we were on.
_____ (e) said, "Bev's right, let's get back on the track."

24. When the others broke for coffee, I . . .
_____ (a) wanted to join them.
_____ (b) stayed where I was.
_____ (c) said, "It's too early."
_____ (d) felt it was a good time.
_____ (e) wanted to finish what we were doing.

25. Whenever Theo gets hostile with us, I . . .
_____ (a) realize the group needs to re-examine what it is doing.
_____ (b) realize he needs help from me.
_____ (c) realize he's getting too serious for us.
_____ (d) realize he and I are at odds again.
_____ (e) realize someone else should help him in this situation.

Second Stage

This stage involves us in interpreting your rankings on the questionnaire. To do this, transfer your answers from the You in Groups Questionnaire in Figure 49.1 to Figure 49.2, First Answer Sheet. The instructions are at the top of Figure 49.2. If they aren't clear to you, the following examples may help you.

In Figure 49.1, say you answered question one by ranking statement a-2, b-4, c-5, d-3 and e-1. Transferring these to Figure 2, line 1, you would have for that line: e __1__ , d __3__ , a __2__ , b __4__ , c __5__ . What you are doing in transferring your answers is sorting your responses into the five main dimensions of the way you respond in groups. An explanation of these main dimensions appears in Figure 49.3, Interpretation for Dimensions. After transferring your answers simply total each column.

Figure 49.2. First answer sheet[2]

Instructions: Beside each letter, write in your ranking from the questionnaire for each statement and then total the columns.

Statement number	Flight	Fight	Pairing	Dependency	Work
1. Work	e_____	d_____	a_____	b_____	c_____
2. Flight	d_____	b_____	a_____	e_____	c_____
3. Dependency	a_____	b_____	e_____	c_____	d_____
4. Pairing	d_____	e_____	b_____	c_____	a_____
5. Fight	a_____	c_____	d_____	e_____	b_____
6. Work	e_____	a_____	c_____	d_____	b_____
7. Flight	b_____	d_____	a_____	e_____	c_____
8. Pairing	b_____	c_____	d_____	a_____	e_____
9. Fight	b_____	e_____	c_____	a_____	d_____
10. Dependency	b_____	a_____	e_____	c_____	d_____
11. Flight	a_____	d_____	e_____	c_____	b_____
12. Fight	c_____	d_____	b_____	a_____	e_____
13. Pairing	c_____	e_____	d_____	b_____	a_____
14. Work	e_____	c_____	a_____	b_____	d_____
15. Dependency	a_____	e_____	b_____	c_____	d_____
16. Pairing	c_____	a_____	d_____	e_____	b_____
17. Fight	a_____	b_____	c_____	d_____	e_____
18. Work	a_____	d_____	c_____	e_____	b_____
19. Dependency	b_____	d_____	c_____	e_____	a_____
20. Flight	e_____	d_____	b_____	a_____	c_____
21. Work	e_____	d_____	b_____	c_____	a_____
22. Pairing	a_____	d_____	c_____	b_____	e_____
23. Dependency	c_____	d_____	e_____	a_____	b_____
24. Flight	b_____	c_____	a_____	d_____	e_____
25. Fight	c_____	d_____	b_____	e_____	a_____
TOTAL	Fl_____	F_____	P_____	D_____	W_____

---

[2]These five basic kinds of behavior in groups were identified by W. R. Bion in *Experiences in Groups* (New York: Basic Books, 1959).

Explanation of Totals

The totals have a possible range from a minimum of 25 to a maximum of 125. The highest total you have is the dimension you use most frequently. The second highest is the one you use next most often, and so on. To gain insight into the meaning of each of these, see Figure 49.3, which explains the five You in Groups dimensions.

Two other things to note about your totals are: first, the closer your total is to 125, the more dominant that dimension is for your reactions in groups; second, the questionnaire, although it has five dimensions, divides into two aspects: work and emotional states. The work state is represented by the work dimension alone. The other dimensions— dependency, pairing, flight, and fight—represent the emotional states. During any group activity, both the work and emotional aspects are in operation at the same time.

It is helpful to remember that a group is always engaged in work. It is always to some extent, implicitly or explicitly, involved in meeting task demands that originate from within or outside the group. Such work represents the consciously determined, deliberative, reality-oriented, goal-seeking aspects of the group's activities.

At the same time that a group is engaged in work, it is also concerned with certain emotional issues that are seemingly illogical, are not under conscious control, and whose purposes are not understood by the group.

These emotional issues in our culture are buried. Work is the main thrust of all groups and hence, in responding to the questionnaire, work for many people (more than 50 percent of the population) will turn out to be the main dimension. You should keep this tendency in mind in looking at your totals.

If work has the highest total, you should look at your second-ranked item as the characteristic of you in groups that is most significantly unique to you. If there is a large gap in your totals between work and your second largest total then you can deduce that work is really a dominant personal characteristic with everything else secondary to it.

Again: to get a greater insight into the characteristics of each of the five dimensions, see Figure 49.3.

Third Stage

So far you have learned how you react generally as a person in groups. The questionnaire can tell you more than how you act in groups. You can learn how you react specifically when the culture of the group is one of the five dimensions outlined in Figure 49.3. To do this, use Figure 49.4, the Second Answer Sheet, and follow the directions to transfer all your answers from the First Answer Sheet, Figure 49.2, to Figure 49.4.

Figure 49.3. INTERPRETATION FOR DIMENSIONS

FLIGHT
Flight is expressed by behaviors such as:
  Withdrawing;
  Attempting to divert the group from its task by irrelevant behavior;
  Daydreaming;
  Avoiding work;
  Avoiding confrontations with others;
  A tendency to avoid interactive situations;
  Removing oneself from tasks or groups;
  Joking.

How Others See Flight People
Flight people (those with high scores on flight) are perceived by others in their group as:
  1. Not wanting to keep the group together;
  2. Not wanting to be liked by others in the group; and,
  3. A handicap to the group's productiveness.

Impact on Group Performance
Pure flight groups are unable to function effectively. In mixed groups, flight people tend to reduce a group's effectiveness. Flight groups are relatively unproductive compared to pairing and fight groups.

Pure Flight Group Tendencies
When the primary dimension of the group is flight, the group shows a tendency to avoid digging into a problem. The products show a narrow range of ideas, over generality within a rigid organization, little attention to the relationship between the cause and the effect in the problem, and little emotional commitment to act on their proposed solutions. Flight tendency causes this type of group to achieve task completion fastest of all five pure group types.

FIGHT
Fight is expressed by behavior such as:
  Attacking others, as well as issues;
  Hostility;
  Aggressiveness;
  Being critical;
  Anger;
  Resentment;
  Resistance;
  Contentiousness;
  Enjoyment of competitive situations;
  Competitiveness.

How Others See Fight People
No specific perception emerges when other group members try to describe how they see fight-type people. The group members cannot agree on how they see fight people probably because of the different effects fight behavior has on each person in turn.

Impact on Group Performance
Fight people help others to hear suggestions that are made because of the aggressiveness with which they push and attack things.

The overall impact of fight people on group productivity is proportional to the complexity of the task. Fight people have a negative impact on group productivity if the task is simple. Hence in simple task situations they should restrain themselves. In complex task situations their impact is positive and hence they should take a progressively more active part as a task's complexity increases.

Fight is an important component to build into a group. It acts as an energizer. It makes a group work harder on tasks. When the fight dimension is operating with other group building dimensions, such as pairing and high work, fight is productive. In combination with flight, dependency and people with low work characteristics, fight is often destructive.

Because aggression, contention, and competition are necessary in any task situation, fight is an important component for group productivity.

Pure Fight Group Tendencies

One might suppose that a pure fight group might have a tendency to be so explosive in nature as to self-destruct. This doesn't come true. In fact, a high fight group seems to have greater problem-solving capabilities than any of the other types of groups. This is because the fight group differs from the other types in ability to dig into a problem, to raise issues, and to settle them one way or another. Its products show the widest range of ideas employed in problem solution, a high level of specificity within a flexible organization, much attention to the relationship between cause and effect in the problem, and a high amount of emotional involvement and commitment to act on its proposed solutions.

PAIRING

Pairing is expressed by behaviors such as:

Supporting other members;
Showing warmth;
Friendliness;
Sensitivity to others;
Expressing intimacy;
Partiality toward others;
Ability to introspect and look at themselves critically.

How Others See Pairing People

People scoring high in pairing are perceived by others in their group as:

1. Serving to bind the group together;
2. Expressing feelings of warmth;
3. Wanting others to like them.

Impact on Group Performance

Groups without pairing members have an extremely difficult time getting started on tasks and tend to be relatively unproductive. People who pair in a group serve to cement the group together.

Groups made up only of pairers prove to be generally productive, although the task's complexity affects their productivity. When tasks are complex, pure pairing groups do not perform as well as one might expect from their ability to do simple tasks well.

Pairing people in groups help to make the wheels turn smoothly but they can't provide adequate fire power by themselves.

Pure Pairing Group Tendencies

When the primary dimension of the group is pairing, the system of control differs from the others in its ability to create and organize its ideas into a flexible but specific solution.

Figure 49.3. (Continued)

Its products show a wider range of ideas, more specific solutions, more attention to the relationship between cause and effect in a problem, and more involvement in and commitment to its proposed solutions. The products of the pairing group tend to show an organization that is neither rigid nor loose in the extreme.

DEPENDENCY

Dependency is expressed by behaviors such as:

Appealing to a leader for help;

Demanding structure;

Expressing weakness or inadequacy.

Dependent groups exist in order to find support and direction from something outside themselves: the leader or external standards or their own history. By contenting itself with posing questions and problems that it expects the leader to answer, a dependent group places all its reliance on the leader to sort out and answer *all* its questions and difficulties.

How Others See Dependent People

People scoring high under dependency are seen by others in the group as:

1. *Not* showing leadership in getting the task done;
2. *Not* aware of the requirements of working with people;
3. *Not* understanding the feelings of individuals;
4. Difficult types of people to deal with; and,
5. People who hinder the productivity of the group.

Impact on Group Performance

By watching a dependent group over a period of time, one sees that although there is no need to doubt the capacity of the individuals in the group for doing work, the group, as a group, is quite opposed to the idea that it is there for the purpose of doing work. Dependent groups react as if some principle would be violated if they were to work. Hence, their impact on performance is negative in every way. Dependent people in groups hinder productivity, no matter how you measure productivity.

Pure Dependent Group Tendencies

When the primary dimension of the group is dependency, the group shows a tendency to confine itself to what it believes to be the ideas approved by the authority (the leader or some other authority figure). Its products show a narrow range of ideas, a high degree of specificity within a rigid organization, little attention to the relationship between cause and effect in the problem, and little emotional involvement in, or commitment to act on, its proposed solutions.

WORK

Work is expressed by behaviors such as:

Conscious determination to do the task;

Deliberateness;

Reality seeking;

Purposeful, goal directed;

Task oriented;

Committed to self development;

Use of a rational or scientific approach to problem solving;

Learning easily from experience.

How Others See Work People
Others perceive work people as:
1. Showing leadership in getting the task done;
2. *Not* expressing warm feelings to others;
3. People who go all out to get the task done with an almost complete disregard of anything else.

Impact on Group Performance
The work group's capacity for cooperation, productivity, and perseverence is immense. The work dimension is the best indicator of the five dimensions of high productivity.

Groups formed around the work dimension are the most successful of all types of groups. In complex tasks work groups have a need for more interpersonal skills than they have. The reason for this is that pure work groups can't deal successfully with the frustrations of trying to deal with complex and apparently insoluble solutions.

Pure Work-Group Tendencies
One can often get groups of high work-oriented people together but this type of group is never pure. The other four dimensions are always present in some form or other. Participants develop these other four skills instinctively and they tend to involuntarily, automatically, and inevitably come into play in work groups.

Pure work groups are totally concerned with reality. They are willing to work on whatever task is at hand. They work in a coldly rational fasion and approach tasks as scientifically as possible. As mentioned above, complex tasks can frustrate the pure work group. Hence it is worth remembering that a pure work-type group will, under complex task situations, perform less adequately than one would expect from the group's name.

Once you have done all five steps, you can study the answers to the fifth part to learn your predominant mode of reacting in each of the five dimensions. For example, let us say your answers across the flight row were, Fl-6, F-9, P-9, D-4, and W-21. This means in the fifth step your answers to (A) part would be in *flight* situations in groups: the *first* reaction mode I use is Work, the *second* reaction mode I use is Fight or Pairing. (If there wasn't a tie here, only one would be stated.)

Conclusion

At this point you have only done the questionnaire and interpreted your own personal scores. In the next column we will provide you with information on the question of productivity and its relationship to the five dimensions. I will also provide a lesson plan for you to consider if you decide to use the You in Groups questionnaire with some of your classes.

Figure 49.4.   SECOND ANSWER SHEET

To learn more about your personal reactions in each of the five modes:

1. Take the first answer sheet for You in Groups.
2. Transfer the five numbers for each flight statement in turn into the larger part of the five boxes across the first row. The flight statement numbers are 2, 7, 11, 20 and 24. When you have done this, you will have five numbers in each box, leaving the small triangle empty.
3. Add the five numbers in each box together and insert the total into the triangle of that box.
4. Complete the other four rows.
5. Insert your highest number under FIRST and the second highest number under SECOND for each of the five dimensions in turn:

Dimension, Statements	Mode	FLIGHT (FI)	FIGHT (F)	PAIRING (P)	DEPENDENCY (D)	WORK (W)
FLIGHT 2, 7, 11, 20, 24						
FIGHT 5, 9, 12, 17, 25						
PAIRING 4, 8, 13, 16, 22						
DEPENDENCY 3, 10, 15, 19, 23						
WORK 1, 6, 14, 18, 21						

(A) In FLIGHT situations in groups,   the FIRST reaction mode I use is _____
                                           the SECOND reaction mode I use is _____

(B) In FIGHT situations in groups,   the FIRST reaction mode I use is _____
                                           the SECOND reaction mode I use is _____

(C) In PAIRING situations in groups,   the FIRST reaction mode I use is _____
                                           the SECOND reaction mode I use is _____

(D) In DEPENDENCY situations in groups,   the FIRST reaction mode I use is _____
                                           the SECOND reaction mode I use is _____

(E) In WORK situations in groups,   the FIRST reaction mode I use is _____
                                           the SECOND reaction mode I use is _____

50

Reactions to Group Situations: Part 2

This article provides you with a lesson plan for the material presented in the previous column and a set of notes about the dimensions used in the You in Groups questionnaire that you might find useful.

LESSON PLAN

- Start the lesson by distributing the You in Groups questionnaire.
- Tell the class:
  a. To follow the instructions. (This may seem like a silly thing to say, but people flounder unless you say it clearly. Reading or explaining the instructions to the class shouldn't be necessary; it often just confuses the issue. The instructions are generally clear to everyone if they are read carefully and followed.)
  b. No one will collect the answers or see their answers. (This is to reassure the people in the class that they will not be judged by others and they may answer freely.)
- It takes the individuals about half an hour to do the questionnaire.
- You can assign this task as homework or as pre-course work to allow you to save over half an hour of class time.
- If you assign this task to be done during class, you can wander around the room and make sure everyone is putting in five rankings for each question: occasionally someone only chooses the top statement.
- In using this and similar questionnaires, I have found it advisable to have them done before the course starts as pre-work or as the first thing that happens on the course. This way, your input does not affect the students' answers.
- Do not do this next step orally: do it visually via a flip chart, blackboard or an overhead projector, because the class will need to refer to it throughout the group activity.

- Ask the class to form small groups of from four to six people each and take their questionnaires with them.
- Visually display the following direction:

If:

W = Work
F = Fight
Fl = Flight
D = Dependency
P = Pairing

Look at the questionnaire and decide in your group which one of the above classifications describes the dimension of behavior expressed in each of the statements. There are six decisions to be made per numbered item: the incomplete statement plus the five completed statements, (a) through (e).

- Allow time for the participants to read the visual, *plus* study and consider what you are asking them to do. Try to avoid getting plagued with questions before the group starts to work; move to the side or back of the room and answer questions individually if a student really needs help. Chances are that the class will start without any verbal explanations from you.
- The purpose of this activity is for the group to learn the definitions of the five dimensions. This way, when they score their own personal answers from the questionnaire, they will be able to interpret their results.
- You may have to tell the groups to decide each end statement separately or independently of the original statement unless the partial statement makes absolutely no sense.
- When the group has started to work, you should stay out of sight until you think the first statement is finished before you wander around from group to group providing feedback.

Group Feedback Techniques

- When you check a group's answers, don't tell the group which answers are right and which wrong. If the group has some of the answers correct, say, "You've got part of it right" and keep on moving.
- If a group is badly lost, you may have to provide some input but this rarely happens with this material.
- If you feel a group wants help, you can point out one thing they have correct, tell them you know they can do it and leave them.
- If a group, after checking a question a second time, is still wrong, your behavior can vary depending on the group's progress:

First: if the group is the fastest group, simply say that it still has only part of it right; or if you can remember its previous answer and this new answer is an improvement, say, "That's better, but you've still got problems," and walk away.

Second: if the group is the slowest group, give them a clue—tell them which answers are right. (But not, of course, if there are only two wrong—then the group will simply reverse the incorrect ones).

By using these two techniques, you can balance the classroom so that the end-timing of the activity is not too out of balance.

• Groups have the most trouble distinguishing dependency from pairing. Don't let this discourage you; eventually they will get the difference between these two.

• It will help you in checking answers to make an answer card. I use a 3" x 5" card with the answers organized as shown in Figure 50.1. If you try to use the First Answer Sheet in the previous article, you can't provide your feedback as fast or as accurately as you'd like to. You could also photocopy Figure 50.1 and glue it to a piece of cardboard to carry with you during class.

• You do not need to have the whole class do all twenty-five questions. Each group should do at least twelve so that they will have a clear understanding of the dimensions when the scoring is done.

• Groups usually want feedback after they have completed the first question. Then, after they have done the next two questions—if they have done the three well—you'll find little need to go back and provide feedback on a regular systematic basis.

• This activity will take about one hour in most class situations. Some groups may have finished all twenty-five by then, and the rest of the class will have done at least twelve.

Interpreting the Questionnaire

• Hand out the First Answer Sheet.

• Tell the class to follow the instructions on the top to start to interpret the answers. These instructions are clear and should not require explanations.

• When people finish the First Answer Sheet early, allow them to talk with their neighbors who have also finished.

• When everyone has finished, ask the class: "What do the totals tell you? What does the highest total mean? The lowest?"

• At this stage, you probably have found that almost everyone has Work as the dimension having the highest total.

This may or may not be true because Work is seen by most people in this culture as a desirable way to behave, and this may affect their answers. Whether or not it is true, ask people who have Work as their highest dimension to look at their second highest totals, which will give them further data regarding their behavior in groups. People who have

Statement	a	b	c	d	e
1	W	P	D	W	F	FI
2	FI	P	F	W	FI	D
3	D	FI	F	D	W	P
4	P	W	P	D	FI	F
5	F	FI	W	F	P	D
6	W	F	W	P	D	FI
7	FI	P	FI	W	F	D
8	P	D	FI	F	P	W
9	F	D	FI	P	W	F
10	D	F	FI	D	W	P
11	FI	FI	W	D	F	P
12	F	D	P	FI	F	W
13	P	W	D	FI	P	F
14	W	P	D	F	W	FI
15	D	FI	P	D	W	FI
16	P	F	W	FI	P	D
17	F	FI	F	P	D	W
18	W	FI	W	P	F	D
19	D	W	FI	P	F	D
20	FI	D	P	W	F	FI
21	W	W	P	D	FI	F
22	P	FI	D	P	F	W
23	D	D	W	FI	F	P
24	FI	P	FI	F	D	W
25	F	W	P	FI	F	D

Figure 50.1. Transfer to answer card

other dimensions in the highest spot should recognize that this is a rather unique situation.

Do not ask the participants to disclose their answers publicly. Remember, you already stated that this would be private, but disclosing will certainly go on and you don't have to discourage it.

- Next, tell the class, either verbally or visually, that the scores they now have will tell them the overall tendency of how their basic traits, drives, and emotions react in groups.

- You can then tell the class that their answers can be further interpreted to show them how they react specifically to each specific dimension.

- To allow them to figure out how they react to each specific dimension, pass out the Second Answer Sheet.

- While you are passing it out, tell the class to follow the instructions exactly.

- Wander around the room and if someone is having trouble follow-ing instructions, help. You should have done the second scoring your-self because the directions have five different steps and do require some care in application if one is to do the interpretation correctly.

A FINAL ACTIVITY

When everyone has completed the Second Answer Sheet, you can close off the lesson with the following activity.
- Ask the class to form groups and try to answer this question:
Assume that five groups are made up of people whose main dimen-sions are, respectively: Flight, Fight, Pairing, Dependency, Work. Ar-range these groups in descending order from the most productive to the least productive.
- Don't expect groups to get this order correct. This is just a fun exercise for them to work on.
- The answer to this exercise is:
WORK is the most productive;
FIGHT is the next;
PAIRING is the next;
FLIGHT is the next;
DEPENDENCE is the least productive.
- Showing or telling this answer will cause a lot of discussion: Two things that I have found are:
Flight groups seem to people to be less productive than Dependence groups. You should have an answer ready for that reaction. I use the statement that if a group is truly dependent it never gets started at all without direction. I also add, "Once started, they constantly stop work because they are totally dependent on someone to lead or guide them." The Flight group at least starts and attempts to do something even though it scatters easily. I also indicate that the class should read the Interpretation for Dimensions handout, which I then pass out, for more information on this group-productivity question.

Improving the Final Activity

An improvement to the lesson plan for the final activity plan has been developed by Marit Stengels, Royal Insurance Group, Toronto.

Marit, on her first use of the material, found the class fouled up this activity, as was predicted. She then, for her second attempt, changed this spot by inserting "Hung Jury: A Decision-Making Simulation" from Pfeiffer and Jones's *The 1974 Annual Handbook For Group Facilitators* (p. 64). This is a group structured experience that allowed her to give the final activity to her class with a different base from which to answer it. Marit asked her groups to rank order the five modes in terms of what was the most productive to the least productive mode in the group's efforts in doing the Hung Jury activity.

Some further information on group modes and productivity that you might find helpful when using the You in Groups material is outlined in the accompanying table and its footnotes.

GROUP COMPOSITION	Productivity: Simple task	Productivity: Complex task
High Work	+	+
High Pairing	+	$-$[1]
High Fight, Low Pairing, Dependence	+	+
High Dependence	$-$	Mediocre[2]
High Fight	$-$	Mediocre[3]
High Fight, Low Work	$-$	+[4]

Footnotes

The general order for productivity in descending order is: Work, Fight, Pairing, Flight and Dependency.

1. The pairing groups fail in doing complex tasks because the difficulty of the task requires the group to have strength at doing tasks. Pairing groups are strong interpersonally but weak in the task accomplishment, work area.

2. The reason dependent group performance on complex tasks is mediocre is because, though the members get along well together, there is little problem solving ability. When disputes, disagreement or contradictions arise, the members easily give in to one another with no depth of exploration. The members of this type of purely dependent group completely accept each other's ideas without any sort of reality check, which leads to mediocre results.

3. No rational explanation exists for this mediocre ranking, though a strong Flight type leader may be the cause. If the leader is strong and right, performance of this group will be good as desire to get the task over with will lead to acceptance of the leader's ideas. It is also possible that with complex tasks, when frustration occurs, it may be useful to have a mechanism like Flight built into the group to deal with the tensions.

4. On simple tasks, High Fight with Low Work turns out to be counter-productive, as fighting out issues of tasks isn't required but the group has a high Fight tendency and hence becomes unproductive. In the complex task the fight nature of the group helps it, as it leads to greater exploration of ideas and hence to better task, problem, solution. It helps overcome the frustration of trying to cope with complex often apparently irreconcilable issues.

From the foregoing one can see that the nature of the task affects a group's productivity as well as the composition of the group.

In conclusion the most useful characteristic to build into a group is Work, while minimizing Flight and Dependency.

NOTES

The following is a collection of notes on groups and on the five dimensions used in the You in Groups questionnaire. These notes may prove useful to you. They are small parts of much larger books on the subject of groups. If you find these quoted notes useful you will certainly find the books they come from even more interesting.

Note 1: "In almost any group there are some members who are helpful and creative. Others are 'problem members.' These are seen as selfish, monopolizing, off-target. The usual reaction to such individuals is to dislike them. The trouble is that if the group ties up its energy in disliking these individuals, it has little to work with. Many a group mostly does process work rather than task work, and the process work is all directed to trying to control these difficult characters.

"So what to do? Observations of groups that grow into effectiveness, even in the face of these troublesome people, show us a probable way out: through realization that (1) there is no use in working on them because we are not really going to change them anyway—since they are so far out of touch with the realities of group expectations and influences—and (2) the problem is not really 'What is wrong with them?' but rather "What is wrong with us that we can't cope with them?" The turning point comes when the members of the group finally realize that it is their own anxiety, cued off by this member, that is immobilizing them."[1]

Note 2: "Group interaction can be described in terms of two aspects: work and emotionality. The emotional dimensions of a group are Fight, Flight, Dependence and Pairing."[2]

Note 3: "A group is always engaged in work. It is always to some extent, implicitly or explicitly, involved in meeting task demands that originate from within or outside the group. The work dimension represents the consciously determined, deliberate, reality-oriented, goal seeking aspects of the group's activities. At the same time that a group is engaged in work, it is also concerned with certain emotional issues that are seemingly illogical, are not under conscious control and the purposes of which are not understood by the group."[3]

---

[1]Reproduced by special permission from *National Training Laboratories, Emotional Dynamics and Group Culture*, by Dorothy Stock and H. A. Thelen, No. 2 of the Research Training Series, pp. 241, 91, 187, 188, 67-88, 119, 120. Copyrighted by NTL Institute 1958.

[2]Ibid., p. 91.

[3]Ibid., p. 187.

Note 4: "The relative dominance of work aspects over emotional aspects or vice versa may vary from group to group."[4]

Note 5: "If I, on some level, perceive another member as having similar needs and interests and as working toward establishing group conditions congenial to me, I am likely to feel friendly toward that person. If, on the other hand, I perceive someone else as interfering with my interests in the group and as working to establish group conditions that I find uncongenial, I am likely to dislike that person.

"To illustrate, an individual who characteristically withdraws from close personal contact with others is likely to prefer others with similar needs, since these members together can meet one another's needs in this respect. The same person is likely to reject those members who are constantly urging the group to become more intimate and reveal more personal material, since these are the members who are, in effect, forcing him to enter into a kind of relationship distasteful to him.

"To translate this commonsense illustration into our theoretical terms, we would say that this flight member (who flees intimacy) is likely to prefer other flight members and to reject pairing members. It is possible to imagine other flight members who might reject flight persons as well as pairing persons. This might happen, for example, when the member is so disturbed in such conflict about his own flight needs that he is equally threatened by members who wish to escape close contact with others, since these would keep his conflict in the foreground.

"The general assumption offered here is that members will be likely to prefer others who satisfy their own needs and are likely to reject others who interfere with their needs."[5]

Note 6: "Consider two groups—one having a preponderance of members who express fight readily and who act together to maintain a fight culture in the group, and the other which can similarly be characterized as predominately 'pairing.' We might expect such differences as the following to exist between these two groups:

"(A) The groups will differ in their efficiencies when dealing with any particular task problem. Each will be more efficient than the other with respect to different kinds of problems.

"(B) Both groups will be able to deal adequately with certain task problems but will show differences in the way they attack these problems.

"(C) The two groups will have different capabilities for dealing with "process" or interpersonal problems. In the second group, ambiguities

----

[4]Ibid., p. 188.

[5]Ibid., pp. 67-68.

in the limits to expression and/or management of hostility might never be dealt with, since when fight situations arise the pairing members will tend to move the group out of the flight dimension.

"(D) Considering the individual members, a person with strong predispositions toward pairing will be somewhat isolated in the first group and find little support for his needs. The same will be true of a fight person in the second group.

"(E) The two groups will differ in the standards they develop with respect to the tolerance and encouragement of fight and pairing. In the first group the limits imposed on fight will be much broader than in the second group. The second group will show higher tolerance for pairing than will the first group.

"One would not generally expect to find compositions in which *all* members show strong predispositions for fight or for dependency, etc. Yet it is not unusual for a group to tend toward a preponderance of one or another of the emotional dimensions; and such a tendency will have a significant influence on the course of the group's operation. . . ."[6]

"Our prediction, then, is that a group that includes a wide range of dimensions will deal more explicitly with a wider range of emotional issues. A group whose range of dimensions is narrower will deal with a more restricted range of emotional issues, and it will tend to deal with them in a less explicit way. If this is true, it follows that a group of the first type will provide opportunities for a wider range of learnings than will a group of the second type."[7]

Note 7: "One approach to effective grouping would be to define the demands which the group is expected to meet and then to decide which of these were most important, and then build the group to meet these demands."[8]

Note 8: "Groups work on tasks, defining roles, recruiting or training leaders, organizing, dissipating individual anxieties, and making possible the unique potential of each individual. It takes a "strong" group to cope with all of these functions."[9]

---

[6]Ibid., p. 119.

[7]Ibid., p. 120.

[8]From H. A. Thelen, T. H. Hawkes, and N. S. Strattner, *Role Perception and Task Performance of Experimentally Composed Small Groups.* Chicago: University of Chicago Press, 1969, 4. Copyrighted by The University of Chicago Press. Reprinted by permission of The University of Chicago Press.

[9]Ibid., p. 4.

Note 9: "The most effective group is one in which members have much in common, where each can contribute his unique strength to help the group meet its needs, and in which no one member's talents are precisely duplicated. Such groups tend to be small."[10]

Note 10: "Groups whose members rated high on Fight, Pairing and Work or any combination of these three would be relatively effective and groups whose members rated high on Flight and Dependence would probably be relatively ineffective."[11]

Note 11: "A climate of interpersonal warmth, (provided by Pairing), supports individual creativity."[12]

Note 12: "(On Forming Groups.) If you want to assign simple tasks and wish to concentrate all a group's efforts on its task, you should try to place in each group at least one individual who is oriented to work. Low work-oriented participants should be distributed among the groups. If you wish to avoid forming a group which would adversely affect productivity in a simple task situation, you should not combine individuals expressing tendencies of Fight, Flight, or Dependency.

"In complex task situations, interpersonal tendencies seem to be closely related to productivity. Interpersonal strengths do not of themselves guarantee productivity. Instead, you should look for individuals with aggressive or affectionate leadership strengths who would be likely to carry a group through to completion of the task. The support which such leaders need could be provided by one or more individuals rating high on Pairing or Dependency. In complex situations, groups whose members have tendencies towards Dependency or Flight will accomplish little more than maintaining themselves as a group. People with these ratings should be distributed among the groups.

"In other words, in a simple task situation a strong leader can cause a group to be productive, but in a complex situation frustrations are likely to arise which could undercut the leader if he has little support from his group. It should be noted that the tendency toward Flight is likely to have different effects in task situations of differing complexities. In a simple task situation it can be disruptive, but in a complex situation it could provide the aggressiveness needed to cut through the frustrations involved in the more difficult task."[13]

---

[10]Ibid., p. 4.

[11]Ibid., p. 65.

[12]Ibid., p. 82.

[13]Ibid., pp. 142-143.